# BEYOND REASONING

This book tells the story of Peter Cathcart Wason, offering unique insights into the life of the pioneering research psychologist credited for establishing a whole new field of science: the psychological study of reasoning. And this was just one of the major contributions he made to psychology.

Covering much more than Wason's academic work, the author, Ken Manktelow, paints a vivid and personal portrait of the man. The book traces Wason's eclectic family history, steeped in Liberal politics and aristocratic antecedents, before moving through his service in the Second World War and the life-changing injuries he sustained at the end of it, and on to his abortive first attempt at a career and subsequent extraordinary success as a psychologist. Following a chronological structure with each chapter dedicated to a significant transition period in Wason's life, Manktelow expertly weaves together personal narratives with Wason's evolving intellectual interests and major scientific discoveries, and in doing so simultaneously traces the worlds that vanished during the twentieth century.

A brilliant biography of one of the most renowned figures in cognitive psychology, this book will be of interest not only to students and scholars in thinking and reasoning, but to anyone interested in the life and lasting contribution of this celebrated scholar.

**Ken Manktelow** was formerly Professor of Psychology at the University of Wolverhampton, having begun his academic career with a PhD on reasoning, examined by Wason himself. He is the author of several books and articles on the topic.

# BEYOND REASONING

## The Life, Times and Work of Peter Wason, Pioneering Psychologist

*Ken Manktelow*

Routledge
Taylor & Francis Group

LONDON AND NEW YORK

First published 2021
by Routledge
2 Park Square, Milton Park, Abingdon, Oxon OX14 4RN

and by Routledge
52 Vanderbilt Avenue, New York, NY 10017

*Routledge is an imprint of the Taylor & Francis Group, an informa business*

© 2021 Ken Manktelow

*British Library Cataloguing-in-Publication Data*
A catalogue record for this book is available from the British Library

*Library of Congress Cataloging-in-Publication Data*
A catalog record has been requested for this book

ISBN: 978-0-367-65127-5 (hbk)
ISBN: 978-0-367-64574-8 (pbk)
ISBN: 978-1-003-12796-3 (ebk)

Typeset in Bembo
by MPS Limited, Dehradun

# CONTENTS

# LIST OF FIGURES AND TABLES

**FIGURES**

## TABLE

# PREFACE AND STYLE NOTES

This book is about one of the most influential research psychologists of modern times, but one whose name is little known outside the subject: Peter Cathcart Wason. He left a large legacy of ideas, findings, methods and people, and some of these ideas have filtered from psychological science into public culture. His work is still being carried on. Perversely, he would struggle to survive in the academic world of the present day, even though his contribution to knowledge is immense: he is principally responsible for establishing a whole field of research, for determining what its concerns are and how they are pursued, and for the production of ideas that have influenced not just other psychologists but people more generally. This state of affairs says as much about that world as it does about him. He was a scientist of extraordinary creativity, but who needed the right environment for this creativity to thrive and work its magic. In his own time, he found it, but in the present time, he would not. He would not be allowed to. The loss would be ours as well as his.

He himself attempted to write an account of his life and work centred around his most famous creation, a reasoning problem known in the business as the Wason selection task. I shall describe this task in due course, and need only note for the present that some people have claimed that it is the most widely used experimental test in the psychology of reasoning, in the psychology of thinking more generally, or in the whole of experimental psychology. It is impossible to judge these claims accurately even when looking at just the published scientific literature: there are simply too many papers, articles, books and conference proceedings to count, or to devote one's life to counting, and there is a never-ending stream of new ones, even today. We can say for sure that it's one of the most popular, at least, and who knows, it may be Number 1. It hardly matters: whatever the case about the numbers, the fact is that it brought Wason fame both in the field and beyond, so he tried to set down the nature and consequences of this fame in a first-hand account. However, he was a punctilious writer, was never completely satisfied with what he set down and, infuriatingly for this one, consigned his manuscript, which he wittily titled *Living with a problem*, to the flames. His title was apt because, as we shall see, the selection task was not the only problem Peter Wason created, or had to live with.

In telling the story of his science and his life, I shall usually refer to him just by his surname, Wason, unless the context dictates otherwise. This is partly down to a convention used in the academic world, where your surname is the label you are known by (so it helps to have an unusual one). What using this naming convention means is that the various other Wasons who wander through these pages, and there are plenty of them, will tend to be called sometimes by their first names only, sometimes by both names, sometimes by more even than that; there was a lot of traditional naming in the Wason family. It should, I hope, be clear which one is in focus at any given time. Secondly, where words or phrases appear in double quotes, they are from Wason's own words, unless otherwise indicated; single quotes are used for terminology, figures of speech and the like. Thirdly, references and sources are given at the end with pointers to the relevant passages; I have not used parentheses, superscripts, footnotes or other text references, for the avoidance of clutter.

Finally, the customary credits that go with telling this kind of story. Firstly, to two people without either of whom this project would have foundered before it set sail. Wason's elder daughter, Armorer, is the keeper of his archive and has been more than generous with it and with her time in guiding me through his personal history and that of their extraordinary family. She read the first draft with great care and provided copious notes. And then there is Phil Johnson-Laird, Wason's one-time pupil and later main collaborator, the name most often associated with his own. Johnson-Laird kept an archive of his correspondence from Wason spanning the years 1964–2001, and turned the whole lot over to this project; it was a glory-hole of information about Wason's personal as well as professional life.

Sarah Wason, his younger daughter, was also extremely helpful and supportive of this attempt to tell her father's story, as were (in alphabetical order to avoid agonising over precedence) those who gave up hours of their time to talk to me about Wason: Bob Audley, Phil Brooks, Brian Butterworth, Jonathan Evans (for his knowledge of chess as well as psychology), the late Vittorio Girotto, William Hartston, Maria Legrenzi, Paolo Legrenzi, the late David Lowenthal, Jonathan Penrose, Richard Rawles (who was able to access valuable material from Wason's employers), Tim Shallice (who connected me to several of Wason's other contemporaries), Diana Shapiro, Neil Smith, Ryan Tweney, John Valentine, Liz Valentine and Norman Wetherick. Others who made a contribution were Susan Carey, Noam Chomsky, Leda Cosmides, Jane Evans, Daniel Kahneman, Matteo Legrenzi, David Over, David Shanks & Antonietta Esposito (head and administrator respectively of the Psychology Department at University College London), who helped me locate Wason's and Penrose's PhD theses, and David Wason; and a website called thepeerage.com, an invaluable resource for tracing some British family trees. Several of the people named above were kind enough to read through a first draft and offer their comments, as also did Bill McGrory and Laura Murdoch. I thank them all for the errors they found and the improvements they suggested. Thanks are also due to Alex Howard, Cloe Holland and the rest of the Taylor and Francis crew, and to Linden Ball for liaison. Lastly, a tip of the hat to the person who should perhaps have been first on the list: Aidan Feeney. He was the one who suggested that I do this.

*Ken Manktelow*
Ash Canterbury Kent
May 2020

# 1

# CREATION

## A remarkable thing

Peter Cathcart Wason was a remarkable man, and in 1966, at the age of 42, he did a remarkable thing. He was a research psychologist. He had been invited to contribute a chapter to a modest little paperback called *New Horizons in Psychology*, a collection of 21 surveys of the latest in psychological research, and he produced one, with the single-word title of 'Reasoning'. There were several ways in which this was a remarkable thing to do. For a start, Wason was not at that time an eminent psychologist; he was not even a regular university academic, but a research associate attached to a university department, on a temporary contract paid for by an outside funding agency. Then, hardly any of his own publications had even been on reasoning. In fact, there was very little psychological work on reasoning by anyone to report on at that time, as Wason acknowledges in the very first sentence of his chapter; but as this was a book about 'new horizons', perhaps that would have been expected. He reviews such psychological work as had been done to that point, which included his own: a single publication that had appeared six years before.

The second of these first-person bits was tucked away in a two-page section headed 'Errors in Deductive Reasoning', and this is the most remarkable thing of all. It is a rather vague description of a novel reasoning task that Wason had invented some years earlier, along with a number-free report of some results, and a tentative hypothesis to account for them. Within a very short time, this little report was followed by a more formal scientific paper from Wason, then more and more, from him and from others, all using this new problem. Hundreds upon hundreds of studies followed, by scientists all around the world; the problem is still being used today. Wason's chapter became one of the most influential book chapters in the history of psychological research, and led to insights which have permeated not just the research community, but general knowledge about how the human mind works.

This was neither the beginning nor the end of Wason's inventiveness either: his first ever published research paper was featured on the front page of a national newspaper; his early research on language influenced government policy and also made the national press; he introduced two ideas that have not only influenced psychology but have permeated our collective consciousness; and he came up with several other novel techniques and ideas as well, both before and after this new problem, all fired by his lifelong, insatiable curiosity about the human mind.

We are all curious about how the mind works, and in that sense, we are all psychologists, of some kind. We spend a large part of our mental lives trying to explain, predict and influence what other people think, do and say. We even try to do this with our own thoughts and actions: remember those times when you have wondered to yourself, why did I do, or say, or think that? But you cannot actually call yourself a psychologist (in many parts of the world) unless you officially are one: it is a legally protected title, usable in a professional capacity only by those who have a recognised qualification. It takes a lot for official psychologists to influence the rest of us, but that is what Wason did.

Research psychologists do just what I've said that we all do: study and try to explain the human mind and human behaviour. But they do something extra. The difference is that they have a set of skills and conventions, in the shape of methods and theories and modes of communication, which enable them to do it systematically. A systematic approach is necessary if you want good explanations, because not all good explanations are available to everyday observation or intuition. In other words, you need to employ some science. Psychological research, therefore, is a branch of science, concerned, like any other, with finding things out, explaining them and testing those explanations to produce good theories that not only account for the observed facts, but predict new ones.

Only rarely do the theories and ideas that emerge from science cross an invisible but sturdy barrier into the wider culture and consciousness. Occasionally, when they do, people's ideas about humanity, and even about themselves, are changed profoundly as a result. Think of Charles Darwin's theory of evolution by natural selection, published in 1859, which changed the 'folk biology', the everyday understanding of the living world that people who are not biologists carry around with them, for instance; or, from closer to home, Stanley Milgram's experiments on obedience a century later, which showed, against the expectations of both laypersons and experts, that large proportions of people can be led gently into acts of cruelty for no good reason.

More recently, and less disturbingly, a view has begun to seep into the collective consciousness, our 'folk psychology', that we have two distinct and different ways of thinking, perhaps even two minds battling it out inside the one head. It is known by psychologists as the dual-process or dual-system theory of thought. This view was given its greatest recent boost by the publication in 2011 of a best-selling book by the Nobel prize-winning economic psychologist Daniel Kahneman, called

*Thinking, fast and slow.* The book's title sums up the idea of the two minds: a quick, intuitive, automatic process and a slower, reflective, effortful process.

The emergence in present-day psychology of the idea of the two thinking processes, fast and slow, is interesting because firstly, it is not really a new idea at all: it can be traced back a long way, even as far as the ancient Greek philosophers of over 2,000 years ago. Plato, for example, discussed the familiar experience of *akrasia*, or weakness of the will: you know you shouldn't have that extra drink, or that you should clean out the catbox, and yet you decide to have another one, or to find something else to do instead. There is the decision about the deed on the one hand (the need to do or not do it), and your thoughts about what you actually did (that what you ended up doing was not what you should have done) on the other. Of course, it's not always negative: we can choose something and then, on reflection, be glad we did. The point is that the two thoughts – the initial decision and its later evaluation – are two quite distinct processes. So distinct, indeed, that we may not have any awareness of what made us make the initial choice at all. To compound the problem for our folk psychology, only the slow reflective process tends to be conscious; the fast process often happens without our being aware that the mind is doing anything: it is effortless and automatic.

The difference between ancient Greece and the present day as far as the dual-process idea is concerned is that since the 1970s, it has been subject to extensive scientific testing, as well as theorising, such that we can now have whole books and college courses on the subject. That didn't happen in classical Athens. The scientific study of two-minds thinking in the modern era began with the work of Peter Wason, and it used the little problem he outlined in 1966. Even the term 'dual processes' in this context is a Wason coinage. There is another point worth noting that arises from an account of Wason's singular importance in our contemporary understanding of the human mind: nowhere in Kahneman's book does the name of Wason appear. This fact has caused something approaching outrage in some quarters.

The aim of this book is not just, or not even, to put right this egregious wrong; academic credit wars in any case only tend to exercise those directly involved. Wason was remarkable not only for this particular contribution to human understanding, although that would be reason enough to admit him to a scientific hall of fame. As would his other discoveries, inventions and ideas. But apart from this – quite a big 'apart' – he was a singular character from an extraordinary background, who lived in turbulent times and did things which changed the lives of many people. He lived a large life and his whole story will be told here, not just that of his science. His science was characterised by extraordinary creativity, to a degree that is very rare. Creativity retains a certain mystery, even though psychologists have studied it intensively. We know quite a lot about the conditions that foster it, but the nature of the creative spark itself remains intangible. Wason's character, background and history enable us to get somewhere near an understanding of how he did what he did, and why. That history begins before him.

## Family matters

Just like everybody else, Peter Wason came to realise, as he went out into the world beyond home and school, that his home and schools, along with his family and origins, were not typical. In fact, he came to see that he had lived, as he later put it, an upstairs–downstairs existence, with himself and his people decidedly 'up'. There is no getting away from the issue of class if you are British, particularly if you are English, and Wason's awareness of class, which came upon him with a thump in his late teens, would influence his outlook profoundly.

His paternal line (see Appendix 1 for this part of a detailed family tree) was steeped in Liberal politics, although this was an aspect that had faded away by the time of Wason's infancy, and he would not follow it. His father, Eugene Monier Wason, was a quiet man who worked as a civil servant, a Divisional Inspector, at the Ministry of Agriculture in Bath, Somerset. He would go around the local farms checking the livestock for disease. He liked nothing more than to be left alone in his home workshop, turning out well-crafted pieces of oak furniture, and also passed his time reading history. As was pretty common in those days, in the early 20th century, he did not communicate easily with his children – three sons – and they did not feel close to him. He despaired of his youngest, Peter's, complete lack of practical skill, at woodwork or anything else. Monier, as he was known in the family, liked to cultivate a rather down-at-heel appearance, and once, when he took a wrongly delivered letter to the house next door, he was dismissed with a curt "Not today, thank you" – having been mistaken for a tradesman. Wason himself, years later, in his 60s, had a similar experience when trying to buy a shoe brush: the shop assistant immediately said, "I'll go downstairs and see if there's a cheaper one." Wason found this hilarious, perhaps in part because of the reminder of his father's experience, which had passed into family legend. Wason's own look in later life was more rumpled academic than studiedly shabby, it should be said, although the resemblance to his father's sartorial preferences – Wason was a very reluctant suit-wearer – is clear.

Monier Wason seems not have been politically engaged at all, but the opposite applies to his immediate forebears. His own father was Eugene Wason; or rather, the Right Honourable Eugene Wason, Liberal MP for Ayrshire South, elected in 1885, and later for Clackmannan and Kinross. Eugene retired from the Commons in 1918 at the age of 72, but not before he had been appointed as Privy Councillor, which brought the 'Rt Hon.' title with it; the Privy Council is a body of establishment figures, largely but not exclusively political, set up to advise the monarch, since then as now, all Acts of Parliament must obtain the monarch's formal approval, the Royal Assent. Membership of the Privy Council is by appointment only, by the King or Queen on the advice of the Government, and it is likely that Eugene's appointment was as a result of his being a highly active parliamentarian: he spoke in the House on numerous occasions, and also served on select committees with the likes of Winston Churchill and Andrew Bonar Law, who would both become Prime Minister. The Liberal Party was in government for much of the time he was in the House, and won a landslide majority in the general election of 1906 – the last time it would form a majority government.

Eugene Wason had a brother, John Cathcart Wason, always known as Cathcart. He too was a Liberal MP, also in Scotland, for Orkney and Shetland. He was elected in 1900, the year of his 52nd birthday. This sounds quite late to be a newly elected MP, but the date is deceptive: he had certainly lived a life, and a political life at that, before then. Around his 20th birthday, he moved to New Zealand and bought a tract of land on which to build a 'model' farm and village, and a mansion. He named it after Corwar, his father's Ayrshire estate. His aspirations for this model community were scuppered when the railway that he expected to be built nearby did not materialise. In the meantime, he had been elected to the New Zealand parliament. He had various spells as a representative before leaving in 1899, selling up his landholdings and returning to Scotland the following year. He was married, to Alice Seymour Bell, but they had no children. Unlike his brother, he did not make many contributions to parliamentary debates, and never ascended to the same Establishment heights. Perhaps this also had something to do with his reputed habit of spending his time in the House knitting. Cathcart's eccentricities were a source of comment in Parliament: a note from him to Winston Churchill on the subject of Irish Home Rule and passed to the Prime Minister, Herbert Asquith, was annotated by the PM with the words "he is well known not to be quite sane". Both men were hard not to notice in the House at the time, being both around 6ft 6in (2m) tall. Eugene was also stocky with it – he must have been a giant – but Cathcart was slim. A cartoon by the famous caricaturist F.H. Townsend in the now defunct magazine *Punch*, from 1913, depicts the pair of them dancing a Hogmanay jig on a table (see Figure 1.1). That such a thing exists attests to the impression they made.

**FIGURE 1.1** 'The Brothers Wason' cartoon, by F.H. Townsend. The caption accompanying it read: "HOGMANAY IN LONDON. At the New Year's Eve Supper, given by the Senior Liberal Whip by way of consolation to the Scottish Members, the Brothers Wason bring down the house." Courtesy of Armorer Wason.

Eugene's and Cathcart's father, the Scottish Corwar estate holder, was Peter Rigby Wason, known as Rigby, himself an MP, this time for the English constituency of Ipswich, in the early 19th century. He was also a barrister. Rigby's time in Parliament was chequered: elected in 1831, he held the seat until 1837, but along the way he was defeated in the general election of 1835, although that result was declared void; Rigby was returned in the consequent by-election. After defeat in 1837, he stood again in the election of 1841, and won, but that election was also declared void (these were interesting times to be an MP), whereupon Rigby appears to have taken the hint: he did not stand again, but reverted to his station as a Scottish landowner.

Wason was proud of his family background, and liked to talk about his forebears, especially when, as an academic, he took overseas trips to conferences, universities and so on. But he was not much impressed by his grandfather, Eugene, despite – or perhaps because of – his political achievements and Establishment credentials. He was much more taken with his great-uncle Cathcart, especially with his eccentricity: the knitting in Parliament comes to mind. He did, however, particularly admire their father, Rigby, for his radicalism in advocating for the working class 200 years ago. This was not a common political position, before the advent of the Labour Party in the early 20th century. Wason became a Labour supporter, and regarded himself as a radical, on the left of the party. He kept a portrait of Rigby in his study.

There is one other historical note about Rigby Wason that we cannot let pass. In 1836, at this time of political ferment in Britain, a group of Whigs and Radicals gathered to set up a social and dining club to act as a counterbalance to the Carlton Club, the social centre of the Tory Party. It was to be called the Reform Club; membership depended on one's support for the Great Reform Act of 1832, which abolished the 'rotten boroughs' – some had only a dozen electors – and extended the franchise to all male householders living in dwellings worth at least £10 per annum. This was the first time a general franchise rule had been instituted in England. Initially, Whigs had been barred from membership, but they later joined forces with the Radicals to form what became the Liberal Party. Rigby Wason was one of the Whigs involved in establishing the Reform Club. While today it no longer requires members to be loyal to the Liberal (or Liberal Democrat) party, "it continues", its website says, "to maintain its liberal and progressive traditions." That would explain why it started admitting female members in 1981, only 145 years after its founding; to be fair, this put it ahead of most of London clubland. It is located on Pall Mall in London, just off Trafalgar Square and hence a short trot to the Houses of Parliament. St James's Palace is at the other end. It is a nice area. Should you find the idea of joining appealing, you will need to be proposed and seconded by current members, and then succeed in being elected. The joining and annual fees are not cheap, I think it's fair to say. You will be in good company, though: members have included political magnates such as Winston Churchill and David Lloyd George, literary luminaries Arthur Conan

Doyle and Henry James, broadcasting titan David Attenborough – and less happily, one of the Cambridge spies, Guy Burgess. Wason recalled dining there on several occasions, although he was not a member, and his father and grandfather, and the eccentric Cathcart, did too.

We have not heard the last of people called Rigby, Cathcart or Eugene Wason.

Peter Cathcart Wason – as he got older, he increasingly took to using his illustrious middle name on his publications – struck everyone who met him, especially abroad, as almost the very model of an old-style English gent, and, to complete the stereotype, an eccentric one at that. Already we have seen that in reality, one half of his ancestry was not English but Scottish, so on this score alone, he might more properly be thought of as British. He himself was a decided internationalist in his outlook, and took a great interest in world affairs in his adult life. In fact, this internationalism had some of its antecedents in the other side of his family history.

In 1911, Monier Wason married Kathleen Jessica Woodhouse. The Hon. Kathleen Woodhouse, that is: she was the daughter of Sir James Thomas Woodhouse, former Liberal MP for Huddersfield in Yorkshire from 1895 to 1906 and senior civil servant thereafter, who was made the first Baron Terrington in 1918, and Jessica (Jessie) Reed, known to Wason as Grandmother Terrington (see Appendix 2 for details of the maternal line of Wason's family). The barony is hereditary: it passed to Sir James's eldest son, Harold Woodhouse, on his death in 1921. Harold was married, to Vera, one of the first female MPs (a Liberal, again) to sit in the House of Commons, but they had no children, so the title passed to his brother, Horace Marton Woodhouse. Wason knew him as Uncle Horace. Horace, the third Baron, had two sons, and in an echo of the previous generation, the title passed from the elder, James, to the younger, Christopher Montague (Monty) Woodhouse. This time, it was because of the male primogeniture rule in the aristocracy: James Woodhouse had three daughters but no son, and daughters were (and still are) prohibited from inheriting their father's title. The current sixth Baron Terrington is Monty's son.

Breaking with the Liberal seam, Monty Woodhouse was a Conservative MP, for Oxford. Before that, he had been a war hero, serving in the Special Operations Executive in Greece in the Second World War (in peacetime, he was an eminent Greek scholar), where he undertook successful and spectacular sabotage missions against the occupying German forces and helped lead the Greek resistance. He was an outspoken opponent of the Greek military dictatorship of the early 1970s, which occurred during his time in the Commons, and as such was out of step with many of his party colleagues. Less heroically, in 1953, working for MI6, he helped organise the overthrow of the elected prime minister of Iran, Mohammad Mosaddeq, who had nationalised the Anglo-Iranian Oil Company, leading to the installation of the Shah as an autocratic ruler. We are still living with the consequences of that operation, since the Shah was himself overthrown in the Islamic revolution of 1979.

Peter Wason was, therefore, the grandson, nephew and first cousin to a line of hereditary peers. 'Middle-class' seems to be selling him a little short in the British social scheme.

Besides her two noble brothers, Kathleen Woodhouse also had a sister, Gladys, and she married into an extraordinary family: her husband was Charles Fitzgerald Blood, 'Uncle Fitz' to Wason. The Blood line – that is not a pun – can be traced back to Captain Edmund Blood in the 17th century (and beyond). Capt. Blood had two sons: the Very Rev. Neptune Blood, who lived a long life between 1599 and 1692, and was Fitzgerald's direct ancestor, and Thomas Blood, who died in 1645. Thomas Blood's son, also called Thomas, was the notorious Colonel Blood, who is famous to this day as the man who in 1671 tried to steal the Crown Jewels from the Tower of London, and came very close to actually pulling it off.

The Blood family, in its several branches, were long-standing members of the Anglo-Irish nobility, based in County Clare. One member was another very long-lived relative, Sir Bindon Blood, who lived from 1842 to 1940 and was a distinguished soldier, a General, as well as a military civil servant in later life; at the age of 94, he was made Chief Royal Engineer to the British Army. Winston Churchill dedicated a book to him. Wason's Uncle Fitz, Fitzgerald Blood, called his own son Bindon, and he was also a military man, although Wason, his first cousin, thought him unhappy in that role. Fitzgerald also came from a long line of Co. Clare landowners, and kept a grand house at Ballykilty, near the small town of Quin. These people, and this area, would figure large in Wason's childhood and young adulthood, and in his worldview and identity thereafter.

# 2

# HELL AND HEAVEN

## The happiest days

Peter Wason was born on April 22nd, 1924 in an upstairs room at the family home, Grafton Lodge, on Weston Road in Bath, Somerset. He was delivered by the family doctor, Dr Dunen, who was mysteriously called 'Old Fullo' by his father. "Another little soldier!" cried Monier, a reaction that came as a relief to Wason's mother, who had thought he might be disappointed not to have a daughter, after two sons. 'Little' was the word: Wason's two brothers were considerably older. Rigby James Monier (Jim) was the eldest, born in 1912, and then there was Eugene Romer, born in 1914. Wason never really got to know his brothers until they were all adults; all were packed off to boarding schools from the age of eight. The two older ones were very different people: Jim a real eccentric, something of a loner, although he did get married, to Mildred Mons Thomas in 1943. They had one son, Ivor. Jim taught himself foreign languages and later became a freelance Russian translator. Wason got to know him well and like him a lot when they were grown men, especially after the Second World War.

Eugene, by contrast, was, in Wason's words, "exceptionally debonair and dashing in an Anthony Eden, Ronald Colman kind of way" (Eden was a Conservative MP who succeeded Churchill after his second term as Prime Minister, while Colman was a British-born, Oscar-winning Hollywood actor). Possessed of considerable charm, he worked for the Secret Service, probably MI5, during Second World War, having been exempted from the military on medical grounds, and went on to a journalistic career, rising to editor at several local and national newspapers. He had been editor – by his own account, unhappily – of the *Sunday Mail* in Glasgow for two years when his life was struck by tragedy: his wife, Emily, suffered a brain aneurysm while on the phone to Wason's wife Marjorie, and died on the spot; she was found by her eldest daughter, one of four children who were then aged between 11 and 17.

On the advice of his paper's management, Eugene left the *Sunday Mail* and went to London, intending to take up a Fleet Street post that had been found for him. Instead, following an ad in the trade press, he took the children with him to what was then, in 1958, Southern Rhodesia (now Zimbabwe), and began a five-year stint on a paper also called the *Sunday Mail*. That led to his becoming managing editor of the *African Daily News* in 1964, just over a year before Ian Smith's Rhodesian Front government made its Unilateral Declaration of Independence (from Britain), in a last-ditch attempt to preserve White minority rule; the British were trying to steer the country towards majority rule. There were 200,000 Europeans and 4 million Africans in Rhodesia at the time. The paper's editorial line changed, on Eugene's initiative, to reflect the perspective of the Black nationalist majority, and was banned for subversion for its pains by Smith in August 1964, as were the African nationalist political parties. Eugene Wason wrote a book about this experience, *Banned: the story of the African Daily News* ten years later. In it, he recalls how the banning of the paper was reported in the London press, and how he received a telegram from his brother, Peter: "Well done. A great fight for freedom". Following his departure from Rhodesia, he fetched up in another political hot spot, as editor of the Belfast Telegraph, just in time for the outbreak of the Troubles in 1968. He was respected by both sides in Northern Ireland, Unionist and Republican, for his even-handedness; indeed, he struck everyone as a decent, moral man. He liked to tell how he had a letter from Sinn Fein in one pocket of his suit and one from Ian Paisley, loyalist firebrand and founder of the Democratic Unionist Party, in another.

Their mother Kathleen was, Wason said, energetic and amusing, kind but a bit overwhelming. Quite unlike his father, in other words, although they appeared to him to be very fond of each other, leading largely separate lives. She was a good golfer, at one time captaining the Somerset Ladies' Team at Sham Castle. One of her close friends was the Archdeacon of Bath – there was a picture of him on the mantelpiece – who ministered at Bath Abbey; Wason found its rather 'low church' services "dreary". On Tuesdays, she would give the nanny the day off and walk with little Peter into Bath, through Victoria Park, to the toy shops to buy model farm animals. He keenly anticipated these weekly moments of closeness with his mother, but came to resent the distance between them that was the rule the rest of the time, a distance that would only get worse when his schooldays arrived. Once, she gave him a florin (10p – worth about £6 today so a generous sum) to give to a beggar: "That will allow him to buy marmalade for his breakfast," she said, which is either the kind of slightly silly thing you say to a small child in a strange situation, or a rather other-worldly reflection of their social standing. Nanny looked after the boy for the other six days of the week, and Wason remembered his various nannies differently: some were kind, some were stiff and strict.

In addition to the nanny, there were two live-in servants, sisters, Ethel the cook and Alice the parlour-maid. They were fondly remembered and with the family a long time; they used to bring Peter fossils from a local coal-pit, where their father was a manager. There was also a gardener with whom the young boy was on friendly terms; he was a First World War veteran who had been gassed. He was called Richards, and Wason called him Rich; Richards called Wason Pete. Another carer took Peter to the kindergarten at a nearby girls' school, Hermitage House. He was made a fuss of by the older girls there, and remembered one of them coming to the house to visit and their dozing off together in a hammock one afternoon. This made quite an impression on him, and he looked back on the episode as a moment that led him to treasure female company later on.

Even though he did not get on well with either of his parents, he came to regard his home life as relatively idyllic, once he was "deported", as he put it, aged eight, to boarding school. At home, he was solitary: not lonely, but happy in his own company, and he developed hobbies and collections, for things such as Oriental curiosities and then books, especially second-hand books. These included poetry, mystical literature and chess books: he became passionate about chess as a schoolboy, and both of these passions, for chess and literature, would never leave him.

As with many kids down the ages, homely pleasures were magnified and contrasted by Wason's experience of school. He was happy at the kindergarten, and not just because of the attention paid to him by the girls there. He enjoyed learning to read and write, and at the end of his first term received one of the very few positive reports from a teacher that he got throughout his education: "very neat at scissor work", it said. He was amused by this report and remembered it for the rest of his life. But, again as with so many schoolchildren, he could make no headway in maths and quickly stopped trying – the subject, with its rigid drills and formalism, simply held no interest for him, as it lent no room for discovery and exploration. He developed a conscious coping strategy of not drawing attention to himself so as not to have to keep working on the problem, and would just watch the rain falling outside; it had a comforting quality, he recalled. University tutors in what became Wason's academic discipline, Psychology, encounter this problem in perhaps a majority of their students even in the present day: psychologists need to use statistical analysis as part of their research skills, and many students just struggle through courses in it as best they can, learning little and retaining less. The more enlightened among Psychology tutors try to follow Wason's childhood attitude to maths and ally it to some real research and data collection, rather than just teach the tests. Discovery and exploration: these would become the hallmarks of his approach to science 30 years later.

## Deported

His boarding school, Kingwell Hall Preparatory School in Timsbury, Somerset, a few miles south-west of Bath, was a shock after the Hermitage House experience. It had been set up in 1921 by two joint headmasters, C.G. Roach and F.A. Lacey, and then taken over in 1925 by the man who was headmaster there in Wason's time, Sydney Allen, known to the boys as 'Syd'. Wason did not hold back when describing Syd or his school in later life. Allen, he said, "was a vicious sadist who seemed to beat boys almost at random", with implements such as a cane or a slipper. He described suffering three such beatings, once owing to a report from a master for not paying attention and daydreaming, the avoidance technique he had developed at Hermitage House to cope with the perceived sterility of maths; another for talking to a friend in the dormitory after lights-out. Once, he tried to flee from the school, and when returned to it, was beaten again. There may have been more. He saw another boy whose buttocks and thighs had been lacerated by a similar assault, sobbing quietly in a changing room. Wason himself was crying so much after one beating that he had to be comforted by one of the other masters.

No-one complained then – it was just how things were – and there is no hint of this experience in the two letters home he wrote which have survived; such letters were, in any case, censored by Syd. However, we now have an expression for this kind of thing, of course: child abuse. It has another, sexual connotation, and there is a strong suspicion of that where Sydney Allen is concerned too. On school trips to local places of interest, most of the boys would go in a charabanc (a kind of open-topped coach), but "favoured boys" would go with Allen in his car. This need not necessarily arouse suspicion in itself, but it certainly does so retro-spectively when we learn, as Wason did, that in late 1939, around the time of the outbreak of the Second World War, Sydney Allen had hanged himself – at the school – apparently after what were euphemistically called 'carryings-on' with some local boys had been exposed. The school itself had moved to a grand Victorian pile near Bradford-on-Avon, just south-east of Bath, by then. After a series of postwar mergers with others, it finally closed down in 1990.

The "pervading atmosphere of danger" (Wason's words again) at Kingwell Hall was not all-pervading: there were aspects and moments which were looked back on fondly, such as the good friends which he made, but did not keep up with, and sports: he once scored a goal in a football game against a school in Bath, whose team included the son of Emperor Haile Selassie of Ethiopia, coincidentally named Wasan. The Imperial family were fugitives from the Italian invasion of Abyssinia, as it then was, and had been set up in a large house in Bath by the British Government. He continued, however, to struggle with school work, and not just with maths; and he continued to deploy his avoidance technique to cope with his intense lack of interest. His Latin teacher took to calling him 'scatterbrain' or 'featherbrain' owing to his persistent inattention, soubriquets he recalled with relish in autobiographical writings 50 years later, as he looked back on his achievements as a research psychologist. He similarly recalled his maths master (one feels a touch of sympathy for this man), a Russian émigré, intoning 'You can't add an apple to a banana', a slogan that Wason decried then, and forever after, as an "obvious falsehood", uttered with all the assurance of a Zen koan.

Given his later success as a university academic, we naturally wonder why he was so unsuccessful as a school pupil. He is not alone in this paradox: the best-known case is of that popular doyen of genius, Albert Einstein, failing the general part of his college entrance exam. Einstein, however, excelled at maths from an early age; Wason excelled at nothing – nothing on the school curriculum, that is.

He excelled at chess. The difference in both cases is passion. Einstein had an early passion for maths which made him expose himself to more and more of it, a self-reinforcing process that turned him into a prodigy. Nothing at school had such an effect on Wason, and so he continued to drift. The problem was one of motivation, exacerbated by the regime of punishment operating at his school and at most others at the time, a regime in which children could have physical injury inflicted on them for not learning satisfactorily. Further evidence for this as the root of Wason's educational difficulties comes from an episode in which his mother promised him a reward (a toy yacht) if he would do really well at school. He was seized by the thought of this yacht, knuckled down, and came top of the form. Upon acquiring the handsome red-sailed boat, which he was allowed to select for himself, he sank back into his educational torpor. He alleviated it by reading, and playing chess, and reading about chess.

The efficacy of reward, and the uselessness of punishment, in promoting learning was a message emerging contemporaneously from the Behaviourist school of psychology, which was reaching its peak at the time, headed by the work and ideas of B.F. Skinner in the USA. Wason and those around him at home and school were not aware of this, of course; neither was most of the wider world. The proposition is quite simple (simplistic, in fact): if you have a given behaviour and you want your child, or your dog or cat, to do more of it, provide a nice experience whenever it is done. This is called positive reinforcement. Punishment, on the contrary, is where a behaviour is followed by a nasty experience. That will cause the child (or dog, or cat) to do less of it. The snag is that the punishment contains no information about what should be done instead, and it is always possible that the undesired behaviour that has been suppressed by the punishment will be replaced by one that is equally, perhaps even more, undesirable. The only remedy is to reinforce a desirable one in its place, and this step is easy to miss. The continuing prevalence of regimes of punishment which lack that necessary step in all kinds of societal settings today is testament to how little effect scientific knowledge can sometimes have on human life.

Wason needed to pass the common entrance exam in order to gain entry into public (i.e. private) school for his secondary education, and after the inevitable struggle, finally did so. There were family traditions on both sides as to which school to attend: boys from his mother's family tended to go to Winchester, those from his father's to Rugby. Winchester was ruled out because Wason was not, understandably in view of his school performance, deemed clever enough, Rugby because he was not thought tough enough. His aunt, Minna, was a friend of the wife of one of the housemasters at Stowe School, however, which had a reputation as being suitable for 'delicate' or 'difficult' boys. Wason was sent to Stowe (Figure 2.1).

Even with his upbringing, Wason was awed by Stowe: it is centred on a former stately home, in Buckinghamshire, that of the Dukes of Buckingham and Chandos; and here is another, albeit distant, family connection, through the fabulous Colonel Blood, whose patron was the then Duke of Buckingham. There

**FIGURE 2.1** Stowe school. (From Wikipedia, Creative Commons Share-alike Licence 2.0)

are several other impressive buildings besides the main house, some in which various school functions are carried out, some merely ornamental, together with the extensive grounds and playing fields that come with a country estate. Stowe is not an ancient public school, like Eton or Harrow, or Winchester or Rugby: it was established as recently as 1923, under the headship of the man who was head when Wason was there, J.F. Roxburgh. It was set up as a more liberal, progressive educational institution than some of the more traditional British public schools, and became rapidly successful, producing a host of luminary alumni. It was expanded in 1934 with the addition of Walpole House (note the Liberal connection: it was named after Horace Walpole, a Whig MP and son of the first British Prime Minister, Robert Walpole). Wason was placed in Walpole House.

He initially took well to the radical change of regime from the one he had experienced at his prep school, and after the first week wrote home, rather incautiously, that "life [was] one round of pleasure". His sporting side emerged again, and he became adept at fencing, even representing the school at one time. Academically, though, he began to drift again, completely blocked by maths and physics, although he did enjoy chemistry and biology. His best subject was English, and he retained an affectionate memory of his English masters, the Shakespearian scholar Wilson Knight, T.H White, author of the Arthurian novel sequence, *The Once and Future King*, and John Davenport, a friend of Dylan Thomas and devotee of 20th-century poets such as Ezra Pound and T.S. Eliot. Davenport gave Wason a complimentary school report, declaring him intelligent and amusing. Literature, and modern poetry in particular, would become an important facet of Wason's life, and the seeds of that love were nurtured here. He also continued to play chess, though not as seriously as he would have liked; the school had no chess-playing culture to speak of, possibly because of its newness.

There was one significant negative influence of Stowe as well, in the sense that it forced him to look elsewhere. Wason was searching for "spiritual nourishment", and was not getting any from the school, whose approach was decidedly low church, as Bath Abbey had been earlier. He took up his interest in mystical literature again, along with a friend, David Duck, and went on book-buying trips to London to build up a library of such works. This led to an interest in, and gravitation towards, Roman Catholicism. This was not welcomed, at home or at school, and particularly irked his mother; there is a suspicion that part of the attraction of the Roman church for Wason was precisely this, as a way of irritating her, since they did not get on, perhaps as a result of the lack of contact between them in his early childhood. Although his adherence would lapse in the coming years, he would return to the Church late in life.

Once again, he struggled to pass the necessary qualification to proceed to higher education, and was sent to a 'crammer' college in Kent, which had a thatch-roofed Catholic church nearby, whose masses he attended. It did the trick and he passed upon his return to Stowe. One other event of lifelong significance occurred during this period: he began to smoke a pipe, something that he continued to do almost until his dying day.

## Away, from school and home

Away from school, there were regular holidays split between Ireland and Swanage, Dorset, and occasionally the Isle of Wight. Wason remembered these as "a life of bliss and luxury" which would soon be swept away. The latter two were with members of the Wason side of the family. In Dorset, his Aunt Minna would hire out an entire prep school, called Hillcrest, during the summer holidays, and the extended family would encamp there. Minna Wason had become Minna Crombie on her marriage to John Crombie, Liberal MP (yet another one) for Kincardine in Scotland. They had two children, John Eugene, who had been killed in action in 1917, and Mary Fenella. Fenella was a notable person in her own right, and Wason loved her. She married John Paton and they set up home at his grand house, Grandholme, in Aberdeenshire. They had six children in a span of 11 years, the elder two, Fiona and Sheila, referred to by Wason as "the glamorous Paton girls", being thought of among the family as possible future brides for him. Perhaps not coincidentally, given such a concentrated sequence of pregnancies and births, Fenella opened the first family planning clinic in the city of Aberdeen in 1926, under the influence of, though independent from, Marie Stopes, the biological scientist (she was an eminent palaeobotanist by the time she was 30 and the first female member of academic staff at the University of Manchester) and eugenicist, and birth control pioneer. Stopes visited the clinic in 1934. It became integrated into the nascent National Health Service in 1948, just a year before Fenella's early death, at 47, from cancer.

Marie Stopes was herself a guest at Hillcrest one year, along with her son, the interestingly named Buffkins. This was actually Harry Stopes-Roe, a contemporary of Wason's at Stowe, although their paths never crossed there; he went on to become an eminent philosopher, and chair of the British Humanist Association. He would be estranged from his mother when he became engaged to Mary Wallis, the daughter of the inventor of the 'bouncing bomb', Sir Barnes Wallis. It was not this connection that incurred her disapproval; rather, it was on eugenic grounds: she feared her future grandchildren might inherit Mary's short-sightedness. She did her best to prevent the marriage, failed, and ultimately disinherited him. Perhaps this family rift might not have happened had Harry married Fiona, Wason's glamorous Paton cousin, as Wason suspected was the intention of her family, at least. But it clearly took a lot to placate Marie Stopes. Wason recalled Stopes as "quite fierce", and she certainly did not take kindly to contradiction: in addition to her spat with her son, she was almost ruined by an unsuccessful lawsuit – it went all the way to the House of Lords – against a Christian author who attacked (in print) her birth control clinic, insulting her in the process; and Wason remembered her and his mother having a heated argument at Hillcrest over wind directions and compass points, of all things.

On the Isle of Wight, the family, usually without Wason's father, stayed with Monier's elder brother, Rigby. Wason described this Rigby Wason, and his wife, Gwen, as beyond question his favourite aunt and uncle. Rigby had been born in 1871, so would have been in his 60s at this time; Gwen was 19 years younger, but would die 2 years before him. In stark contrast to his brother, Rigby was loquacious, but there is one thing in particular that makes him stand out in Wason's family story: he was an avid collector of puzzles. Indeed, he had a whole room devoted to this collection, and Wason was captivated by them. Rigby liked to give people mathematical problems to solve, but would get irritated if they succeeded, and produce another one in the hope of stumping them. In view of Wason's later career as an inventor of cognitive tasks – puzzles by another name – it is hard not to see this relationship as crucial to his intellectual orientation.

Of perhaps greater significance to him at the time, however, were his stays in Ireland, and his exposure to that side of his family's history and culture. He and his mother stayed with his aunt Gladys (his mother's sister) and Uncle Fitz, Fitzgerald Blood, at their home at Ballykilty, near Quin, County Clare. As we have heard, the Blood family was Anglo-Irish, Protestant nobility with a centuries-long history in Co. Clare. It was here that Wason became acquainted with their son, his first cousin, Bindon Blood, the unhappy soldier (as a boy, he had contemplated an alternative career as a historian, and should perhaps have followed it), who tried to teach him how to fire a shotgun. The bang terrified Wason, and he occupied himself after that with hunting for the spent cartridge cases instead. The Bloods were part of a circle of Anglo-Irish aristocracy which included the Studderts of Ballyhannon and the Inchiquins (family name O'Brien) of Dromoland. Wason's grandfather, the first Baron Terrington, was rumoured to have had a mistress from the Studdert family.

There was another family with which Wason's was friendly, the O'Hallorans, who also lived near Quin, but these people were not included in this circle because, as Aunt Gladys confided under her breath, *they were Catholics*. This kind of discrimination was perhaps another factor in Wason's rebellious gravitation towards Rome. The O'Hallorans were never invited to one of the collective picnics held by this gilded group. Despite this snub, Wason enjoyed these picnics,

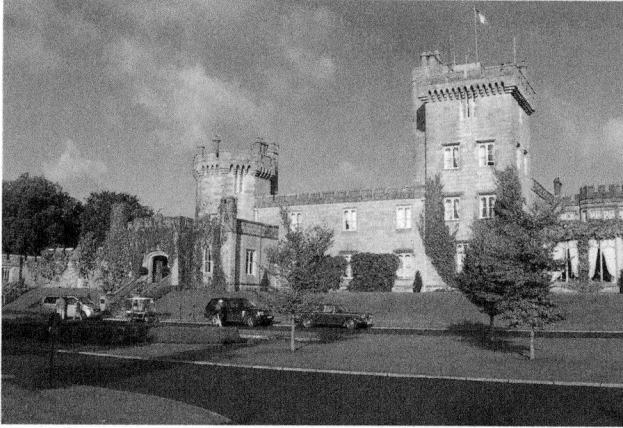

**FIGURE 2.2**  Dromoland Castle in recent times, as a hotel. (Public domain)

revelling in the conversation that accompanied them, and other walks around Clare. His mother once took him to the Studderts' home, Hazlewood House, or what was left of it: it had been burned down by the Irish Republican Army some years before, one of many great houses and castles which met that fate. She reminisced about being taken by her father, the Baron, to dances in its ballroom. Her mother's deep affection for Ireland – she said that she had been given the name Kathleen because of the Terringtons' Irish connections – transferred itself to Wason. He became sympathetic to the Republican cause, even voicing support for the armed campaign. He was struck by how the ordinary people of Ireland seemed to bear him, a scion of their nation's oppressive neighbour, no ill will at all. He struck up deep friendships with some of the workers at Ballykilty; one in particular, Paddy Ryan, would go with Wason hand-in-hand to fetch water, and sing to him the republican anthem, *The wearing of the green*, as they went. Wason even as a boy resented the disdainful way they were treated, especially by Uncle Fitz.

Dromoland Castle, the Inchiquins' seat, was largely rebuilt in the 19th century, and had an impressive art collection. The castle was sold in 1962 by the 16th Baron Inchiquin and is now a (very) upmarket country house hotel (see Figure 2.2), which has hosted Nelson Mandela and two US presidents, among other notables; the 2004 EU–US summit was held there. But on September 3rd, 1939, Dromoland was host to 15-year-old Peter Wason, who was playing tennis. It was the day when Britain's Prime Minister, Neville Chamberlain, announced that a state of war now existed between Britain and Germany, since Hitler's army had failed to withdraw from Poland, invaded two days beforehand. Lady Inchiquin, an accomplished violinist who played Beethoven on a Stradivarius, came outside and told everyone not to stand close together, because of the risk from bombs, adding "If a bomb should fall on me, I should run a mile". One cannot help but admire such many-layered other-worldliness; Ireland was in any case, and would remain, a neutral country in the new world war. To Wason's distress, it was at first decided that his family, but not he, should do their patriotic duty and return to England; he would be subject to a form of evacuation, something that befell tens of thousands of British city children once the bombing raids started in earnest in 1940. But they relented and he did go back, after all. It very nearly didn't end well.

# 3

# END OF A WORLD

## The home front

The idyll of home and holidays – but not school – that Wason recalled would have been coming to an end in any case, as. he reached his middle teens and the threshold of adulthood, but it was cut off conclusively because this period of his life coincided with one of the most ominous in human history: the inexorable rise of Nazi Germany and the seemingly unstoppable slide towards another European war.

Always accompanied, from the beginning, by thuggish, paramilitary elements such as the Brownshirts and Stormtroopers, the National Socialist German Workers' Party had emerged as an almost conventional election-contesting political party, albeit extremely right-wing and eternally anti-Semitic, in the 1920s, and in the general election of 1930 returned the second largest number of seats to the Reichstag, at 107 – up from just 12 in the election just two years previously. This still represented only 18% of the popular vote. Paramilitary violence against other parties increased: their meetings were frequently disrupted by Nazi gangs. It was not all one way: communist militias were similarly aggressive. In the first election of 1932 (there was another after a no-confidence motion), the Nazi vote doubled, and they became the largest party. The parliament remained deadlocked, though, between right-wing and left-wing coalitions: the Communists had also increased their vote, especially among the working class; Nazi support was largely in the middle classes. After a period of instability and fresh elections, Adolf Hitler was sworn in as Chancellor in January 1933. Another general election was called two months later; despite a sharp increase in violence and intimidation on their part, the Nazis won only 44% of the popular vote. Hitler and his lieutenants immediately set about dismantling every democratic structure in Germany, banning first the Communist Party then others, and bringing every political and quasi-political organisation into its orbit, and under its control. Those that were not forcibly 'co-ordinated', as the official euphemism had it, saw the way things were going and jumped before they were pushed; vast numbers of civil servants joined the party just to keep their jobs. Hundreds of political murders were recorded.

By the late 1930s, it was becoming clear that the Nazi hegemony was not going to stop at Germany's borders; those borders were not recognised by the regime in any case. Anti-Semitic purges, which had been going on for years, when even world-famous orchestral conductors such as Bruno Walter and Otto Klemperer were pushed out and fled the country, became widespread; Jews were turfed out of their homes, jobs and schools, and began leaving Germany in great numbers – if they were lucky. The prospect of another war, so soon after the Great War of 1914–1918, was felt generally in Britain to be inevitable at the time, despite the Prime Minister Neville Chamberlain's 'peace for our time' meeting with Hitler in September 1938. Only those who wanted to be convinced were convinced that it promised any such thing.

The onset of the Second World War a year later had an immediate effect on the Wason household at Grafton Lodge in Bath. First of all, and to the family's regret, their two long-standing servants, the sisters Ethel (the cook) and Alice (the parlour-maid) left, and the family engaged temporary staff. Then Wason's maternal grandmother Jessie, Grandmother Terrington, moved from London – it was not just the capital's children who were evacuated – to stay with them. Wason thought her a sweet old lady, never in a bad mood. She brought with her a butler called Fussinger (his first name remains a mystery), who attended to her every need, even filling her fountain pen for her. Wason thought him the almost American-stereotypical English butler: tall, aloof and always immaculate in evening dress. His father, rather mockingly, pointed out the mirror Fussinger had in the pantry to check his appearance before entering the dining room. He was in fact Swiss, but his name was Germanic enough for the British authorities, who had him shipped to an internment camp on the Isle of Man, along with thousands of others, whether or not they were sympathetic to the Hitler regime – or German, for that matter. This did not last long, however, because Fussinger was fortunate in his choice of employer. Grandmother Terrington was the wife of the first Baron Terrington, and her second son, Horace, was the third Baron, having succeeded upon his brother's death early in 1940. This was Wason's Uncle Horace, who was a senior civil servant and Deputy Speaker of the House of Lords: a person of substance and a good one to have on your side. Uncle Horace was quick to exert his influence and have Fussinger released.

Grandmother Terrington also had two lady 'companions' while at Grafton Lodge, Miss Carmichael and then Miss Vaisey. Wason liked them both, but Miss Carmichael irritated his mother with her peculiar quirks of speech: she had a tendency for needless abbreviation of names. This must have amused him, although he knew better than to show it. This slightly Victorian arrangement stopped in early 1942, however, when Grandmother Terrington began to ail and was moved to a nearby nursing home. She died later that year. This meant that Fussinger had to leave the household, which he did rather gracelessly: his parting shot to Wason's mother was the ominous-sounding "You'll get a rude awakening soon". Despite this fit of petulance, Uncle Horace rode to the rescue again, and secured Fussinger the post of head carver at the Reform Club on Pall Mall. Wason had lunch there later in the year, but no flicker of recognition passed between them.

Wason's mother put her team-captain skills to use for the war effort, and became the leader of the local branch of the Women's Land Army ( WLA). This body had been formed in the First World War, when women were drafted into all kinds of industry to replace the millions of men who had joined the armed forces: women took over many of the roles of farm labourers, and thus became 'land girls'. It was revived in June 1939, before the start of Second World War, clearly in response to the imminent threat and the sense of the inevitability of the coming conflict. The WLA was not formally disbanded until 1949, long after the end of the War, owing to the economic privations experienced by Britain as a consequence of its struggles in securing victory, exacerbated by the terrible winter of 1947. She also took evacuees from Fulham, London, into her home. This became public knowledge when she fell foul of the law in April 1941: she was charged with illegally importing rationed meat from Ireland. She had done so through her sister Gladys at Ballykilty. Her argument that the meat did not qualify as rationed goods did not persuade the Bench, and she was fined £2 (about £120 today). If she had imported canned meat, she would have been in the clear: this was not rationed, an anomaly that baffled the magistrates. In any event, the Chair of the bench, one Mr P. Browning, was moved to remark that it was not a bad case. No doubt that was some consolation.

Fussinger's parting remark took on extra but, as the family acknowledged, unwarranted import on April 25, 1942, three days after Wason's 18th birthday. On this night, Bath was on the receiving end of one of the Luftwaffe's Baedeker Raids. These were so called, by both sides, after the German travel guides of the time, and were deliberately targeted at historic towns and cities with little or no military significance but great cultural value: "We have chosen as targets the most beautiful places in England", crowed a Nazi radio broadcast the following week. The aim was explicitly to demoralise the civilian population of Britain. The raids were initially mounted in retaliation for the Royal Air Force's (RAF) almost total devastation of the historic German towns of Lübeck and later Rostock, with their huge stock of ancient wooden buildings (something of which the chief of the RAF, Sir Arthur 'Bomber' Harris, was well aware; indeed, that was the reason these towns were targeted), which alarmed the Nazi high command. This destruction in itself was the result of a strategic shift by the British from precision bombing of military targets, which had not proved effective, to what was called area bombing: laying waste to whole districts in which notable targets were contained, along with their civilian populations. The Luftwaffe had already used such tactics, but the RAF area campaign, deploying a new generation of heavy bombers, was proving much more destructive than theirs, as Lübeck and Rostock showed; much German air power had in any case been redirected eastwards, following Hitler's opening of the second front against the Soviet Union the previous June.

Bath was the second picturesque English city to be attacked, following Exeter on the two nights before; York, Norwich and Canterbury would follow in this first wave of Baedeker raids, and although the raids lessened in intensity, towns and cities with more cultural than military significance would continue to be hit until well into 1944.

On the night of April 25, 1942, Bath was all but defenceless, as Exeter had been, and the bombers did their work with impunity and without losses. They came in waves, and in the second wave not only dropped bombs, but descended to rooftop height and strafed the streets. During the first wave, Wason and his mother sheltered in a ditch on the edge of the nearby Victoria Park, along with one of their temporary staff, an Irish maid called Mary. The Archdeacon and his wife came and joined them in the ditch, while bombs fell all around and terrified them all. Monier Wason stayed in the house, and steadied his nerves with whisky. In the morning, Grandmother Terrington, at her nursing home, asked if there had been a thunderstorm during the night.

The Luftwaffe had not finished with Bath: they returned on the following night, and the Wasons, with Mary again and this time including Monier, found a ditch to shelter in on Weston Fields, a short distance from the house. Mary had brought a silver meat-cover, which she used as a helmet; when she took it off, she saw that the fires and flashes were reflected in its shine. "Oh, isn't it pretty!" she remarked. Wason saw the first aircraft drop a stick of bombs on a cottage, killing everyone inside; it then turned and machine-gunned the country roads. Over 400 people in Bath were killed in these raids, and the destruction was still visible a decade later, as photos taken in the 1950s attest (see Figure 3.1). On returning to Grafton Lodge after the All Clear siren, they found it had not been hit, but some of the other houses in the street had been, and their friends, Admiral and Mrs Bevis, were trapped in one of them; they were eventually rescued. You can see the traces of the damage in Weston Road today, where incongruous modern buildings now replace those destroyed in the War.

The Baedeker Raids as a whole in fact destroyed mainly domestic buildings, some 50,000 of them during the course of the War; remarkably, Bath Abbey and similar monuments such as the cathedrals of Exeter, Norwich, York and Canterbury survived with only minor grazes at worst. They were well protected by fire marshals, so only a direct hit from a high explosive could have done for them. Coventry's medieval St Michael's Cathedral was not so lucky, of course, sustaining just such a hit and being left as a burned-out shell, although Coventry was not a Baedeker target, being a major industrial centre, and was bombed earlier, in November 1940. The medieval streets and buildings in Coventry's old centre did not survive either, although the war only finished off what had already been partly cleared by pre-war planners. It is a common myth in Britain that post-war planners simply completed what the Luftwaffe started; sometimes, it was the other way round. Other Baedeker cities, including Bath, were similarly disfigured by

**FIGURE 3.1**   Bath in 1958, still showing war damage. Photo by Ben Brooksbank. From Wikipedia, CC as Fig. 2.1.

British as well as German hands; the common factor post-war was an obsession with cars and traffic management, as well as the more laudable aim of slum clearance and new housing. Only the burghers of York seem to have realised what they had and kept planning damage low.

## Private's progress

Later in 1942, Wason enlisted in the armed forces, without waiting to be called up. He had been thinking of going into medicine, though how he was to gain entry to a medical degree with his poor educational record was uncertain, to say the least. The War put paid to that aspiration in any case. He felt the need to make a contribution to what most already thought was a just war, even though the Holocaust was not yet widely known about. He may also have been spurred by hints that he might not have seemed robust enough for service life: the organist at Bath Abbey, a family friend, whose own son had volunteered, had said as much, as Wason's mother related to him with "evident pleasure". Upon turning up for his initial medical examination, among a large assorted group of fellow volunteers, he was seen by none other than 'Old Fullo', Dr Dunen, who had delivered baby Peter, 'another little soldier', 18.5 years earlier. Wason opted for the Army, and the doctor suggested he might like to stay behind with the big guns (hinting again at a lack of confidence in Wason's fitness for front-line service). Perhaps recalling his earlier experience when his cousin Bindon Blood had had him fire a shotgun, scaring him witless in the process, Wason declared that he didn't like bangs and should go wherever he could be most useful. He was aware of the prospect of psychological tests, and was already fascinated by them.

He began his war service as a private (Figure 3.2), in a training centre at Nelson Barracks in Norwich – one of the Baedeker cities, damaged earlier in the year. Passing through London on the way there, he bought his first Dunhill's pipe; the first of many. It cost him 25 shillings (£1.25), about £70 in present values. Pipe-smoking would come to be a source of comfort in what was about to happen to him, and for the rest of his life thereafter. It was at Nelson Barracks that Wason was struck by the contrast between his present situation and his previous universe of boarding schools, grand houses, noble families and servants. Apart from these servants, he had never had much to do with working people before, let alone lived among them, and was taken aback by the revelations that came with doing so. They sent part of their Army pay home; he received an allowance from his father. They swore profusely, and he found communication with these "very rough" people difficult, at first.

He and his fellow public school boys were conscious of the class difference, so tended to detach themselves, and to regard the 'common' soldiers with something like disdain. It seemed to be up to these 'others' to break down the social barriers, which they tried to do. These men went out of their way to help each other, something that astonished Wason: he had simply never been taught this kind of selflessness. They even helped him; when assigned an especially physically demanding job, an older soldier took over, saying "That's no job for you, mate, let me do it for you". He was both touched by and interested in this behaviour: it is his first recorded psychological observation. He made them laugh when, having to fire a rifle, he succumbed to his well-established fear of bangs and shut his eyes – but scored a bulls-eye anyway. When his rifle jammed and he called out "oh, Sergeant", he was greeted by laughter and mickey-taking cries of "oooh Sergeant". The barriers were beginning to come down. Mickey-taking – gentle mockery – was then and is still a social signal in Britain: you have to show you can take it as well as dish it out, and if you do, you're 'in'.

At one time, he got a call from the training centre's padre, who had received a letter from Wason's old chess opponent, the Archdeacon of Bath, suggesting he receive holy communion. He did so, once only, in the company of a single other

**FIGURE 3.2** Officer-Cadet Wason in uniform. Courtesy of Armorer Wason.

soldier. The same padre once addressed the soldiers, concluding with "Never forget that the greatest thing next to the Church of Christ is the British Empire". This patently failed in its intended inspirational message, judging by the faces of the assembled troops.

The psychological tests which so interested Wason, together with interviews, led to his being recommended as a suitable candidate for the RAC. "You're obviously going to be an officer", said his sergeant at a farewell drink, and Wason was transferred to the notoriously tough (then and now) Catterick Camp in Yorkshire, the British Army's largest garrison, just before Christmas 1942. Wason was now a trooper rather than a private, in a squadron rather than a platoon, distinctions which are clear in the military and cloudy everywhere else. Conditions were Spartan, and freezing cold, but Wason liked the nearby town of Richmond, an ancient market town with a Norman castle, which might have been a Baedeker target but never was. He also enjoyed some of the exercises; long marches were enlivened by reciting poetry to himself, something he enjoyed doing all his life. He learned to drive, and command, a Sherman tank.

He gravitated to a canteen called the Zetland, run by the Church Army, and there started finding people to play chess with. Two of the canteen's other habitués, one a non-commissioned officer and one from the Church Army, were players, and recruited him for a match against the Pioneer Corps. This was a non-combatant, behind-the-lines body of men, concerned with logistical and engineering matters and general support for the front-line troops, an indispensable part of any army. Because they did not bear arms, so-called enemy aliens – a category that would have included Grandmother Terrington's butler, Fussinger – were allowed to serve, and in time, this came to include a large number of liberated Germans and Austrians, especially Jews. Wason was caught out by this when it came to the chess match. He, along with, one suspects, most of the regular army, looked down on the Pioneer Corps as menials, and so he expected an easy ride. But when their team arrived, several were carrying wooden chessboards, so they were clearly serious players, and they turned out to be Czech intellectuals. Their country had, in the eyes of many, been betrayed by the Allies before war broke out and ceded to Hitler, as part of the 'appeasement' process, and so these people were part of the expatriate resistance movement. Wason suspected that they had not been allowed a combatant role because of communist sympathies. One of them was a champion player, later killed on bomb disposal duty in England. The Pioneer Corps team of ringers duly thrashed Wason's team, winning every game.

In the Spring, after his 19th birthday, Wason was looking to move on. He saw a notice on the regimental bulletin board inviting applications to join the Royal Electrical and Mechanical Engineers (REME). He applied, and was sent for an interview in Leeds, conducted by senior officers from across the Services. The first question came from a senior Naval officer, and gives us some idea of how these things went when you were from the right background:

> Are you any relation to Admiral Wason?
> Yes sir, he is my uncle.
> Apart from chess, I see you are interested in poetry.
> Yes sir: modern poetry.

Wason recalled this kind of exchange in later life with a mixture of amusement and contempt for the influence of privilege in upper-class life. Such social lubricant did not work on this occasion, in fact: he was not selected for the REME. He, therefore, did what had been expected of him, and sought a commission in the Royal Armoured Corps (RAC). The interview that followed, conducted by his commanding officer, Lieutenant-Colonel Fanshawe, had a familiar ring:

> Are you related to General Wason?
> Yes sir, he is my cousin.
> If you become as good a soldier as General Wason, you won't be doing badly.

It is worth taking a moment to consider these two relatives, since we have not come across them to this point, and they enrich the flavour of Wason's extraordinary family. Admiral Wason was Rear Admiral Cathcart Romer Wason, born in 1874 in Scotland, died 1941 in Somerset. He served as a captain in the Royal Navy in the First World War, in the Persian Gulf, and was decorated twice for gallantry. Upon retirement, he returned to his estate in Wason's home county of Somerset, becoming a magistrate and going into business. But he is notable for something else entirely: for fathering Cathcart Roland (Roly) Wason (1907–1998).

Roly, Peter Wason's first cousin, was another almost fantastical character, perhaps the richest fruit on the whole tree (along with Colonel Blood, the almost successful thief of the Crown Jewels). After Rugby School, where despite being academically undistinguished he became head boy, he graduated from Cambridge with a first class honours degree, with distinction, in classics and ancient history. At the age of 24, he was appointed Professor of Archaeology ('professor' is not such an exalted title in North America as it is in Britain, where 'lecturer' would be used) at the University of Toronto, Canada, leaving after just a year to take up a lectureship at the University of Edinburgh; his stay there was even shorter. By this time, he was disillusioned with the educational system and a committed Marxist, although, unlike a later set of Cambridge radicals, he did not throw in his lot with the Soviet Union. Rather, after a series of extensive travels across Europe in exotic cars (they included a Bugatti) with his wife Margherita (with whom he had eloped to Gretna Green, and who would be worthy of a portrait in her own right), he gave up the academic world and became an expert lens grinder in Glasgow. Along the way, having become involved in running the local Labour Party, he rejected offers of candidacy as an MP, viewing the process as corrupt. He gave well-attended lectures to his fellow-workers and others on music and history.

Leaving Glasgow, he tried, and failed at, fruit farming in Somerset (he had inherited his father's estate), and then moved in the 1950s to the heavy industrial area of North-East England, as works manager in an engineering firm. When that firm went under, he and his wife became, of all things, bus conductors in Hartlepool. This is a now extinct species of worker whose task was to collect fares and control the stopping and starting of buses by ringing bells, in the days before driver-only-operated buses. He then graduated to be a bus driver, and wrote a regular column on his experiences for *The Guardian*, called, with admirable directness, *Bus Driver*. These were followed by a book, *Busman's View*, its flyleaf describes Roly, at the start of this part of what can only be loosely be called a career, as "a middle-aged unemployable, stranded with his wife and small children in a small provincial town" and with a mild disability. And that is just about all the biographical information the book contains, apart from a dismissive passing note about his education.

After their spell on the buses, Roly and Margherita spent the last years of their working lives as schoolteachers before retiring to Somerset. He once invited the London committee of the Communist Party there for their annual picnic. They were met by a banner hung across the street reading:

> WE, IN BRIDGWATER, SOMERSET, FEAR GOD AND HONOUR THE KING. DOWN WITH COMMUNISM.

Margherita died in 1992 and Roly, having acquired his first computer and begun to communicate with the world via the internet on his 90th birthday, died in 1998.

General Wason, the other relative, invoked by Wason's commanding officer, was Major-General Sydney Rigby Wason (1887–1969), and was in fact Monier Wason's first cousin, hence Wason's second cousin. As the interviewing officer had said, he was indeed a soldier of some renown. He was a decorated officer (a captain) in the Royal Artillery in the First World War: he was awarded the Military Cross (and two bars) for conspicuous gallantry in leading raiding parties across no man's land, and for conducting reconnaissance observations while under fire. He ascended to Brigadier at the Larkhill School of Artillery on Salisbury Plain between the wars. At the outbreak of the second war in September 1939, he was part of the British Expeditionary Force (BEF) which was deployed to France and which met disaster at Dunkirk in the Spring of 1940. The famous evacuation, spun in Parliament by Winston Churchill as a "miracle of deliverance" and celebrated in Britain to this day, began on May 26th, but Gen. Wason did not immediately leave. Rather, on that day he assumed command of forces on the southern flank of the BEF while its previous commander, Lt Gen. Adam, moved to secure its eastern perimeter. He was

Mentioned in Despatches for this. Back in London, now in a desk job at the War Office, he was dismissed by Churchill because he objected to women serving in anti-aircraft batteries. The Prime Minister may not have been making a feminist point; his own daughter was one such, so Churchill seems to have taken Sydney Wason's argument as a personal slight. General Wason did not even receive the compensation of a knighthood, an unusual snub for someone of his rank and record.

# 4

# SERVICE

## Training days

Wason attended a War Office Selection Board over a weekend, and reported being exhilarated by the experience. This was because of the use of psychological tests and techniques, with which he had already developed a fascination. They included Murray and Morgan's Thematic Apperception Test (TAT) and Raven's Progressive Matrices, an intelligence test; the leaderless group exercises were based on the theories of another psychologist, Kurt Lewin. The TAT is a psychoanalytically based 'projective' test in which people have to give their interpretations, following structured instructions, of ambiguous, intriguing pictures. The assumption is that doing so will reveal unconscious thoughts and motivations, just as talking to an analyst is supposed to do. This approach to psychology, deriving ultimately from Sigmund Freud ('psychoanalysis' is the term for Freudian psychotherapy), would turn out to have a profound effect on Wason's own thinking, and to his approach to psychological research when that became his metier, although he was not uncritical of Freudian theory.

Part of the selection process involved interviews, one by an army psychiatrist with the rank of Major, and one by the chair of the selection board. The psychiatrist was interested, inevitably, in Wason's childhood, and finally asked him whether he had any questions. Wason asked him what the difference was between a psychiatrist and a psychologist, a question that every member of each profession must get used to answering. This impressed the psychiatrist, who told Wason – despite not having seen any of the test results – that he was the most intelligent candidate the board had seen. Such is the power of impression formation, as social psychologists call it. It bedevils personnel selection even now, leading to frequent but neglected calls for less emphasis on interviews. He was also impressed, as others had been, by Wason's fondness for chess, despite the fact that Wason was not, at that stage, a serious competitive player. The chairman, a friendly type, asked him which two books he would take with him on a long march, and when Wason replied Plato's *Republic* and Thomas a Kempis's *Imitation of Christ*, he slapped himself on the knee and shouted "Capital!"

Wason was thus selected for officer training. He himself expressed puzzlement at this, and that puzzlement is revealing. We can ask how someone not from his – and his interviewers' – cultural and social background would have fared in this situation: would their answers have warmed the panel's hearts, as Wason's so clearly did? Would success at the psychological tests have outweighed a failure to reveal yourself in the interviews as 'one of us'? We cannot know for sure, of course, but we can have a strong suspicion. Are things different today? Again, without sending people through the process as a kind of mystery shopper, it is hard to tell, although one wonders why the privileged would willingly give up their privileges, and the Sandhurst accent is regularly heard today when senior military officers give media interviews. Wason's reaction to this experience, combined with his earlier interviews with military commanders, evolved into long-term reflection on class and the privilege his background had conferred on him.

Wason's answers reveal too that he was far from being the hopeless educational case that his accounts of his schooldays might lead us to imagine. Despite his litany of educational failure, he had an inner self-confidence about learning. He was an avid and enquiring consumer of books – these are impressive leisure reading choices for someone of 19 – and perhaps his experience of English teaching at Stowe, and the inspiration provided by masters who were themselves genuine literary scholars and authors, had fuelled a hunger for learning, which books, along with chess and psychology, helped to satisfy. He had also been on a spiritual search as well, as shown by his dissatisfaction with the Christianity he had been exposed to at home and school hitherto (he wrote 'Catholic poetry' as a teenager); the mere fact that he felt this dissatisfaction attests to someone who was already thinking deeply about, to use a rather weighted word, the soul. So a lot of his reading was on this topic; he was not a one for pulp fiction or romances, although he did read Conan Doyle and the Empire tales of George Henty and his like. And it is not too great a step from thinking about the soul to thinking about the mind.

Leaving Catterick Camp late in 1943, Wason found himself on the path to the Royal Armoured Corps' (RAC) Officer Cadet Training Unit (OCTU) at Sandhurst, on the Surrey-Berkshire border near Camberley. Officer training is a function still performed there, at what is now known as the Royal Military Academy. First, he had to pass through the Pre-OCTU unit at Blackdown, also in Surrey. There he learned drill, under the supervision of non-commissioned officers (NCOs) from the Brigade of Guards (Wason respectfully remembered Sgt McAlpine, with his penetrating gaze) and also how to ride a motorcycle, which he took to readily. There was more tank-driving as well, but he could not get to grips with driving an Army lorry, and never acquired a car driving licence, then or later. He was now mixing routinely with people from outside his former social range, and recalled two close friends at Blackdown: Taffy Giniver, "a large, amiable ex-policeman from South Wales", and Jake Waters, whose politics were strongly left-wing. He was impressed with Waters, regarding him as clear officer material owing to a natural presence, and socialised with him and his girlfriend, also a left-winger, when away from the base. Wason and Waters met again after leaving, firstly during the forthcoming Normandy campaign, and then by chance at Charing Cross Station in London after the War. And that seems to have been that as far as their relationship was concerned; as with his friends from school, he seems not to have known how to keep up with them after their paths diverged.

On to Sandhurst. The regime there was tougher than at Blackwood, tougher even than Catterick, although now, since they were officially officers, albeit in training, their NCO instructors had to call them 'sir'. These professional soldiers were, in the time-honoured phrase, tough but fair. 'Losing your name' was part of the process of military socialisation:

What's your name, sir?
Officer-cadet Wason, sir.
Well, you've lost it.

No place for individualism in the army, especially an army at war. There was more drill, and once again Wason quite enjoyed it; he found ways to wheedle himself out of parts that he dreaded, such as jumping over a gap in a broken bridge high off the ground: telling the sergeant that he had already done it seemed to work, though one wonders how. Perhaps the sergeants knew a lost cause when they saw one. Battle training in Snowdonia followed, under live fire from trained marksmen. They heard that only one officer-cadet had been killed by it. This was supposed to be reassuring, presumably. Wason had to lead a night march with map and compass, and did so without mishap. Group solidarity, promoted by shared challenge and a sense of common purpose, assured that they returned to Sandhurst in good spirits.

The period of traineeship was coming to an end, this being marked by the passing-out parade, attended by family, with the band playing Auld Lang Syne and the adjutant parading around on a white charger. At the end of the ceremony, the King's Commission having been conferred on him, Wason was now, at the age of 19, a Second Lieutenant in the RAC; some of the others went on to join other regiments. He and his comrades were saluted by the "famous and fearsome" Regimental Sergeant-Major, who the day before would have been bawling orders at them; now, he was outranked by Wason and the other fledgling officers. Wason and his mother, who had been at the parade, stayed with a relative in Camberley before going back to Grafton Lodge; he had a week's leave. He spent a good part of it back in the bookshop in Bristol where he sought out his books on mysticism, poetry and chess.

## On the march

As 1944 came around, Wason was posted to the 53rd Training Regiment of the RAC in Dorset, familiar ground for him from the holidays spent at Hillcrest, the prep school hired by his Aunt Minna in the 1930s. It was his own 'phoney war': not much happening, undemanding duties and use of the officers' mess, which was to the common soldiers' canteen what business class is to economy. One of these duties was censoring the troops' mail; Wason found little worth wielding the blue pencil for, and was amused by the oft-used clichés, such as 'Well, darling, I must end this epistle now': they jarred against his love for good writing. He rode an army motorcycle around the county, visiting old haunts such as the school at Swanage that his Aunt Minna used to hire for holidays, and new ones such as, naturally, the bookshops of Bournemouth. He bought mainly chess books, and was deepening his knowledge of the game, studying the games of master players, learning the finer points of chess theory and attempting to improve his own play in matches. He discovered the regimental chess club. He was also back in the hands of servants again, having been assigned an elderly batman and later a young bat-woman from the ATS (the Auxiliary Territorial Service, a women's company in the Army, similar in function to the Pioneer Corps).

All the time, there was the background awareness that the Allied invasion of Europe would be coming soon. The waiting RAC troops at the Dorset camp did get the occasional explicit reminder. Once, when Wason was Officer of the Watch, a worried-looking sergeant told him about some butterfly bombs, hanging in the trees. These were vicious little anti-personnel devices, an early type of cluster bomb, dropped en masse in large containers: their outer casing when it opened resembled a pair of wings. They could be fitted with a time fuse or a booby-trap fuse that would activate if the device was handled; the sergeant was obviously aware of their reputation. They caused numerous civilian casualties, especially as the Nazi forces retreated after the D-Day landings, and indeed con-tinued to do so, as cluster weapons still do, long after hostilities had ceased. These ones must have been dropped by a German plane. On another occasion, there was an air raid on the camp, just after the general officer commanding the RAC, Maj-Gen. Fanshawe (the one who had recalled Gen. Wason) had visited. Coincidence, or a tribute to the German intelligence operation? No-one was quite sure.

The Allied operation to liberate Europe stopped being impending on June 6, 1944: D-Day. Wason was wakened by the roar of planes passing overhead, which lasted the whole day. The Normandy bridgehead, they learned from the radio, had been established, and the group of Second Lieutenants wondered when they would be on the move, and what part they would play. It was at least ten days before Wason found out. They were transferred to Colchester, Essex and told to send their service dress (they would now be in battledress) and personal items home. Wason kept two chess books and the collected verse of Yeats to take with him to France. They wrote letters home, and managed to get them sent by the unlikely means of passing them through the carriage windows (you couldn't do that now: train windows no longer open) to the driver of a train that was moving slowly alongside theirs. It worked: Wason's mother later confirmed that she had received hers.

The train took them to the Channel port of Newhaven, and they marched from the station to the docks singing martial songs. A band played, a singer sang; women waved handkerchiefs at them from windows as they marched past. A V1 flying bomb passed overhead, but its engine did not cut out (which was when the thing would plunge to earth and explode); as it was a 'revenge weapon' (the V in its name, and that of the even more terrifying V2 rocket, stood for Vergeltung: vengeance) it was probably heading for London. Hours passed and then they marched on to a landing craft and headed out to sea. They were lucky: it was a calm and uneventful crossing, with no opposition, two things that could not have been said for the first wave on June 6th. Wason watched the outline of Beachy Head receding behind them. Their craft was one of hundreds, spread out over the Channel literally as far as the eye could see. It was a sight which imprinted itself on his memory. They landed at Gold beach, the central of the five landing sites, and the concern entirely of the British Army, backed up by Dutch and Polish elements. The army's main objective was the seizure of Bayeux and the securing of the Caen-Bayeux road. It had been intended to accomplish the former on the first day, but Bayeux did not fall to the Allies until the second, when a British unit entered the town unopposed, the Wehrmacht having made a strategic withdrawal. It was thus spared the damage that other towns and villages suffered.

After some protracted and what felt like aimless marching, Wason's company encamped in a field just outside Bayeux, and another little phoney war period ensued. It was here that he ran into Jake Waters again, and swapped his Yeats for Waters' copy of the *Faber Book of Modern Verse*. The collection of newly commissioned officers began to erode, as each day one or two would be assigned as troop commanders, a troop in this case consisting of three tanks. Wason was sceptical of the usefulness of the tank training he had experienced at Sandhurst: it seemed to have been designed for North Africa rather than Northern France. In any case, when his turn came, it was not to be for a front-line role, but as a liaison officer to the Eighth Armoured Brigade, a role that Wason dismissed as that of a "glorified office-boy". Were there doubts once again about his suitability for a combat role, or was it simply that he was next in line? Parsimony favours the latter but no-one, least of all Wason himself, would have been surprised by the former.

His duties involved listening to the radio, sending and receiving in code, and taking information to and from the headquarters of the three regiments that comprised the Eighth Armoured Brigade, and Divisional HQ, to help the commanders develop a picture – a mental model as modern psychologists would call it – of the disposition of allied and enemy forces. He was given a scout car with a driver to enable him to shuttle between these various parties. Wason thought that the Brigadier, Errol Prior-Palmer, was becoming irritated by his ineptitude. Once, while visiting one of the regimental HQs, his car had to traverse a crossroads which was under shellfire. He told his driver to take it as fast as possible to minimise the chances of being hit. They nearly were, and took shelter in a ditch. A military policeman told him angrily that his approach had thrown up a cloud of dust which served only to pinpoint them as a target; he should have taken it slowly. He had been lucky. Another time, having misread a map, Wason and his driver realised they were heading for enemy lines, something which surprised a British soldier taking cover. One of his friends did a similar thing, but in his case, the soldier was German. He seems to have got away with it.

The near-miss had killed a cow; the farmer came out and said, mournfully, "C'est la guerre". You can almost see the shrug. Dead cows, blown up like balloons and with their legs in the air, were everywhere, and the stink of death was too. There was the occasional sight, and smell, of human death as well, although Wason had missed the fierce fighting and mass casualties that had occurred here a few days before. In a recently recaptured village, he witnessed something that became common and notorious as France was liberated: the humiliating of two women, by having their heads shaved in public, presumably because they had had relationships with German soldiers. The women ran away in tears, to the jeering of the crowd, and the local priest turned to Wason and shrugged. C'est la guerre, encore.

This was all in the area adjacent to the Normandy bridgehead, and it was not for some weeks that they broke out and began the advance through France in pursuit of the main force and the retreating Wehrmacht. They were largely unopposed, and greeted joyfully by the local population, who offered them flowers and wine whenever they stopped. One place where the Germans did make a stand became known as the Falaise Pocket; the retreating army was battered from the air as well as on the ground, and thousands died, along with the farm animals, and a great many horses in harness. When Wason's troop passed through, even though the fighting had ceased, progress was slow. It was a hot August day; the smell was appalling, and everyone held handkerchiefs, and in some cases gasmasks, to their faces. Many of Wason's comrades, but not he himself, to his regret, 'liberated' the prized Luger pistol from fallen German soldiers; they all acknowledged its superiority to their standard issue Smith & Wesson, although ammunition for it was scarce.

The company crossed the Seine at Vernon, a pretty town with an ancient castle and an arched bridge (see Figure 4.1): on the other side, just a few miles away, is Monet's house and garden at Giverny, which bears no mark from the war. Vernon, on the contrary, is still visibly scarred. Progress was now rapid. US forces had entered Paris on August 24th, following an uprising of the Free French, and accepted the surrender of the German garrison the following day. On September 3rd, the fifth anniversary of Britain's declaration of war, Wason, now with the Guards Armoured Division, entered Brussels. Once again, there were scenes of wild jubilation, which went on for three days or more; some who had seen both thought that the crowds were even more jubilant than those in Paris. The people must settle down soon, said a local man to Wason. Wason had a few days of leave in Brussels before being stationed at Leopoldsburg, not far from the Dutch border, south of Eindhoven. This was where the disastrous airborne-led raid on Arnhem, codenamed Operation Market Garden, was co-ordinated. It was carried out during

**FIGURE 4.1**    The bridge over the Seine at Vernon today, looking towards the east bank. Photo by K. Manktelow

the week beginning September 17th, its aim being to capture a series of bridges over the Rhine. Although some were captured (some were destroyed) and important towns such as Eindhoven and Nijmegen were liberated, the operation foundered at the last bridge, at Arnhem – the infamous 'bridge too far'. Wason was in the area at the time, but not involved in the action; once again, he was at Brigade HQ, in Nijmegen, not on the front line. This inability to do anything for the beleaguered paratroops upset Wason, and he would recall this frustration sorrowfully for years afterwards. Although the HQ was attacked from the air and by shellfire, Wason emerged unscathed. He and another officer were billeted in a house occupied by two women. He played chess with one of them, quite a good player, he recalled. One of the women said that they would like to sleep with the two young British men, but that their husbands would not like it. Wason did not recollect his reply, and gave no clue as to what happened next. Nothing, I suspect. In any event, it became another humorous, self-deprecating story that Wason would delight in retelling.

The British advance on Germany had been stalled by the debacle at Arnhem, and the company settled in for the winter in an area near Nijmegen between the rivers Waal and Rhine known as the Island, in an atmosphere of gloom. Another phoney war period began. Wason sent to Dunhill's in London for a new pipe, one with a large bowl, paying 45 shillings for it (£2.25 – today, the same model retails at £550). He was becoming weighed down by anxiety about his own lack of aptitude for the tasks faced by a soldier in wartime. His commander, Brig. Prior-Palmer, told him "We all like you, Wason, but you've got no *nous*", and reiterated that he would be reluctant to give him a troop command. Far from being disappointing, this was reassuring to him, and a source of more humorous recollections in later life. In November, he was to be sent to the port of Ostend, probably to go back to England, to a role more suited to his abilities, although it was not made clear what this would be. Perhaps someone had thought him a suitable candidate for the code-breaking enterprise at Bletchley Park: proficient chess-players were among the types sought after for this work. This would not have been divulged to him or his superiors as such, of course, secrecy being a prime concern. He would simply have been recalled home. In any case, he never found out the reason for his transfer.

### For you, Tommy...

A jeep arrived to take him to Ostend, driven by a sergeant whom Wason did not know, a nice man but, as quickly became apparent, a terrible driver. Early in the trip, he almost drove into a wall, and if Wason had been able to drive, he would have taken the wheel; his failure to learn back at training camp had returned to haunt him. As they were entering Turnhout, after quite a long drive, about 60 miles (95 Km), the sergeant swerved on to the wrong side of the road, perhaps forgetting that he was not in England, and going quite quickly, crashed head-on into a US Army truck. Wason was trapped in the jeep; his kneecaps were smashed and both femurs were broken, and he also had head injuries, though less serious. "Let's get this guy fixed up", said an American voice, and Wason was lifted on to the road, in great pain; this action, he was convinced, saved his life. The sergeant seemed to have got off lightly and merely looked shocked. Wason never saw him again. A Royal Army Medical Corps officer appeared and injected Wason with penicillin, fixing after he had done so a yellow label to his tunic with PEN written on it; a vivid memory. A monk offered, and Wason gladly accepted, Extreme Unction, one of the Last Rites, and the crowd of soldiers around him became visibly impatient. "You've got a real Blighty one there sir", one said; a wartime expression denoting an injury serious enough to get you sent home, to Blighty (military slang for England, deriving from Urdu and the days of the Raj). An army ambulance arrived and he was taken away, drowsy and free of the pain; he must have been given something else, probably morphine, in addition to the penicillin. He fell into unconsciousness.

When he came round, he was in a military hospital in Antwerp. He underwent an emergency operation, and woke to find his whole lower body in plaster. Catheterised, he spent the night "in some discomfort", which may be putting it mildly. A Canadian padre appeared and dispensed cigarettes to the patients, but no pipe tobacco, to Wason's chagrin: his new, expensive Dunhill pipe had, miraculously, survived the crash, although two others were destroyed. The next day, he was stretchered on to a plane and flown, slowly and bumpily, to Swindon, where he was met by some Queen Alexandra nurses and put on a train, in a first-class compartment, and taken to Nottingham, to the City Hospital, where he would spend the next few months in traction, immobile. He was well cared for there, and, in common with many young men who found themselves in hospital as wounded servicemen, he fell in love with one of the nurses. Indeed, he carried a photo of her in his wallet for the rest of his life; there is no name on it.

On the train trip to Nottingham, the pain had come back, and the analgesia he was given was not as effective as what he had been given at the field hospital in Antwerp. Despite that, he was guiltily euphoric: for Peter Wason, the war was over. Not that it ever would be, entirely: the whole tenor of his life would now be different, very different from that of the athletic youth who had fenced for his school, played tennis in Ireland while Chamberlain spoke gravely to the nation, and played football against an Ethiopian prince: he would be on analgesia, and suffer varying degrees of infirmity, for the rest of his days, a near 60-year span. He never fully recovered.

Within six months, he had exchanged his crutches for a stick, something else that would remain a permanent fixture for him. He was not yet 21. As his birthday approached, he was taken on a Red Cross train from Nottingham to Bath, and driven in an ambulance through the city's Victoria Park, where he had played as a child, arriving at Grafton Lodge in time for tea. In Bath, he was treated at the Royal United Hospital and then at a nearby orthopaedic cottage hospital, and it was there that he had his 21st birthday. Ethel, the family's old cook, and the nurses at the hospital both made him cakes, and they went to the pub in the evening. Two weeks later, while he was still a patient, it was VE Day.

A few weeks after that, he found himself back at Ballykilty, his favourite place on earth and the best possible one for further recuperation, of body and soul. He was there when the general election result was announced, in July, the one that de-livered the first ever majority Labour government, under Clement Attlee, in one of the greatest British electoral landslides ever recorded: Labour increased its re-presentation from 154 seats at the previous election, in 1935, to 393, while Winston Churchill's party, the Conservatives, collapsed from 386 seats to 189. The Liberals and Liberal Nationals (the Liberal Party, home to so many of Wason's family predecessors, had split in 1931, thus ensuring an exclusion from government that would last nearly 80 years) fell from 54 seats between them to 23, with both party leaders losing theirs. This turn of events lifted Wason's mood considerably, since he had become a socialist, partly as a result of his experience of the war and of the people he had served with. But he kept his elation to himself, since everyone else in Uncle Fitz's household was shocked and saddened by Churchill's unseating, and could not understand the electorate's apparent ingratitude. In fact, the population were far from ungrateful to Churchill for his heroic role in leading the wartime coalition government and the nation; it was just that they also had vivid memories of life before the War, in the 1930s, a period of worldwide political turmoil, economic depression and mass unemployment. The Conservatives had been in power then, and the people judged that they were not best placed to lead the country into the new postwar world. There was a more collectivist spirit abroad.

Wason was still in the Army at this stage, but in November 1945, the War now well and truly over (VJ Day, the end of the war in Asia, had been in August), he was asked to attend the Army Medical Board for assessment. He was honourably discharged after almost exactly three years' service and given ten years to recover, supported by what he recognised was a generous disability pension, his sense of self and his worldview bent into radically different shapes.

"Do you like playing golf?" asked the Medical Officer.

"No," said Wason, "But I want to go to Oxford."

# 5

# THE MOST IMPORTANT MOMENT

## Going to Oxford

"I want to go to Oxford". On the face of it, this looked more like a fantasy than a realistic aspiration. As Wason himself was only too ready to admit, his educational experience had, almost from first to last, been a story of constant and unalloyed failure. He had barely scraped through his common entrance exam to get to Stowe, following his 'featherbrain' years at the hellish Kingwell Hall. He barely scraped through again when it came to his matriculation from Stowe, needing the assistance of a crammer college, and the solace of its picturesque neighbouring Catholic church, to secure the results needed for progression to higher education. Despite this constant stream of setbacks, however, he never doubted that he had a good intellect. His interests were pursued vigorously and he became deeply knowledgeable about them. He also was not impressed by many of those who tried to teach and instruct him, at school and in the Army, and so was not damaged by their low opinions of his abilities.

Although it seems strange to say it, he had an enormous stroke of luck when the Second World War intervened. Of course, it ended painfully for him; indeed, it left him an invalid, and not many people would agree to having to sustain serious physical injury in order to secure a place at university. It seems certain, however, that without his experience of the War, and its personal outcome, he would have needed something like the galvanising effect that his mother's promise of an exciting present had had on his prep school performance to get any further in his education. And it is far from clear what that could have been. Some currents were now, though, running in his favour. He had, for one thing, been to Sandhurst and found some success there, which would certainly figure in his credit column. He had been a commissioned officer for most of his three years in the Army and had seen action, albeit mainly at a distance. He had been exposed to a wider sample of humanity than he had encountered before, and to a range of experiences that those who have not had them can barely imagine. Besides which he was far from being uneducated; it was just that he was almost entirely self-educated. He was interested in, and could rouse himself to study, only that which was interesting to him; anything that did not engage his passion he simply tuned out of, not bothering, as most people would, to do just enough to get by and get the job done. He needed pressure, or the prospect of immediate reward, to engage with topics that did not immediately fire his passions.

Anything that did engage him, on the contrary, would engage him for hours, for years – for life. Hence, his burgeoning skill at, and knowledge of, chess: he not only played, but since boyhood had read extensively about the game, and delighted in thinking about chess problems written down in books (people who write about chess problems in books, newspaper columns or, today, on websites are known as 'problemists'). He took a chess set, and two chess books, with him into the Army, and played whoever would give him a game; this did rebound on him at least once, when he and his team were thrashed by some proper players, the Czechs from the Pioneer Corps. A stinging experience. Besides chess books, he also took works of literature with him, and at least once exchanged one with a comrade; he was by this time very well-read, especially in modern poetry. Indeed, the only teachers he had admired at Stowe had been his English masters, especially John Davenport, the friend of Dylan Thomas who had given Wason that extreme rarity, a complimentary school report. A particular literary favourite was the Irish poet W.B. Yeats, his Irishness being part of the attraction. He had also built up a library of works on mysticism and religion, and was a practising, though not devout, Catholic: it was the aesthetics of the liturgy and the services – and the irritating effect on his mother – that attracted him, rather than any profound faith in God. Finally, perhaps as a byproduct of these other interests, he had discovered a native fascination with psychology, especially Freudian and post-Freudian psychoanalysis, an interest magnified by the use of psychological tests, including the psychoanalytically inspired TAT, in his officer training. He had also begun to be intrigued by aspects of human behaviour such as he had observed among his comrades, with their very different backgrounds and perspectives compared to what he had been used to in his youth.

Thus, he emerged from the Army physically broken, but intellectually fortified. How to turn this unofficial education into something that would pass muster for university entrance? Two factors would aid in this aim. Firstly, as we saw in the case of his interviews when applying for officer training, he had some persuasive attributes as far as the selection process was concerned. One was precisely his extensive literary knowledge, along with his chess proficiency. There is no record of a university admissions interview, but he must have had one: they are still part of the process at Oxford and would have been then too. Another was his social background, which if one needs a label might be called lower-upper class. There was no tradition in his immediate family of university education: neither of his parents, nor his brothers, had been, so Wason's desire to go up may well have been a surprise to them. But most other young men from this part of society would certainly expect to go to university, and not just any university either, but one of the gilded pair, Oxford or Cambridge; the choice between the two was largely down to family tradition, as it was with schools. The academic interviewers, even though less impressionable when it came to cultural knowledge than perhaps senior army officers might have been, and a good deal more knowledgeable about their subjects, would still have recognised someone who, despite what his school reports might have said, clearly had what it took to get on in university life as it was then, both intellectually and socially. There is some suspicion that Uncle Horace, the third Baron Terrington, may have had a hand in oiling these wheels too, although there is no documentary evidence of this. All we can say is that if he had been seen lurking in the background, no-one would have been at all surprised.

There was in addition a purely pragmatic factor which probably clinched for Wason his coveted place at Oxford. He had been honourably discharged from the Army with what he himself recognised as a "generous" disability pension, and allotted ten years to receive it, so he was financially secure in his own right. As an officer who was a wounded war veteran, he was also entitled, under a government scheme, to take a shortened course in an honours subject. Which subject? There was only one in the frame. He therefore enrolled at New College to read for a BA in English, in the New Year of 1946, the start of Hilary term in the Oxford argot. That means he was starting later than the usual October–December first term (Michaelmas), and was also exempted from taking 'mods' exams, interim tests which are usually held at the end of the first year and, although graded and classed, do not contribute towards the final degree assessment.

Despite its name, New College is ancient, having been founded in the late 14th century, originally for the education of priests: their numbers had been more than decimated by the Black Death, which had arrived in England only 30 years before. The plague claimed the lives of over 40% of Oxford's citizens in 1349, and there is no reason to suspect the proportion of the priesthood to succumb would have been any lower. The 'New' comes from the fact that it was the second Oxford college to be dedicated to St Mary. It was the first college in England to be sited around a central quadrangle, a design which has inspired educational institutions around the world ever since. On its edge are cloisters, as you can find in a medieval abbey or cathedral. The College's buildings are extraordinarily beautiful, inside and out, as indeed is its setting, in the centre of, though largely hidden from, the city (Figure 5.1). Although it has expanded over the centuries, it is currently home (they lodge in its buildings) to only just over 700 students. Today, there are both male and female students, but in Wason's time they were all male, as they had been since the College's foundation; women were only admitted in 1979. New College was like most of the older universities and colleges in Britain in this respect: the progress towards women's equality in university education has happened largely within living memory.

If Wason had been awed by his first encounter with Stowe School, he must have been equally impressed when enrolling at New College. He was in many

**FIGURE 5.1**  New College Oxford. From Wikimedia Commons, originally from Flickr by Snapshotsofthepast. Licensed under CC-BY-SA 2.0

ways a different person now, of course: not an 11-year-old boy, but a young man, almost 22, and an invalided war veteran at that, not a naïf straight from school; that was what he had been when he went into the Army. When he arrived, it was not much more than a year since the trauma of his injury and the months spent recuperating, first in hospital in Nottingham and then at his home in Bath and its neighbouring orthopaedic hospital, and in his beloved Ireland. It would still have been fresh in his mind, and the pain in his legs would have given him regular reminders, to keep it there. Awed or not, arriving at Oxford had one particular impact on Wason: a feeling of liberation. "It was not until I got to my universities" (here and when he became an academic in London), he remembered, "that I could really breathe". This is a common feeling among students, of course, away from home and hovering parents for the first time, but it must have been acute in his case, and that of the many officer veterans like him who were taking advantage of the enlightened provision of fast-track degree places for them.

Acute also because Wason was casting off an unusually heavy set of shackles, even setting aside the physical and psychological damage bequeathed him by the sergeant's fateful mistake at Turnhout. Outside a prison or a closed monastic order, there are few more constrained people than a serving soldier, and he had also come from ten years in two boarding schools and a home life where, as a young child, he had a mother whose company he enjoyed only on Tuesdays and a father who, as a practical man, despaired of his youngest son's complete impracticality and kept himself distant from him. No wonder he quickly came to love Oxford.

Liberation was only the half of it, as far as the transformative experience of Oxford was concerned. It was here that he was to meet several of the people who changed his life. The first of these was his tutor, who had perhaps the most profound effect of anyone on his intellectual style. This was Lord David Cecil.

In the parade of extraordinary characters that march through Wason's story, Cecil is somewhere near the head. Edward Christian David Gascoyne-Cecil was a genuine aristocrat – no lower-upper for him – the second son of the fourth Marquess of Salisbury (so the 'Lord' designation was a courtesy title, not a peerage); his mother was the daughter of the Earl of Arran. The third Marquess had been Conservative Prime Minister at the end of the 19th century. Physically delicate, especially as a child, Lord David went to Eton and Christ Church College, Oxford, reading modern history, and became academically brilliant; his first class degree was only the start. He became a Fellow of Wadham College, Oxford straight after his graduation in 1924, and transferred to New College 15 years later, where he remained, apart from a one-year hiatus, until his retirement in 1970. He turned down the offer of a professorship at Cambridge to stay there; an Oxford chair came along in 1948 in any case. He published his first book at the age of 27, *The Stricken Deer*, a prize-winning biography of the 18th century English poet William Cowper, who gave us one of those sayings that has passed into common usage: 'variety is the spice of life'. He went on to publish more than 30 books, the last one in 1985, the year before his death at the age of 83. They included not just biographies but critical studies of novelists, poets and painters, and a history of his own family, *The Cecils of Hatfield House*. The house was built by the first Earl of Salisbury just over 400 years ago and remains the family seat, although it is open to the public.

Cecil's fame rested not just on his literary output, but also on his manner, and this extended to his manner as a tutor. The historian David Kynaston puts it this way: "If there was a quintessential mandarin of the late 1940s, it was [Cecil]". If you had to sketch an outline of an aristocratic Oxford 'don', especially an arts don, of the period, you would draw someone like him (see Figure 5.2). He was tall, slim and elegant in his movements – people remarked on his long, delicate fingers,

**FIGURE 5.2** Lord David Cecil in 1939. From Voxsart. Reproduced under licence from the National Portrait Gallery, London.

always rendered as such in painted portraits, the expansive use of gestures when he spoke, his compulsive thumb-twiddling. And his speech: many profilers have attempted to capture its quirks and cadences, and not always in complimentary terms. He spoke very rapidly, as if struggling to keep up with the speed of his thought, with frequent repetition of certain phrases and the odd impediment: r as w, th as f. He would often finish a sentence an octave higher than he started it. The philosopher Sir Isaiah Berlin, a contemporary and friend, attempted to sum it up. Cecil's voice, he said, sounded like a crate of hens being dragged across a field. You can judge this for yourself by listening to the surviving 6-minute clip from his 1969 appearance on the BBC's *Desert Island Discs*, obtainable from the Radio 4 website. The equally lordly sounding presenter, Roy Plomley, describes his output, to his face, as "fairly small: a book every three or four years". I would like to have seen his face at that moment, although he does not audibly demur.

Cecil gave weekly lectures on literature and, according to another famous friend, the novelist L.P. Hartley, poured his whole being into them, turning each into a dramatic performance. Not surprisingly, they were very popular, and attended not only by undergraduates. The broadcaster and author Ludovic Kennedy, like Wason an undergraduate in the postwar years, remembered him as "an astonishing communicator", and not just for his lecturing style. He also conducted tutorials, mainly on the novel, Byron and Shakespeare. Students would usually read their essays to their tutor, and according to Kennedy, Cecil always listened sympathetically. He chain-smoked, and wanted to know what his students thought, ready to enliven the discussion with effortlessly retrieved quotations, or instantly located passages read from volumes drawn from his bookshelves. Occasionally, he would take the paper from the student and stand in front of the fire, reading rapidly, dropping each page to the floor as he finished it. He was, according to Teresa Whistler, another 1940s student, "very unexacting" as a tutor.

Not everyone was as enchanted by Cecil's manner and methods as these pupils were, however. The novelist Kingsley Amis, also, briefly, tutored by Cecil as an undergraduate student in the 40s, savaged him as a "posturing quack" and found him impossible to pin down for supervisory sessions to discuss his thesis. Cecil was notoriously late for tutorials anyway, but may have taken lateness to active avoidance in the case of Amis. Amis came from humble South London origins and had been a serving soldier in the War, after a year at Oxford during which he had joined the Communist Party, as did many left-leaning intellectuals at the time (Amis would lean much further to the right in later life). Soviet Russia was, of course, one of the Allies against Hitler, and the one whose sacrifices outweighed all others'. Perhaps he bridled at this upper-class aesthete, exempted from military service. In any event, returning to his studies in 1945, Amis transferred to another tutor and had his thesis failed by Cecil. They clearly had no time for each other, literally and figuratively. Wason also recounted having difficulty with Cecil's tutorials: Cecil had a disconcerting habit of indicating disapproval during the reading of Wason's essays by jumping up and opening the curtains, if they were closed, or closing them, if they were open. Wason reckoned the supervision had not gone too badly if this happened only once or twice.

Wason came to admire Cecil deeply, and was for a while a peripheral member of his circle. He had at the time, and would later develop, character traits that recalled aspects of Cecil's personal style; Cecil may have overtly influenced him in this way, where these aspects did not simply resonate between the two men. Both came from privileged backgrounds, Cecil's much more so than Wason's, of course: there is no Wason family seat, for instance, and the barony held by the Terringtons ranks well below an earldom in the hierarchy of the British aristocracy. Both had hard times at their schools, Cecil largely through ill health, Wason through his deliberate retreat from anything that did not spark his passions (which meant almost everything on the school curriculum). Cecil would remark later, as Wason did, that he only really came alive, intellectually and socially, as a university student. Both were generally, though not utterly, unsnobbish towards those from different necks of the social woods while being at least to some extent aware of their privileged positions; both had nearly illegible handwriting; and both were hopelessly impractical, relying on family, friends, and later, understanding wives to get them through the day. Their experience of friendship was different, however: Cecil had a gift for it, whereas Wason, continuing the pattern of his childhood, made and retained very few close friends throughout his life; he was not a man who sought company, and small talk, that useful social cushion, was practically purgatorial to him. It was not that he was unfriendly, or antisocial: quite the contrary. In company, he was a charismatic presence, witty and warm. It was just that he was for some reason unable to initiate either friendships or social gatherings; people had to reach out to him, and when they did he responded.

But perhaps above all of these elements, in terms of influence, was their mutual approach to their first intellectual love, literature. Each had no patience with 'structuralist' textual analysis, the fine dissection of passages of writing for microscopic traces of meaning and implication against the socio-political analysis of the writer's background or the milieu of the 'text' in question. Rather, they regarded literature as primarily a means of giving pleasure, through telling the story of human feeling, thought and experience. They cherished beautiful writing. For Wason, the medium for this pleasure was principally poetry, while Cecil was more concerned with the novel; Jane Austen was, according to Isaiah Berlin, the love of his literary life. Cecil struggled in his own writing to achieve this transmission of pleasure – L.P. Hartley recalled that the writing process was, for Cecil, "agony". But the pain, all agreed, was worth it when the product was revealed, and despite it, Cecil was prolific, no matter what Roy Plomley thought. Wason's approach to writing, which we shall hear more about in later chapters, was different: contemplative and painstaking rather than agonising. He developed a technique for generating writing that he found worked for him, and urged it on others, also researching into writing in the later part of his career as a psychologist. He was, though, not prolific; not as prolific as Cecil, nor by the standards of many of his later academic peers. He did not set out to be.

Wason's time at Oxford and under David Cecil's wing turned a profit: he took his finals in Trinity (summer) term, 1948 and graduated with a second class BA degree in English, formally awarded in Michaelmas term that year. Lest this sound pale compared with his tutor's starry performance, we should recall Wason's previous, life-long history of academic failure; even to call his school results 'mediocre' would be overstating his meagre achievements. "An unmitigated disaster", he himself recalled it. Add to that the fact that he was still suffering from the effects of his war injuries and his degree was, in this context, a considerable feat. Cecil had succeeded where previous tutors had failed, and turned the unteachable youth into a willing acolyte. Wason applied for an MA five years later, and always used this designation thereafter.

## Talk to her

Life in Britain for most people in the immediate postwar years was almost unrelentingly grim. Most of the photos of the time are in black and white, but even when colour film was used, they did not look much different. There was extensive damage to the country's infrastructure, with hundreds of thousands of buildings destroyed and some towns and cities, such as Plymouth, Hull, Birmingham and Coventry, and much of the East End of London, all but laid waste by air attacks. At one point, London suffered 57 consecutive nights of bombing: almost two months without respite. As we have seen in the case of Bath, such damage was still visible in the 1950s, even later in some places: most children of that generation can recall 'playing on the bombsites', a word that had disappeared from the language by the time their own children had grown up.

The resources were simply not there to furnish reconstruction on the scale that would have been needed for complete restoration. The country was massively in debt for the funds needed to fight the war, mainly to the USA and Canada – these debts would only finally be cleared in 2006 – and the economy was flat on its back. The Empire, the bulwark of the economy, and vital to the war effort, was in the process of breaking up, beginning with the jewel in the crown, India, which gained its independence from Britain in 1947. Continental Europe was also engaged in a process of reconstruction, especially Germany, where the Nazi regime's cruel and futile extension of the war far beyond the point at which defeat was assured had left millions of its citizens dead: more soldiers and civilians died in the ten months after the Stauffenberg assassination plot against Hitler in July 1944 than in the five years preceding it. The country was devastated, the economy in complete collapse, and its territory divided: the eastern part, along with many neighbouring nations, was now under Soviet occupation and would remain so for more than 40 years. Some parts of pre-war Germany, such as the former East Prussia, would never be German again. Any dreams of export-led prosperity for Britain were going to have to wait until not only it but also these shattered countries were back on their feet.

Because of the wartime U-boat blockade and labour shortages on farms and in other industries, rationing of food, fuel, clothing and other essentials had been introduced, and by mid-1942, almost all food items were rationed. People were given ration books filled with coupons which they had to use when doing their shopping, the aim being to keep strictly to allotted quotas and thereby reduce dependency on imports, which had been seriously curtailed by the blockade. Britain imported most of its food when the War started. Rationing had the un-intended but fortunate consequence of actually improving the general health of the British working class. The reason was that it controlled not just demand but supply, and the Government, a wartime coalition of the main political parties, saw to it that the quotas included a range of foods that added up to a balanced diet, something that had been denied to a great many working people before.

The end of the War did not magically lift these shortages; indeed some became more acute than they had been during the conflict, partly because of the need to help the populations of the wrecked countries of continental Europe to survive. A case in point was the relief of the famine in the Netherlands following the 'hunger winter' of 1944–1945, an effort which began, with air support largely from the Royal Air Force, even before VE Day. Food rationing in Britain would only finally cease in 1954. The incoming Labour government in 1945 also im-plemented a number of additional austerity measures alongside its nationalisation programme and centralised economic planning, an example being the banning of midweek sports events after the severe winter of 1947, ostensibly to save fuel; it was the end of the first postwar season of the Football League. Although well-intentioned, such measures were self-defeating and widely resented: people felt as if they were snuffing out what little light there was in their lives. These seemingly never-ending hardships conspired to make the government unpopular, so that the 146-seat majority gained by the Labour Party in 1945 was reduced to 5 in the general election of 1950, and turned into a defeat, by 17 seats, to the Conservatives under Churchill 20 months later. It was an even closer result than it looks: Labour actually secured a quarter of a million more total votes than did the victorious Tories, but the Attlee government, along with the country itself, was by now exhausted, and there was little sense of injustice when the electoral system gave the Conservatives more seats.

In Oxford in 1946, Wason and his contemporaries were insulated from the worst of these privations, although Kingsley Amis did remark on the "bloody cold" winter of 1947, during his final year there. Wason set out to make the most of Oxford life and the feeling that, finally, this was where he belonged. He quickly fell in with a fellow English student, Claude Miéville, and the two became firm friends; the friendship would long outlast their student days. Although they were contemporaries as students, Claude was a few years older than Wason, and poli-tically they were different too: Wason, along with his brother Jim and cousin Roly, had disavowed his family's Liberal heritage and was now firmly aligned with the Left, while Miéville's sympathies were Tory, and he would go on to a career in business. He was also married, to Luki, a non-student. He was a worldly, charismatic individual, extraverted and scarcely ever serious: his preferred mode of conversation was a stream of jokes. He gloried in the third-class degree he ultimately obtained; anything more and it would have looked as if he had actually cared about it. He fancied himself to be something of an artist and craftsman, and was especially keen on photography, taking many pictures of Wason, and of himself and Luki, the people they knew and the places they lived in, during their time together. One stands out: of the young Wason hunched over a chessboard, pipe in mouth, head resting on hand, in rapt contemplation of the game in progress. It is, to my mind, the finest portrait of him, capturing the major interest of his life and the intensity with which he pursued it. That now rather debased term 'iconic' properly applies in this case (Figure 5.3).

Claude Miéville was the kind of person who gave you confidence just by being around him. In the spring of 1947, after a lecture, he and Wason had repaired to that eternal favourite haunt of Wason's, a bookshop. Wason, who already had a girlfriend – in fact it was 'understood' that they were engaged – had seen a young woman, also a fellow English student, and been immediately struck by her. Now here she was, outside the bookshop. Wason wanted to get to know her, but was held back by … shyness, or guilty thoughts of his existing partner? Miéville was having none of this faint-heartedness. "Talk to her," he said. "Ask her out for a drink. If you don't go after her, nothing will ever happen". It was the single most important moment of Wason's life.

The young woman – in fact, like Claude, she was a couple of years older than Wason – was Marjorie Vera Salberg. She came from a colonial family, and had been born in India, in 1921, where her father, Frank, was a chief engineer on the Assam–Bengal railway (so his legacy will still be visible there). As was the way with colonial families in those days, when Marjorie was seven years old, she was shipped

**FIGURE 5.3**  Claude Miéville's portrait of Peter Wason, c. 1948. Courtesy of Armorer Wason

back to England, accompanied by her brother, who was only five, a few nannies and a platoon of similar children, to boarding school; in this case, to Weston-super-Mare, Somerset. This is just a few miles from the home of Admiral Romer Wason and, later, his son Roly, near Bridgwater. Wason used the term "deported" when recalling how he was packed off to boarding school aged eight; it applies more literally in Marjorie's case, as she had spent her whole life in India up to then. She did not return to her parents in the school holidays: that was hardly practicable in the pre-air travel era of the 1920s and 1930s. Colonial children went to relatives or to holiday homes: these were institutions, set up for children like Marjorie, separated from their parents. Marjorie was one of the latter: she stayed in holiday homes, visited occasionally by her aunts, only one of whom she really got on with, who were meant to keep an eye on her. She did occasionally stay with them too. They were maiden aunts, part of the post-First World War generation whose marriage prospects had been blighted by the loss of so many male contemporaries. This had particularly affected the class from which they were drawn, the officer class: a higher proportion of officers were killed than were 'other ranks'. They were usually the first out of the trenches when the charge was sounded, and so the first to be cut down.

Marjorie only saw her parents for a fortnight every three years, when they came over to England, and consequently she hardly knew them. Not surprisingly, she remembered her childhood as an unhappy one – as Wason did his – and from our modern standpoint it is a barely believable upbringing. She suffered health problems, including pneumonia, at school. This was initially ignored, and she then had to be rushed to hospital; she convalesced at her aunt's home in Weston-super-Mare. The peak of this exiled experience came one day when she was 16. She was summoned to the headmistress's office. "Salberg", the imposing figure announced, "I have to tell you that your mother has died". She left the room nonplussed, not sure what to feel, wondering: who was this person she had just lost? She may only have seen her mother for a matter of weeks out of the previous eight years.

After this event, she went off to that other conventional educational destination for young women of a certain social standing: the finishing school, with its instruction in etiquette and elocution. At the age of 17, with the war in Europe imminent, she went back out to India: her father was retiring from the railways, he had just lost his wife and she was to help in bringing him back to the old country. The outbreak of war put a hold on that and for a time, Marjorie enjoyed the white British experience of the Raj: parties, picnics, tennis and cool drinks on the veranda. Rather than sit idle for ever, though, she decided to train as a nurse, and did so for three months. The Imperial Japanese army had invaded eastern Asia and refugees were beginning to pour across the border, and Marjorie was posted to help care for them. After two years, and with the Japanese invasion of Burma, which has a border with Assam, proceeding ever closer, the decision was made to risk the return to England.

Safely – or perhaps not so safely – home in London, she volunteered to become a pilot in the Women's Auxiliary Air Force (WAAF); this would have been a non-combat role, as the WAAF's name implies, but there were a few women who supported the RAF by behind-the-scenes flying: delivering aircraft, passengers and freight, for instance, and so freeing male pilots for the air war. But Marjorie did not become one of them: she failed the eye exam. So she enlisted in the Women's Royal Naval Service, known inevitably and universally as the Wrens. Her duties mainly involved driving officers and non-commissioned officers around the south coast at night, and resulted in some of her reputed 23 proposals of marriage. She had received some of them in India before, including from one 'Bats' Barthold, a Spitfire pilot, who liked to buzz the field hospital in Assam where she was serving. More were to follow after the War.

One of her suitors turned into an important influence on her life. She met and fell in love with Sandy Wilson. This was Colin Alexander St John Wilson, a history and architecture student at Oxford in the early war years; in 1942, he joined the Royal Naval Volunteer Reserve, later serving in Europe and India. It is likely that they met through this naval connection. At the end of his war service, in 1946, he completed his architecture degree at University College London. He used to travel to Paris after its liberation and bring back paintings and books on art. This world of culture was a revelation to Marjorie. Wilson persuaded her that she had a mind (although she would not have called herself then, and never would after, an intellectual), and that she should go to his alma mater, Oxford. She took a bridging course and was admitted to St Anne's College, to study English. Sandy Wilson went on to become Professor of Architecture at Cambridge, and to find fame as the designer, along with his second wife, Mary Jane (MJ) Long, of the new British Library on Euston Road, begun in 1962 but only completed in 1997, after which he was knighted. MJ Long was awarded the lesser honour of an OBE in 2009. Wilson died in 2007 and his headstone, in Highgate Cemetery, is a miniature replica of the entrance portal to the Library.

Wason's courage, lent to him by Claude, was rewarded, and Marjorie agreed to go for that drink with him. She returned to her room at St Anne's, and confided to her roommate, Pat: "You're not going to believe this, but I've met a man who doesn't even believe in God!" Wason had by this time decided he was an atheist and, as with his earlier defection from the Anglican to the Roman Church, there is a hint here of another dig at his mother, whose rather austere low-church Anglican faith was important to her but anathema to him. Wason remained ambivalent about his mother throughout his life. On the one hand, he was fond of her, and admired her spiritedness and independence of thought. But it seems as if he could never bring himself to forgive her for his having been cared for largely by nannies in his early childhood, and then sent away to his terrible prep school.

Marjorie and Wason soon became a couple, largely inseparable. Two weeks after her first shocked revelation to Pat about his atheism, she had another bombshell to impart: "It's even worse than that: he votes Labour!" She had plainly never, in her rather cloistered youth, come across either of these things in real life before, not even from Sandy Wilson. Wilson had opened her up to art and culture, and now Wason did the same with religion and politics. She took on all three traits and incorporated them into her mature persona, as Wason had done with David Cecil's influence following his own liberation at university. Art, not just visual art but music too, became central to her identity in a way they never would for Wason, and she would bring up their children with the arts always in the background: concerts, gallery shows, Chopin on the piano at home. She thought herself an atheist now too, and would never go back to any kind of formal religious observance. And she became a more active Labour Party member than Wason ever did, especially after they set up home together. Wason also introduced her to psychology, and they both began seeing an analyst whom they called 'The Grizzly'. It was the start of a long relationship with psychoanalysis, especially for him. He was now experiencing it as a therapy, rather than just reading about it as a window on the mind.

As for Wason's fiancée: in May 1947, New College held a 'Commem Ball'. Commemoration Ball, that is: the colleges held them every two or three years; 'held' because they have become less frequent recently, perhaps owing to some unsavoury and well-publicised incidents. They were quite lavish affairs and would feature serious artists as entertainment – the Rolling Stones in 1964, for instance. But the Ball 17 years earlier, in 1947, became the occasion when Wason broke off his informal engagement. Perhaps he was looking for a way out in any case, as she was a rather County type: conservative (and Conservative), the daughter of a master of foxhounds. Wason could never see himself as being part of that society. He kept a photo of her, nonetheless, and it has 'darling Peter' written on the back. But it was Peter and Marjorie now, and would be until the end. Pictures taken in London by street photographers – they would leap out of the shadows, take your

**FIGURE 5.4**  Peter and Marjorie Wason, taken by street photographers in London in the late 1940s. Courtesy of Armorer Wason

picture and then, if you had a mind to, take some money and your address and then send the picture to you when it was developed (people must have been very trusting in those days) – show them adopting a certain 'Parisian anarchist' look: dark clothing, berets; she very youthful-looking and gamine, he rather gaunt and yes, tall, dark and handsome, walking-stick in hand (Figure 5.4).

Within very short order, the relationship was put on an official basis in that traditional way: telling the parents. After graduation, in the summer of 1948, Wason and Marjorie set off for his second home: Ireland. They did not go to Ballykilty, but toured around, spending a couple of days here, a couple of days there. They had to keep moving because they were an unmarried couple and if they stayed anywhere for more than three days they would have had to show their ration books, which of course had their different surnames on them. In the 1940s, and especially in Catholic Ireland, a known unmarried couple holidaying together, sharing a room, would have caused a scandal, possibly involving the police. They had told Wason's parents that they were going with the Miévilles, but this was a fiction. They could never show them any photographs from this trip, as there would not have been any of these phantom companions, and it was also why they could not go to Ballykilty. It all sounds like a lot of fun.

# 6

# OXFORD TO LONDON, VIA SCOTLAND

## To Scotland

The trouble with fun is that it never lasts. It was the autumn of 1948: those freewheeling university days were gone, and the couple's idyllic, romantic trip to Ireland was already slipping into memory. They may have been cocooned in their new-found love, but they could not just live on that alone. For a while, they did try to, shuttling between Wason's family home in Bath and Marjorie's London milieu. Wason still had his war pension, and Marjorie found work in the publishing industry, initially for a one-man-band literary agent in Kensington. This fellow would put on different telephone voices in an attempt to convince callers that there were more people in the office than there really were, while Marjorie would aid and abet the subterfuge by asking them to hold while she pretended to see if the particular agent they were calling for was in; he was, of course, sitting across the room. She would move on from this farcical setup to work at the rather more sober, though perhaps less entertaining, offices of Oxford University Press.

The sense of dread that many university students feel at the looming end of their days of freedom must have struck Wason foursquare in 1948, and been amplified by his post-graduation jaunt with Marjorie in Ireland. Life as a 24-year-old war pensioner could not have been attractive either, despite the regular income. He had found himself as a student at Oxford; they both had, and they would continue to reminisce about their time there for years afterwards. Perhaps there was a chance to continue in that world? Despite his friendly relations with Lord David Cecil, there was never a serious prospect of doing what Cecil had done, and passing straight to the university's tutorial staff: Wason had, after all, managed just a second class degree, and there were plenty of firsts to compete with. But Cecil had parlayed his love of literature into a stellar academic and publishing career. Reading and writing about books for a living – could Wason perhaps replicate that, albeit in a different setting?

As sometimes happens when a clear pathway through a problem emerges, it became the only possible pathway, and Wason set out along it. But the direction it took was unlikely. In 1949, he applied for, and obtained, a post as assistant lecturer in English at a university 400 miles from London, and from Marjorie: at Aberdeen, in north-east Scotland.

Aberdeen is one of the oldest universities in Britain, with origins traceable back to before 1500; it was the last of three universities established in Scotland in the 15th century. Only Oxford and Cambridge among English universities are older, so there was a period of several hundred years (from the late 15th to the early 19th century) when there were more universities in Scotland than in England. In the years following the Second World War, there was a governmental push on the part of both the Labour and Conservative parties to expand higher education, and by 1950, the number of students gaining degrees had almost doubled, to 17,000, from 9,000 in 1938; four new 'redbrick' universities were established between those dates. However, this effort was partly limited by the lack of qualified teaching staff, even after the most stringent austerity period of the late 1940s. It was therefore not as difficult to find a lecturing post as it would be today if all you had to offer was a second class first degree, even one from Oxford. Such an application would not be looked at twice these days; there are vastly more graduates now as well: almost 350,000 first degrees were awarded in 2010, and according to the Higher Education Statistics Agency, there were over 1.37 million students enrolled in 2017, and that is UK first-degree students only – there were another 230,000 from other countries. Candidates for academic posts today therefore need something else to make their case persuasive, such as a higher degree, preferably a PhD. An Oxford MA is not a higher qualification derived from a course of advanced postgraduate study, and in any case, Wason did not yet have one, and would not until 1953. So in 1949, he was fortunate in his timing, and managed to secure a lectureship without any of these additional attributes.

There is also the question of why this place in particular, so distant from the world he had known. In fact, the distance was not as great as it might appear. One attraction, indeed probably the overriding reason for taking this course of action, must have been family connections. Wason's family on the paternal side was Scottish, albeit from southwest rather than northeast Scotland, and two parts of this side of the family were resident in or near Aberdeen. His elder brother, Eugene, and his new family were living in the city, and would be able to offer him a bed. His uncle, Rear Admiral Romer Wason, had lived in Aberdeenshire and his cousin Roly was brought up there. His beloved cousin Fenella, daughter of his father's sister Minna, had married John Paton. They had all holidayed together at Hillcrest School in Dorset, rented by Minna, in the 1930s. The Patons and their children were living at the stately residence of Grandholme, just outside Aberdeen, and Wason could stay there too. There was an immediate and tragic setback, however. Wason's post at the university started on October 1st, but Fenella, already gravely ill with cancer, died on the 21st. The atmosphere at Grandholme must have been sombre. It was an omen.

Whilst at Grandholme, Wason ran into yet more exotic relatives, near and distant. John Paton had part-Hungarian ancestry, from an old aristocratic family. One of these Continental relatives was the red-haired and dashing Mihold Kemeny. She played Wason at chess, and lost, despite his giving himself a handicap. They stayed up one night in the hope of seeing a ghost reputed to haunt the Grandholme library, but it failed to make an appearance. Mihold had also stayed once at Grafton Lodge, in 1949, and Wason recalled her being propelled along by his mother, arm in arm; despite Wason's now deep relationship with Marjorie, it seems his mother viewed Mihold as a possible match for him. She never did marry, and died in Paris in the 1980s.

Also gathering at Grandholme after Fenella's death, along with Aunt Minna, was another impressive female relative, Armorer of Breadalbane, as Wason always called her. She was married to Charles William Campbell, the ninth Earl of Breadalbane, and one of the largest landowners in Scotland. However, his life was blighted by mental health problems. Wason's mother told him that Charles required Armorer to appear at a certain spot in front of their castle at a precise time every day and drop a handkerchief, which the Earl would observe from a window through a telescope. It seemed he suffered from paranoid jealousy.

Wason regarded Armorer as "beautiful and regal", and liked and admired her – to the extent of later continuing an established tradition by giving his own elder daughter that name. But her regality had another, harder side. The Breadalbanes' only son was known to Wason as John Glenorchy, and Wason liked him: they had met at Newnham Hall during Wason's time at Stowe, and he found Glenorchy quiet and unassuming, a dab hand at card tricks. A lieutenant in the Black Watch, a celebrated Scottish regiment, he had been wounded at the Salerno landings which spearheaded the Allied invasion of mainland Italy in 1944, and developed schizophrenia afterwards. Whether this was because of his traumatic war experience, or was inherited from his father, or some combination of the two, is impossible to know.

In any event, after the psychiatric fashion of the time, he was subjected to 'psychosurgery', in the shape of a prefrontal lobotomy, in an attempt to alleviate his condition. This was a drastic and irreversible treatment, now thankfully obsolete, which involved cutting the connections from the prefrontal lobes of the brain to the neural tissue behind. The prefrontal cortex of the brain is mainly concerned with what neuropsychologists call 'executive function': strengthening or weakening other brain processes, such as when controlling impulses. The surgery did him, in Wason's euphemistic phrase, "no good at all", and he went into a spiral of decline, joined a circus as a bagpipe-player, and married (and later divorced) Coralie Archer, whom Armorer thought unsuitable. She disinherited him, and he ended up penniless, in a homeless hostel in Brighton. He had no children, and when he died in Somerset in 1995, aged 76, his titles died with him (besides being the 10th Earl of Breadalbane, John Romer Boreland Campbell was also 14th Baronet Campbell of Glenorchy – hence his adopted surname – 10th Viscount of Tay and Paintland, and 10th Lord Glenurchy, Benederaloch,

Ormelie and Weick). Several distant relatives currently lay claim to these titles. Armorer Breadalbane herself lived a very long life: born in 1890, she died only in 1987.

Military psychiatry took some time to reform itself after the Second World War, and John Glenorchy was by no means the last to be treated in this way (one dreads to think of the fate of a PTSD-afflicted common soldier, if the aristocratic Glenorchy could be subjected to such 'therapy'). It certainly had not done so by 1952, when R.D. Laing, later to become a self-styled 'anti-psychiatrist' and 1960s counter-cultural hero, visited an army psychiatric unit. He found psychosurgery still being almost routinely practised, alongside other treatments that today sound little short of brutal. There seems little doubt that this experience helped send Laing in the radical direction, as critic and therapist, that he took.

Transferring from Oxford, via London, to Aberdeen would have been dislocating enough even without the tragedy of Fenella's death, but this dark cloud over such a wholesale change of scene got Wason's academic career off to an inauspicious start. It would only get worse. Wason's love of literature, and his approach to its enjoyment, gelling so well as it had done with that of David Cecil at Oxford, failed utterly to equip him for the job of teaching undergraduates. He was, at 25, just a few years older than them in any case, but his task as a tutor required him to do with literary works what he so despised as a reader: analyse, dissect, interpret. To this distasteful activity could be added the bane of every teacher who has ever lived: some – perhaps most – of the students were just not that interested in the subject of his classes. The unteachable Wason now found the experience of being a teacher himself, attempting to put over material in which he was only half-engaged, in a manner that he found uninvolving, to groups of young people many of whom would rather have been somewhere else, thoroughly alienating. He was also still suffering physical effects from his war injuries, with constant pain and restricted mobility. And all this while Marjorie was a day's travel away.

It was all too much, and Wason suffered what he later described himself as a nervous breakdown, seeking refuge in a further round of psychoanalysis. It clarified for him, as if any further clarification were needed, that he was not cut out to teach English. There was only one way out, and Wason took it. "It was intimated", state the rather coyly-phrased minutes of the University Court of March 14, 1950, "that Mr P.C. Wason had resigned from the post of Assistant in the English Department from 31st March 1950". His head of department, Geoffrey Bickerstaff, was sorry to see him go: "He is a man of real ability and his work has been much appreciated". He had lasted less than one full academic year.

## What can Peter do?

This was a moment of crisis in his life. He went back to Grafton Lodge, where a family meeting was held. "What can Peter do?" asked his mother. At that point, there was no clear answer to this question. He still had his war pension and so was not dependant on others to survive, and he still had places he could stay: Bath, Ballykilty, London, where Marjorie was still working in publishing. But this was a period of depression, and depression means more than just feeling down. There is a behavioural aspect to it as well: it becomes harder to rouse yourself to get anything, even the most mundane tasks, done, and the process can become self-reinforcing. The less you get done, the more depressed you become, the less likely you are to get anything done, and so on. Depression would become a psychological correspondent to his physical injuries for Wason: always there, another problem to live with. Waxing and waning, but always there. He would have recourse not only to psychotherapy but to psychiatry, and its accompanying drug treatments, in the long term.

Another possible pathway began to form in his mind, and his own mental state played a part in it. Wason had always been curious about people and about the human soul, or the mind, to put it in less loaded terms; a curiosity that included a somewhat morbid fascination with those who were referred to at the time as the 'mentally handicapped'. This fascination with the ways the mind worked had been with him since boyhood, and had been sharpened by his wartime experiences: the testing involved in officer training, the range of people he met, from "rough" working-class privates to grand brigadiers, the friendships he formed, the places he passed through. He had collected books on mysticism and religion, along with modern poetry, and was fascinated by the rituals of the Church. He was proficient at chess and not only played but studied the game, and he was captivated by his favourite uncle Rigby's puzzle collection. And he was a habitual noticer of curiosities and, especially, paradoxes. There was a way he could put these interests and aptitudes to practical use: by actually studying Psychology.

Once again, he was well-placed to take this turn. He would not get state support for a second undergraduate degree, but he still had his war pension. Added to this, Marjorie's family was wealthy and her father, Frank Salberg, having retired from his chief engineer's post on the Indian railway, was now back in London, living in Lee Green, near Blackheath, readily accessible. Wason could look to them, and perhaps to his own family, for support. And so the plan was formed. Wason would live in London and study Psychology there. Psychology as a subject of study was, like the university sector generally, undergoing rapid expansion. It had been given a boost by the Second World War, which had brought into being the sub-discipline of cognitive ergonomics: the study of how to get the best possible match between the workings of a machine and the mental processes of its operators. Everything from the design of aircraft cockpit displays to the length of shifts that radar observers could undertake before starting to miss signals was subjected to intensive psychological experimentation. Despite its popular stereotype, Psychology was not, indeed never really has been, just the study of mental abnormality or illness, but its purview was starting to include ever wider-ranging aspects of mentality and, especially at that time, behaviour. In September 1950, six months after the Aberdeen debacle, Wason enrolled on the BA Psychology course, with Sociology as a subsidiary subject, at University College London.

To put everything on a comfortable footing, at the start of his second year, the event that had seemed inevitable since Claude Miéville had pushed him forward outside the Oxford bookshop four years previously took place and on September 8, 1951, Peter Cathcart Wason and Marjorie Vera Salberg were married. The marriage had one immediate and unfortunate consequence: Marjorie was forced to give up her job at Oxford University Press. This was because there still existed in some parts of the economy a practice known as the 'marriage bar': a policy of either not employing married women, or dismissing women when they got married. Incomprehensible to most people now, it had several justifications in those days, besides simple blatant discrimination, such as a need to get returning soldiers back into their former employment after the First World War (when women had entered previously 'male' jobs in unprecedented numbers); an assumption that a married woman would be supported by, and should support, her husband; to free up jobs for men, the traditional breadwinners, during the great depression of the 1930s; and because married women would be likely to leave and have children. It was not a peculiarly British affair: marriage bars also operated in, and began to lapse, at the same time in the USA and Australia, for instance. It had begun to die out by the time Marjorie Wason was 'let go', especially in the public sector: the Civil Service, for instance, had abolished the practice in 1947, and the teaching profession had removed it in 1944. The last vestiges went extinct as late as the 1960s but it was only outlawed altogether by the Sex Discrimination Act of 1975. Whether the sentiment behind it has entirely gone from the collective consciousness is moot: you still, even now, hear 'a woman's place is in the home' uttered from time to time, and the related problem of female disadvantage in pay and seniority seems never-ending.

Such financial hardship as might have resulted from the loss of Marjorie's salary was alleviated when her father bought them a flat to live in, in Blackheath, near his own home. Now firmly in place at the second university at which he felt free, and settling into married life, Wason may have had an inkling that the course of his life was now set. If he did, he was right.

# 7

# CURIOSITY PAYS

## Falling into place

The second phase of Wason's experience of university freedom, after New College Oxford – gently setting to one side the Aberdeen interlude – shared several attributes with the first. For one thing, he was, and had been for years, genuinely interested in Psychology: he joined the British Psychological Society even before he began studying it formally. And since he was interested in it, he was stimulated to put the work in to studying it, and that work paid off: he would graduate in 1953 with first class honours. If any of his old schoolteachers became aware of this, their facial expressions would have been good to see. More importantly, though, the same thing happened at University College London (UCL) in the 1950s as had happened at Oxford in the 1940s: he met people who became highly significant in his intellectual development. Two in particular: John Whitfield and A.R. Jonckheere.

Once again, Wason was fortunate in his timing as well as the location for his new pathway. You can always count yourself lucky if you find yourself starting out in science in an era when things are in flux: there are doors opening all over the place; you can even create your own doors. So it was at UCL when Wason fetched up at the Psychology Department there. British Psychology coming into the 1950s had its own culture and traditions, but was succumbing to dominance by the largely American approach known as Behaviourism. This almost self-explanatory term nevertheless needs some explanation. Behaviourism recast Psychology, early in the 20th century, as a strictly empirical science, that is, one whose data were to consist entirely of publicly observable events: events that could, in principle, be seen by anyone. That is how it is in the physical sciences, and so, thought this new school, that is how it should be for Psychology too.

Until this idea was put forward, initially and extremely vigorously by John B. Watson, professor of Psychology at Johns Hopkins University, Baltimore, MD,

USA, psychological data came largely from the introspections of 'observers' trained to look not outwards but inwards: at their own thought processes. You can get a flavour of this for yourself. Take the standard example of a word-association test. You are given the word 'rhubarb'. What's the first idea that pops into your mind? Custard? Did you form an image of a nice warming bowl of rhubarb and custard? Let's say you did, you used your 'mind's eye'. Now it so happens that when I was given the word 'rhubarb' I also thought of custard, but my own thought processes did not include any such mental picture; it was just an abstract thought, arising simply because these words often go together. Under the same conditions, we made two very different observations.

This little imaginary game points up a real, serious theoretical question which exercised many psychologists of the turn of the 20th century, before Watson came along: does thought always stem from sense data and, hence, must it ultimately depend on mental images? Does your report of a mental picture prove it does? Or does my non-pictorial experience (and let's assume, so as not to complicate things even further, that we are both reporting our experiences accurately and truthfully) disprove it? How can you tell? The answer is, of course, that since our introspections are of private thoughts inside ourselves, they are not available for anyone else to examine, and so you cannot tell. You claim one thing, I claim another, and there is no way to arbitrate between us. Behaviourists, rather in the manner of the little boy in Andersen's tale of the emperor's new clothes, pointed out that a true objective science cannot be based on unverifiable, subjective events; any theories arising from such data cannot be proved or disproved, since the data themselves can always be doubted. The emperor, Psychology in its 19th century guise, was naked all along, its scientific clothing just an illusion. Since actions – behaviour – are publicly observable events, Psychology, if it is to be considered scientific, must be a science of behaviour, pure and simple, the behaviourists argued.

Watson, a brilliant polemicist as well as a scholar, pushed the argument further: any psychological term that denoted private, internal experience, such as emotion, belief, thought or even memory, could not, he maintained, serve as a scientific term. Watson picturesquely called such ideas "medieval conceptions", a phrase which always makes me visualise copulations in castles. Or so I claim.

The behaviourists' challenge dealt an almost instant death blow to introspectionist Psychology. The discipline began to put questions of observability and testability in the foreground, and to direct its attention away from thought to behaviour. Psychology and other social sciences have always been slightly obsessed with the scientific method, and scientific respectability, even before the advent of behaviourism. This state of affairs has attracted mockery from 'hard' scientists, such as the Nobel Prize-winning physicist Richard Feynman, one of the greatest science communicators. When physicists get together, they talk about physics; when social scientists get together, they talk about methodology, he joked (or half-joked), in an article cruelly titled *Cargo cult science*.

The Psychology Department at UCL in the early 1950s was changing in this direction, but it did not go over completely to behaviourism. In 1950, its long-serving Professor and Head of Department, Sir Cyril Burt, retired, at the age of 67; he had been in post for 19 years. Burt was a dominant figure not only at UCL but also in British Psychology as a whole at the time: he was the first psychologist to be knighted, partly for his 20 years prior to his UCL appointment when he was a pioneering educational psychologist in London. Following his death in 1971, his reputation was damaged by claims that he had fabricated some of his research data, apparently to support his view that intelligence was to a large degree inherited – politically a highly charged hypothesis, because it has led some theorists of a similar view to argue that there are racial differences in intelligence. You could hardly get a more politically charged piece of psychology than that. Revisionist accounts disputing Burt's alleged fraud have appeared since, and it will now probably never be known for sure whether, or to what extent, Burt was a scientific rogue. He is a diminished figure in any event.

Following his retirement, there was a brief interregnum when Wason's soon-to-be mentor, John Whitfield, took on the headship as a stand-in, before he was replaced by a permanent appointment in the shape of Roger Russell, an American animal psychologist and behaviourist. Russell was Head during Wason's time as an undergraduate and postgraduate student, and he was a popular figure, a rare thing among departmental heads, anywhere. Partly this was down to his personal affability, but it must also have been because he defied expectations. Burt was the doyen of the British psychometric tradition, psychometrics being the measurement of psychological traits and abilities such as intelligence and personality, two of those medieval conceptions. Russell represented the revolution. But far from seeking to turn UCL into a behaviourist redoubt, he instead maintained its catholic take on Psychology; it never did become wholly, or even mainly, a behaviourist department. Animal psychology had been legitimised by behaviourism: since animals behave, animal behaviour could be studied just as well as human behaviour could, using the same methods. For a while, and justified by evolutionary theory, animals served as 'models' for humans, especially where the psychology of learning was concerned (behaviourists were concerned with little else), and most large-scale departments had an animal lab; UCL's did.

Animal psychology took its place there alongside other strands of the subject. But it did not supplant them. Russell seems to have recognised that the more radical behaviourist approach to psychology was even then beginning to decline, and that the experimental study of the mind – what came to be known as cognitive psychology – was starting to make a comeback; that is why the mid-1950s were a period of transition not just for this department but for the discipline as a whole.

Whitfield and Jonckheere were members of the department during Wason's undergraduate time there, and were members throughout his postgraduate roles there and beyond as well. They were not much older than he was: Whitfield was born in 1917, Jonckheere in 1920. With the arrival of these two people on Wason's scene, the elements of his future as a psychologist, and of his defined public persona, were falling into place. Jonckheere joined the lecturing staff in 1951; Whitfield had joined as Reader, a senior research position just a rung below the level of Professor, the year before, following a productive time as a researcher with the Medical Research Council Applied Psychology Unit in Cambridge (it was not part of Cambridge University), beginning during the War, in 1942. In this, and in other aspects of his early working life, his career trajectory was strikingly similar to Wason's, as we shall see. Whitfield had graduated with a first from Cambridge in 1938, in the Natural Sciences Tripos; experimental psychology was part of the Part II of this programme. Although he began research into the psychology of religion as a postgraduate student at Cambridge in 1940, he never completed a PhD, and so was always Mr, not Dr, Whitfield. This was not all that unusual in those days, but would be very unusual indeed in Psychology now.

John Whitfield also shared some characteristics with Wason's previous academic inspiration, Lord David Cecil. His teaching style involved a rather high-pitched voice, as did Cecil's, a decidedly 'posh' accent, and some idiosyncratic pronunciations. This despite Whitfield's Northern origins: he had been born in Stanley, County Durham, and educated at a grammar school in nearby Sunderland. It was a heavy industrial area, peppered with collieries and steelworks. He was reputed to have been the first son of Stanley to go to Cambridge. He did not have Cecil's rapid-fire delivery, however. Quite the contrary: Wason's future main collaborator, Phil Johnson-Laird, remembers him speaking at a slower rate than anyone he ever heard. This may have had something to do with Whitfield's fatal weakness. Recalling his work for the Medical Research Council (MRC) in Cambridge during the War, he hinted later that he had been recruited by the security services at that time, helping to devise disinformation campaigns to spread in Germany. John Valentine, a later student of his, remembers him telling how it was put about there that staring at radar screens led to impotence. Unfortunately, the rumour reached the British forces too, in an example of what we now call 'blowback'. But that was not his weakness. He had fallen under the influence of a senior colleague, a specialist in animal intelligence, and a notorious drinker. Whitfield became a drinker himself and, in his own time, notorious for it. His editorship of the British Journal of Statistical Psychology fell apart under his drinking, even to the extent of some issues failing to appear. He took to conducting tutorials in a pub, the popular UCL watering hole (it still is), the Marlborough; Johnson-Laird recalls attending one there after which Whitfield was so drunk that he had to be restrained by the then head of department, Russell's successor, George Drew, until health professionals arrived and took him away.

This flaw in his character was a double tragedy. For him personally of course, and for his family, but also because Whitfield was academically brilliant: his alcoholism deprived his department and his subject of what would, without it, have been an even more substantial and original body of work.

He began conducting and publishing strictly applied research while at the MRC in Cambridge. He wrote papers on mining accidents, the measurement of opinion, and IQ differences among army recruits related to their pre-service jobs. Some of this work attracted the attention of the BBC: there is a transcript of a two-part broadcast tagged as 'for the BBC News in Hindustani', dated April 1945 – the very last days of the war in Europe. This research led fairly naturally to an interest in the theory and mathematics of the statistics he was reporting on. Statistics is an academic subject in its own right, with whole research teams devoted to it and a now gigantic library of textbooks, research papers and computer packages. Whitfield became a disciple of, and pioneer in, a particular form of statistical method involving putting scores in rank orders – first, second, and so on – rather than reporting them 'raw'. There are technical reasons for why you might want to do this which I shall not divert into. Interestingly, A.R. Jonckheere also became an eminent statistician developing methods for analysing ranked scores around the same time, but quite independently. Whitfield, like Jonckheere, published research papers on this topic and as a result, he was involved with the BBC a second time, as part of a panel discussion programme on scientific inference, along with other celebrity statisticians, broadcast on the Third Programme (now Radio 3) in 1957.

But there was more to Whitfield than high-level statistical geekery, and it was undoubtedly the nature of this 'more', along perhaps with those echoes of Cecil, that led Wason to gravitate to him. Besides his mathematical eminence, Whitfield was also an unusually original thinker; too original for his own good, in the view of some who still remember him. Here are two examples, from papers published around the time that he joined the UCL Psychology department. Before we get to them, a note about what 'published papers' are in the academic world, since I have mentioned them several times already and shall do so again. They are (mainly) reports of original research and theory, appearing in journals some of which are attached to learned societies: Whitfield published some of his mathematical studies in the *Journal of the Royal Statistical Society*, for instance, and there are similar journals in Psychology, as there are in all academic subjects. There is a rigorous process of 'refereeing' involved in getting a paper published, using the system of peer review: your paper is looked at by two or three acknowledged experts in its field and overseen by an editor, who is also an eminence in the area. Their job is to judge that the work is sound and that it adds something worth having to the literature; it is not to say whether they agree with it or not although, being members of the human race, referees sometimes do allow a little bit of personal bias to creep into their judgement.

It is the papers that are rejected that assure the quality of those that appear, and it is common for there to be a ratio of 10, 20 or more rejected to 1 accepted; for the most prestigious journals, the ratio can be higher still. Even the accepted ones have usually been sent back for revision before they are finally let in, and the referees pore over them again. In other words, a paper has to be pretty good before it finds its way into the journals. Even with all these safeguards, bad ones do occasionally slip through, sometimes even leading to a formal retraction by the journal, but they are very much the exception, and often newsworthy for that reason.

With that out of the way, let's look at these two papers of Whitfield's. The first has an immediate come-on title: 'The imaginary questionnaire'. It is in fact a paper about statistics, and about ordinary people's understanding of one statistical phenomenon with which we are all familiar: randomness. Whitfield had previously observed that with questionnaires asking people to give a yes/no answer to opinion questions, their response to a given question is influenced by the previous responses they have given. Obviously, this should not happen: if you say 'yes' to the proposition that there should be, say, legal restrictions on gas-guzzling cars, your 'yes' should not have been influenced by how you answered the question before, which asked about your view on the charitable status of private schools. And yet there is evidence that just such an influence occurs. This is clearly an unconscious bias, and raises the question of how to study it; how could you ever measure it? Whitfield's solution was to try to develop what he called a psychologically 'null' questionnaire, one without such interfering content; but how can you have questions with no content? Whitfield came up with the answer. By giving people blank items: 'Do you prefer ... to ...?' and asking them to fill in the blanks, indicating 'yes' or 'no' to each one (they had to do this 6, 10 or 14 times).

That, I submit, is an original idea. Using it, Whitfield found out that people have a flawed understanding of randomness and bias: they avoid long sequences of yeses or noes, for instance, as they do heads or tails when thinking about tossing coins (sequences of four or five heads, or tails, are far more common than people think they will be). So your answer about cars will be deflected if you have answered 'yes' to the previous four questions, no matter what they were about. This is important in our interpretation of things like opinion surveys, which are often reported in the media. I don't recall ever seeing any note in such reports about how this bias was taken into account or controlled for. If it was not, it may be part of the reason why such surveys sometimes get things wrong, for instance, in election polling. It could also be used nefariously: you could deliberately design multiple-item surveys so as to influence a particular answer, and distort its findings for commercial or political gain, safe in the knowledge that no-one knows about this bias.

Whitfield's other paper has a rather less enticing title: 'An experiment in problem solving'. Despite this plain cover, it nonetheless illustrates his originality. It addressed an issue that Whitfield had identified in studying this kind of thinking: that of assessing how difficult a problem is, so that we can judge people's performance in solving it. This sounds straightforward: everyone knows that some problems are harder than others. But how can we measure that degree of difficulty? One way is purely behavioural: see how many people solve it, how long they take, what kinds of mistakes they make, and so on. Whitfield called this 'phenomenal difficulty'. The other is objective: look at how much information is acquired at each stage of the problem, as the person works through it. Whitfield called this 'stimulus difficulty'. To compare them, he had to devise a completely new method. People were given eight objects to put into spaces, and allowed repeated attempts ('trials') to do so. Stimulus difficulty can be varied by adjusting how many spaces the objects have to be placed in. Feedback as you progress through the task – about which objects are in the right place – steadily boils down the possible options. Whitfield discovered two important things using this method. In the first condition, where eight objects had to be put in eight places, human performance (phenomenal difficulty) closely matched stimulus difficulty. Not so in two other conditions, where there were fewer places to put the objects in: people took twice as many trials to solve the problems as they should have done. The second discovery was that people adopted different methods in the different conditions: they used different strategies. Strategies in reasoning became a hot topic in psychological research on thinking 30 years later. That's how far ahead of his time Whitfield was.

Not many people were studying the psychology of thinking in the early 1950s, and this fact is attested by the tiny number of references in these two papers. Normally, research papers show how the current work is related to previous science, and to do that you cite the relevant literature, leading to a string of other research publications listed at the end. There is just one, a mathematical reference, at the end of the problem-solving paper, five at the end of the questionnaire paper – and one of those is by Whitfield himself (another is by John Maynard Keynes).

## Instant impact

Wason was thoroughly impressed by Whitfield and took some valuable lessons from him. One was that you could build a career on curiosity. Another was that it was possible, indeed desirable, to devise your own ways of addressing research questions. This need for originality perfectly suited Wason's own background and cast of mind. He came from a family in which it was usual to be unusual: remember his great-uncle Cathcart, knitting in Parliament, Uncle Horace the puller of strings, and his favourite uncle Rigby with his room full of puzzles; his cousins Bindon Blood and John Glenorchy, the extraordinary Roly and the beloved, lost Fenella; his brothers, the brilliant but reclusive Jim and the dashing and fearless Eugene. And many more besides. He was endlessly intrigued by the quirks and foibles of everyday life. And amused by them too; both of these psychological effects fuelled his curiosity about even simple everyday things.

John Whitfield had first established himself as a researcher on real-world problems with the Medical Research Council's Applied Psychology Unit in Cambridge. It so happened – and here was some more good fortune – that the MRC also had a research unit at UCL, the Industrial Psychology Research Group. Following completion of his degree in Psychology, in 1953, Wason succeeded in finding a post there, perhaps through Whitfield's influence.

One of his first assignments resulted in an almost immediate impact. In the autumn of 1953, Wason was sent to observe the actions of women working in a perfume factory, wrapping bars of soap. The factory's management had called in the MRC, having become concerned at the rhythmical movements that many of these wrappers made when going about this highly repetitive but intricately skilled task. This 'jig' as these movements were known in the factory seemed extraneous to the task; surely these ritualised jerkings were impairing efficiency, and possibly affecting the workers' health. The jig often consisted of body swaying and completely unnecessary actions such as tapping the soap bar. In one case, the wrapper kept turning her head. These habits emerged gradually after training; the wrappers were trained by non-jiggers, and the training could take months before a person was allowed on to the real production line. It was then that the problem started.

Except that it was less of a problem than common sense might lead us to expect. Wason found that there was a positive correlation between the amount of jig and a worker's efficiency at wrapping: the more they jigged, the more they wrapped. It was nothing to do with the workers' age or length of practice, although two of the more pronounced jiggers had over 20 years' experience at this job (how did they stand it?). Jigging seemed to come about through imitation of 'qualified' wrappers, especially the very good ones: workers sat in pairs opposite each other, so it was hard not to observe what the other was doing. In what would be a characteristic of his research through the coming years, Wason did not stop at collecting objective data, but also sought the views of the workers themselves. This meant the use of introspection, deemed disreputable for the previous 40 years, but beginning to creep back into Psychology, and it was this that revealed the importance of imitation. Not all the jiggers were aware that they jigged; those that were aware often tried to inhibit it but found that they could not.

These very surprising findings were written up, and published by the *British Journal of Industrial Medicine,* a journal of the British Medical Association (BMA) in 1954, under the title *Soap wrappers' "jig"*. The paper's impact was amplified by its appearance on the front page of a national newspaper, the Daily Express (then one of the top-selling national papers), on November 10th (Figure 7.1). *They're doing ... the soap wrapper's j-i-g* chirped the jolly headline. "All it [the jig] does", says the story, in phraseology that would never, thankfully, be used today, "is make you jerk as though you were doing a jungle-drum tribal dance", before going on to give a brief summary of the paper, including direct quotations from the author (slightly misquoting him, in fact) and his subjects. The story appeared just above one telling how *Dartmoor gunman just gives up*, which must have been troubling for those Express readers concerned about the nation's declining moral fibre. The following day, the paper printed a cartoon on page 3 inspired by the jig story (Figure 7.2). There cannot be many academics whose very first publication resulted in a story in the national press – and a cartoon. Wason himself was especially fond of this, his first, research paper, regarding it as one of his favourites among his own publications decades later, after his retirement.

The Express story referred to the wrapping paper's author as Dr P.C. Wason, but it was getting ahead of itself: Wason did not yet have a PhD; perhaps the journalist was deceived by the paper's having appeared in a BMA outlet, and presumed that Wason was a medic. Wason was in fact at that very moment setting out to put this right: he embarked on a PhD research project, to run in parallel with his work at the Industrial Psychology Research Group. It was a study into people's memory for précis of passages of text, following the interesting observation that such summaries contain similar information to the versions produced by people when they try to recall the original passages. It was not Wason's

**FIGURE 7.1** The Daily Express report of *Soap wrappers' "jig"*. By permission

idea to do research into this topic but that of his allotted supervisor: John Whitfield.

A final note about Whitfield. It seems that he was given medical treatment for his drink problem and did succeed in kicking it. However, he did very little research after the 1950s. He contributed an entry to Chambers' Encyclopaedia in 1961 (receiving payment of £5.13.6 four years later!), on psychological measurement, and reviewed his wartime research on accidents for *British Industry*, the journal of the Confederation of British Industry, in 1967, and that appears to have been that. He also did very little teaching; such classes as he gave were mainly on statistics, highly technical and consequently poorly attended. Nevertheless, he held on to his post as Reader in Psychology at UCL until his death, from heart failure, at the early age of 62 in 1979. How he survived in his academic post for so long is a mystery to many: he must have been protected in some way by George Drew,

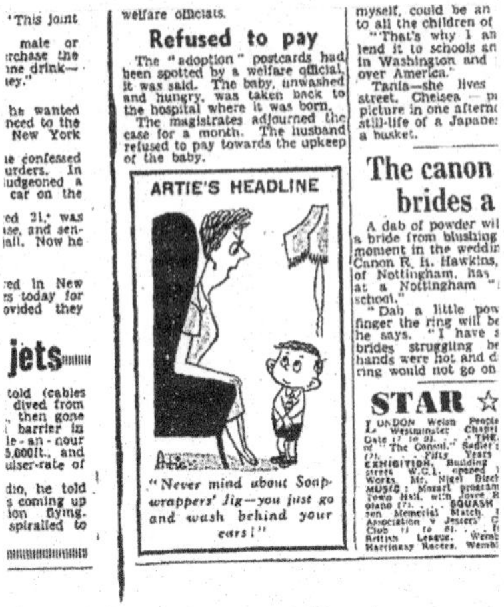
welfare officials.

Refused to pay

The "adoption" postcards had been spotted by a welfare official, it was said. The baby, unwashed and hungry, was taken back to the hospital where it was born.

The magistrates adjourned the case for a month. The husband refused to pay towards the upkeep of the baby.

ARTIE'S HEADLINE

"Never mind about Soap-wrappers' Jig—you just go and wash behind your ears!"

The canon brides a

STAR ☆

FIGURE 7.2 "Jig" cartoon in the Express the following day. By permission

head of department for much of that time, although no-one is quite sure why. It would not happen today. Wason wrote an affectionate remembrance of him in the *Quarterly Journal of Experimental Psychology*, misremembering the title of the problem-solving paper in the process, and considered him a better supervisor than lecturer; the same would later be said of Wason himself. Wason thought highly enough of him to have included, in 1968, 'An experiment in problem solving' in the first book he edited, with Johnson-Laird, called *Thinking and reasoning*, where Whitfield takes his place among the giants of the field.

# 8

# LIFE AND CHESS

## Life support

Those pre-war, dreamy days at Ballykilty must have seemed like a memory of someone else's life to Wason now. Since the Baedeker raid on his home town in early 1942, his life had been a succession of dramas: his Army experience and horrific, if inglorious, injury; his time at Oxford and his meetings with David Cecil and Marjorie Salberg; the near disaster of his attempt to become a lecturer in literature at far-distant Aberdeen. Since his return from there, the changes in his circumstances had if anything accelerated: admission to the Psychology course at University College London (UCL); marriage to Marjorie after one year there while putting in the effort needed to obtain a first class degree; transfer to the Industrial Psychology Research Group and parallel enrolment on a PhD pro-gramme with John Whitfield; a brush with fame, courtesy of the Daily Express.

This would have been dizzying for most people, but for Wason, there was an extra challenge: his hopeless impracticality. It had been a characteristic of his from his early childhood, driving his father, a practical man himself, to despair, as it did his teachers and his Army colleagues and superiors. He really was the stereotypical man who couldn't change a light bulb. Apart from the tension between him and his father, this trait had not caused him a lot of problems before; indeed, he was amused by it, and liked to tell self-deprecating stories about it. He had lived in a succession of situations which all had one thing in common: almost everything was done for him, and he had very few decisions to make. At home as a young child, he had been looked after by nannies and other servants; he went to two boarding schools; he spent three years in the Army. All very controlled, and controlling, environments. But after that, he was no longer in such a cosseted world. One word sums up how he was able to keep his head above water while all these new things were happening to him: Marjorie. She was his life support system.

She not only realised right from the start what she was in for if she was going to be Peter Wason's life partner, she accepted the assignment gladly. Of course, after their wedding, she didn't have much choice in the matter, owing to the marriage bar costing her her job with Oxford University Press and with it some of her economic autonomy (she could still count on support from her father). She threw herself into supporting him, taking on all the management roles that came with their setting up home together; not just housekeeper but financial decisions too, which Wason was happy to delegate to her. Her new family life was something she had never experienced in her own childhood, and she revelled in it. With this support, he was able to commit himself fully to, first, his Psychology degree and then his PhD, alongside his Medical Research Council research work. Without it, one doubts whether he could have prospered in the way he did. That is why, in Chapter 5, I described his meeting with Marjorie, urged on by Claude Miéville, as the most important moment of his life: Marjorie not only gave him love, but enabled him to become what he became. He simply could not have done it without her.

Not that she was some meek housewife, standing by her man; anything but. She was a vivacious, outgoing person, bright and beautiful, but not, as she would admit herself, an intellectual: she did not have the power of sustained concentration. Her cultural passion – a legacy of her previous relationship with Sandy Wilson – was art, which became a lifelong interest. Similarly, having been introduced to socialism by Wason, she joined the Labour Party. He did too. However, while he was content to be a relatively passive member, she became politically active. This was particularly the case when they moved to their flat in the affluent south-east London suburb of Blackheath, near to where her father was living. There, she also did voluntary work at a local school for 'deprived' children, and took part in political activities through the Party. She became well known in the local branch, and came to count MPs among her friends. One of them was the Labour member for the neighbouring constituency of Greenwich, Richard Marsh. He was a prominent figure at the time, a minister in the government led by Harold Wilson, elected with an increased majority in 1966. Marjorie, from her left-wing perspective, began to have her suspicions about Marsh. These were vindicated ten years later, when, no longer in Parliament, he fell, politically, for Margaret Thatcher and transferred his allegiance to the Conservatives. He was rewarded with a peerage.

Marjorie's father, Frank Salberg, was instrumental in helping them move from the flat and buy a house, still in Blackheath. It was fairly modern, with a large garden and a study into which Wason would pile his books, his pipes, his chess sets and his collection of Uncle Rigby's puzzles. They needed a house rather than a flat because, midway through Wason's PhD programme, Marjorie found herself pregnant. Their first child, Armorer, was born in 1956. The name came from Wason's fairly distant but very imposing relative, Armorer Breadalbane, John Glenorchy's mother, who was then aged 66, but still had more than 30 years to live. He must have admired her and thus continued the family custom of traditional naming, as we have seen elsewhere. As well as the new baby, they also had an elderly cat, called Trotsky. He had to go, for safety's sake: there were cases where babies in old-fashioned prams had been suffocated by cats curling up on top of them and covering their faces. Later, they would acquire two whippets. Wason loved animals, especially cats.

Perhaps to his surprise, given his own impoverished experience in this regard, Wason found himself settling readily into family life, and his daughters would remember him as a loving father. Despite this, though, Wason and Marjorie were even at this early stage starting to live their lives on gradually separating tracks. While both abhorred middle-class conventionality – Wason never had any time for 'money men' – Marjorie's rebellion against it depended on her bohemian, unconventional nature; she simply did not care how old you were, what you wore or whether you used the right word for the lavatory. In complete contrast to Wason, Marjorie quickly acquired a wide circle of friends, particularly female friends; Wason had very few close friends throughout his life. He could be judgemental about people in a way that was anathema to her: someone would come round to their house and Marjorie would enthuse about how nice they were. "Nice but dull", Wason would comment, and that was the end of that. Just as with his intellectual pursuits, Wason was only interested in someone if they were interesting. He could not feign it. But if a person happened to fall into that category, he would almost fall in love with them, and converse with a passion. He was an entertaining, humorous and charismatic conversationalist among company he liked, warmly remembered as such by those who are still here.

Partly because of the strains of their new family life, the pressures of his work – a PhD programme running alongside his 'day job' as an MRC researcher – and the increasing divergence of their lives, along with these temperamental differences, they would sometimes argue. Wason also rather looked down on Marjorie intellectually: she was the real scatterbrain, a term that had been used to disparage him at his prep school. For him, the intellect was all-important, and despite the constant reminders of his own physical impairments, in the shape of the eternal pain from his legs and the continuous medication he needed to manage it, he was apt to neglect his physical health. He also had a belief, forged in the period he grew up in, that to be overly concerned with one's physical condition was slightly fascistic. He was much more concerned with his mental health. Both he and Marjorie continued with psychoanalysis, but when Marjorie told the analyst she was pregnant, the therapist refused to see her anymore; perhaps he was holding to the decidedly patronising psychoanalytic view of pregnancy as a period of regression, where the woman reverts to the stage of her own early psychological development. This would have been bad at the best of times, but it was worse than that for her. She was in her mid-30s, which would be late now but was very late then for a first-time pregnancy, and she was about to become a mother when she had had no real experience of mothering herself: nannies before being shipped off to boarding school on the other side of the world at age 7, with very little parental contact thereafter, before losing her mother altogether at the age of 16. There was thus no mother around to help her with the experience of pregnancy. Her husband had had a similar experience of parenting, except that he saw more of his parents when not at boarding school as he did not have to travel far in the holidays and simply returned home. They were both going to have to make it up as they went along. Marjorie was especially happy to take the lead in family matters, compensating for the complete lack of such an experience in her own childhood.

In the late 1950s, the family situation became more complex still, not least because a second child, Sarah, came along in 1958. Wason suffered periodically from depression, and sought psychiatric help. He saw the psychiatrist Peter Dally, who diagnosed him as manic-depressive (bipolar, as we would now say). Dally would later write a book on Virginia Woolf's manic-depression. Wason was quite open about his diagnosis, at least within his own family, and he was not always down; there was a lot of humour in the Wason household, and the occasional rows with Marjorie were quickly smoothed over. Dally, an eminent psychiatrist, consultant at St Thomas's Hospital and with a thriving private practice which included slices of society's upper crust among its clientele, prescribed lithium and other antidepressants, and treated Wason for most of the rest of his life. Wason's morning routine thus included a large round of pill-popping, since he also had to take regular analgesia for the pain in his legs. He was still only in his 30s.

## Chess men

There is another factor which also accounts for the increasing separateness of Wason's and Marjorie's lives. It is related to their temperamental difference, which in other ways could be complementary rather than corrosive. Wason's intellectual style was contemplative, ruminative. He needed a sanctum within which he could sit, fire up his Dunhill and think about problems; a real-life Sherlock Holmes. He would take one of his many observations of some everyday curiosity of life home and wonder about it, eventually, if the mental cards fell kindly, working out a way in which it could be studied. He did not read a lot of psychology after his first degree, and so had to do this without leaning on a battery of existing experimental paradigms. Besides which, at this stage of the development of the subject, there were not many experimental paradigms to lean on in the first place: cognitive psychology, the experimental study of mental processes using behavioural methods, was then in its early infancy. Notwithstanding this accident of history, Wason would turn this 'don't read too much' principle into a kind of commandment, and pass it on, in time, to his research students too, some of whom passed it on to their own students. He was, of course, widely read outside Psychology, so continued as an academic the pattern of his own education: becoming self-educated outside the context of formal learning.

The first such student was someone whom Wason found interesting, and so could deal with enthusiastically: Jonathan Penrose. He was interesting for a particular reason: he was a chess prodigy. In fact, he was a far better player than Wason would ever be, having learned the game from the age of four, under the tutelage of his father Lionel, himself a high-standard player and problemist, and a world-renowned scientist who was Professor and head of the department of Human Genetics at UCL. By his mid-teens, in the early 1950s, Jonathan was beating international champions, later including the world champion: he was the first Briton to do so since 1899. In 1958, during the time he was working with Wason, he won the British championship for the first of ten times, an unsurpassed record to this day. Wason and Penrose had crossed paths briefly while Penrose was an undergraduate – he got his degree in Psychology in 1956 – but it was when he was a postgraduate student that they got together properly: they bonded over their love of chess, and took it from there.

In 1959, a staff–student chess match was organised by the student chess society at UCL. Whether the students knew about Penrose's stature as a competitive player and thought that, as a PhD candidate, he would be on their side, or they simply didn't know about him, is uncertain, but the latter is highly unlikely: his capturing of the British championship the previous year at the age of 25 would have made large waves in chess circles, and even in the wider world. It was billed as a 'friendly' match. In the event, Penrose played for the staff side, along with his father. The staff team leaned on Wason to play a match for them. Amazingly, he agreed, and won his game, against a certain Mr Northage.

This is amazing because it is the last recorded case of Wason playing a competitive match 'over the board', as chess aficionados call a face-to-face game. He played against anyone who would give him a game when he was younger (he was now 35), at school and while on military service, and in January 1947, the Western Daily Press, a local newspaper, reported on a simultaneous match held in Bath between a visiting French grandmaster, Eugene Znosko-Borovsky, and local club players. Wason was one of them. He was one of only five players to avoid defeat against the visiting titan, drawing his game; M. Znosko-Borovsky won the other 16 and lost none. But in recent years, Wason had moved exclusively to correspondence chess: the British Correspondence Chess Association (BCCA) has records of games involving him from around 1949–1950. Correspondence chess (it still exists although it has now been largely, though not completely, replaced by the online version) is where players set up boards and tell each other their moves by post. It is slow going – even a quick game can take two years – but it does have some advantages: you can play people from around the world, and you can have several games on the go at any one time. Wason did both, and was particularly fond of playing against opponents from the then Soviet Union. He suspected, because of the time taken for their moves to come back, that the games were being intercepted by Russian postmen, themselves keen players. Of course, it could have been the Soviet – or the British – postal system, or just the mere distance between them.

There is no one reason why Wason abandoned over-the-board play and devoted himself just to this form of the game; many factors, both negative and positive, conspired to push him in that direction. He was, for instance, terrified of 'blunders': errors that are surprising given the level of skill of the player in question.

Perhaps he had committed one when his Army team had been whitewashed in a match against the underestimated Czechs of the Pioneer Corps during the War, and was stung by the experience. Penrose thought that the physical tension which is part of the over-the-board game was hard for Wason, with his injuries, to bear. These are negative factors that might have pushed him away from the over-the-board game. But there were also aspects of correspondence chess which, for him, were a decided positive: firstly, it enables players to contemplate their moves at their leisure, since they are not playing against the clock, or at least, not so much: correspondence players have the convention that a move should be made within three days. This perfectly suited Wason's ruminative thinking style. He was also not that interested in the competitive aspect of chess either. As with his approach to religion, it was the aesthetics of the game that intrigued him, so he also liked to ruminate over 'manufactured' games: chess problems composed by problemists that had not actually occurred in real games and were published in magazines and books. Penrose liked these too, and they would discuss them together. A second positive factor was the byproduct of the correspondence game whereby it opened up relationships with his opponents, particularly those from behind the Iron Curtain. The closest of these was with Emil from Hungary, who would write to Wason about matters other than chess. He would read these accounts of east European life to his family.

Wason achieved a high standard as a correspondence chess player, ultimately being granted the title of International Master. This is the level below Grandmaster. He won prizes from the British Federation for Correspondence Chess (BFCC) for the best game of the year, and in time returned the compliment: he left the BFCC a small legacy to set one up in his name, initially called the Wason Brilliancy Prize. Owing to the decline of correspondence chess in the face of the online hegemony in the 21st century, there were ever fewer entries, and in 2010, it was combined with the existing Potter Best Game Prize to make up the Potter–Wason prize, which is still awarded.

Penrose duly surpassed him, however, becoming a Grandmaster at correspondence chess, and leading the victorious British team at the Correspondence Olympiad, held over a five-year period (I told you it was slow going) in the 1980s. Penrose had also himself transferred from over-the-board to the correspondence game, but for a very different reason. In 1970, the year after the last of his 10 British titles, won over a 12-year period, he suffered a collapse at a tournament, and never played at a championship over the board again. He was nevertheless, and deservedly, awarded Grandmaster status in this most testing form of the game retrospectively, like a lifetime Oscar, by FIDE, the World Chess Federation (the initials are from the French) in 1993.

Wason published some of his games, and other articles on chess, in the *Journal of international correspondence chess* and in US chess magazines. Neil Limbert, from the British Correspondence Chess Association, was able to retrieve some of his prize-winning games from the BCCA archive. Wason provided his own notes on these games, and Jonathan Evans, an expert chess player himself and also one of Wason's two starriest PhD students (with Johnson-Laird), has reanalysed them. This he did with the aid of a powerful chess computer program, or engine, Stockfish 9, which works by 'brute-force' computation, i.e. using the machine's massive computing power to sort through far more possible moves and positions than a human mind, even that of a chess champion, ever could. These analyses are shown in Box 8.1 and Box 8.2. If you are not familiar with chess notation you can readily skip them, but chess players should find them interesting.

In both cases, Wason's comments are edited down (he made extensive annotations) and combined with the output of Stockfish 9. The game in Box 8.1 was awarded the BCCA best game prize in 1951. Present-day reanalysis shows that it was played at Master standard.

The second game is longer, but is interesting because at around move 33, Wason made a deep positional sacrifice of two pawns which most chess engines would not have made (except perhaps the very latest, such as Alpha Zero or Leela).

There was a degree of mutual admiration that turned to genuine friendship between Wason and Penrose. Wason was a fan of Penrose the chess champion, while Penrose considered Wason a decent, helpful man and mentor, as far as Psychology was concerned. He had high regard for him as a supervisor. Although they drifted apart after Penrose completed his PhD (with John Whitfield as one of his examiners), they did have the occasional contact thereafter. In the early 1960s, Penrose was playing in Bath, and Wason, on a visit to Grafton Lodge, turned up unannounced at the hall, accompanied by his now elderly mother, whom Penrose liked; it was a fleeting encounter. They last saw each other in the 1980s, when Penrose visited Wason at the latter's invitation, to discuss a book that Wason had written with another British chess champion, William Hartston, called *The Psychology of Chess*, which was published in 1983.

Wason and Hartston, a well-known journalist, latterly for the Daily Express, who himself had a background in Psychology, had met at a tournament (Wason was not playing), took to each other, and planned the book over the next few years; it was done quite quickly in the last of these years, aided by frequent lunches together at an Indian restaurant near Wason's office in the Euston area of London. They would discuss the chapter that one had sent the other a short while before. Each found the other stimulating company: Hartston thus fell easily into the 'interesting' category that made him appealing to Wason. Wason once told Hartston that there were two kinds of people in the world: the living and the dead. He was thankful, he said, that they could both be counted among the living.

Despite the fun they had when writing it, looking back in his retirement, Wason at first came to regard this book as not one of his foremost achievements, although he did quickly revise that view. It was the only time he tried to bring his psychological expertise to bear on his major passion. From our current perspective, the authors made a serious misjudgement when they pronounced, in a chapter headed *Artificial stupidity?* (the question mark at least indicates a measure of doubt), that computers would probably never outplay human Grandmasters, and that even

---

## BOX 8.1 WASON'S PRIZE-WINNING GAMES 1

White: Peter C Wason
Black: Rev G E Hewson
BCCA Knockout, best game prize 1951
Opening: French Defence Winawer variation

1. e4 e6
2. d4 d5
3. Nc3 Bb4
4. e5 c5
5. a3 Bxc3+
6. bxc3 Qc7
7. Nf3 Nc6
8. Bd3 Nge7
9. h4

[diagram 1]

This position was reached in master level play as recently as 2008
... h5?!
The reply appears to be novel but not all that good, according to SF9, which prefers h6

10. O-O Nf5?

A mistake. Wason comments that better is 11 ... c4 12. Be2 Nf5; SF9 suggests 12 ... f6

11. Bxf5 exf5
12. dxc5!

[diagram 2]

White willingly triples his c pawns. He intends to win by force and has no thoughts of an endgame

12. ... Be6
13. Nd4 a6?!

Another inaccuracy, according to SF9, which now gives White a winning advantage at this level

14. Bg5 Ne7
15. Rb1 Rb8
16. Rb6 Nc6
17. Qf3 Qc8?

Another mistake, although the game was already lost. Wason comments that if 17 ... Nxe5 18. Qg3 followed by 19. Bf4, winning the knight

18. Qg3 Na5
19. Bf6!!

[diagram 3]

... Rg8
Black declines the bishop sacrifice. If gxf6, Wason intended 20. exf6,

demonstrating wins after 20 ... Rf8, 20 ... Rh6, 20 ... Qd8 and 20 ... Nc4. A great deal of calculation was needed here with the luxury of analysis time available to a correspondence player

20. Rxe6+ 1-0

20 ... fxe6 is met by 21. Qg6+ Kf8 22. Bg5 and Black will have to give up his queen. After 20 .. Kf8 Be7+ leads to mate. The mechanical mind of SF9 recommends 20 ... Qxe6 giving up the queen immediately, but most humans would prefer to resign, as did the Reverend Hewson

Diagram 1

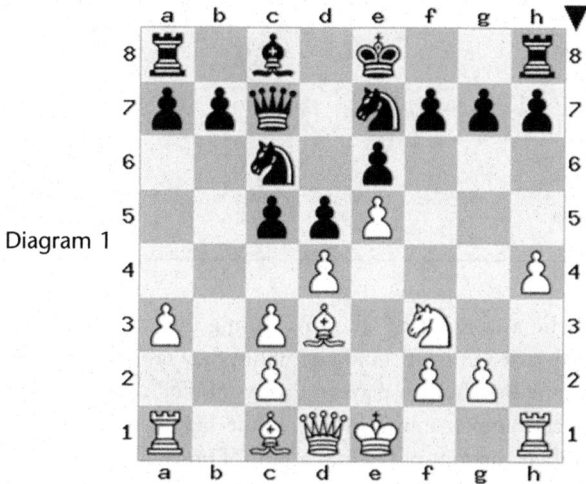

Diagram 2

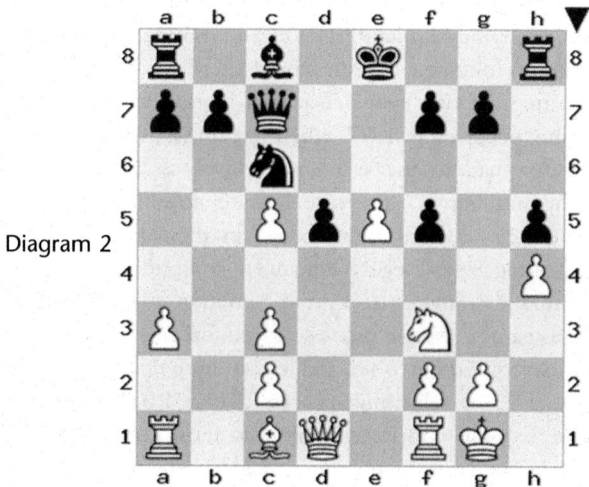

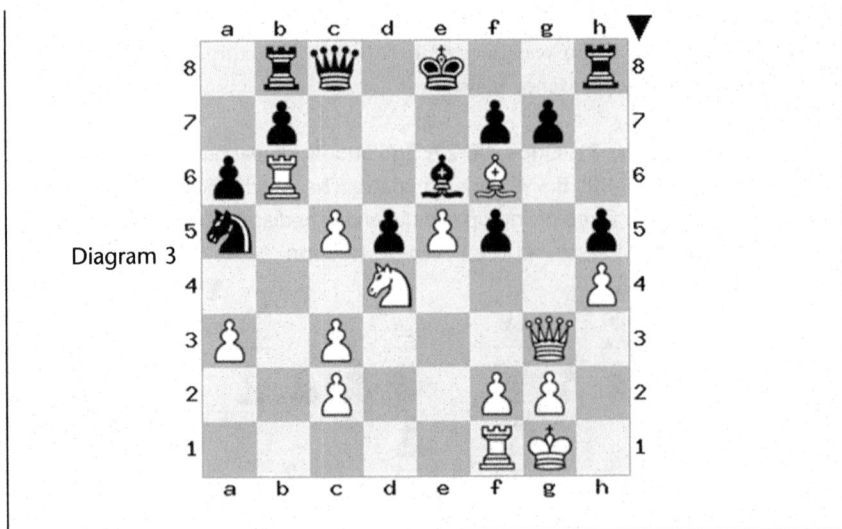

Diagram 3

if they did, it would be as a result of 'cheating': using the computer's vast processing power in a way that a human could not. Thus, they say, even if a computer succeeded in beating the best human players, this would tell us more about chess than it would about the human mind. In fact, while Hartston and Wason were essentially correct in their account of the limitations of brute-force programs, they greatly underestimated the advances in computer power that have occurred, and hence overestimated the engines' limitations. We can forgive them this, of course, since they were writing so long ago. Wason would later have been well aware of their misjudgement, since the first-ever defeat of a world champion by a computer, IBM's Deep Blue, occurred in 1997, when Wason was still an active player.

Programs have always had to use what are known as 'position evaluation functions' to limit the number of otherwise infinite possible positions – they discard those that could never lead anywhere – but these have become more 'intelligent' recently, along with hugely enhanced computing power and the development of machine learning, whereby the computer adapts its approach in the light of its previous games, using a process of 'reinforcement': attaching more weight to moves that have good outcomes and less to those that do not. This, you may recall from Chapter 2, is a learning process that had been extensively researched and described by behaviourist psychologists, most notably B.F. Skinner, in the inter-war period. The latest such engine, called Leela, plays huge numbers of games – millions – against itself on computers around the world and learns as it does so. It makes intelligent moves above Grandmaster standard and is widely admired in the chess world as a result. It is hard now to brand this kind of machine performance as artificial stupidity: the answer now invited by Hartston and Wason's question mark is 'no'.

Hartston was convinced that Wason ultimately preferred correspondence chess to over-the-board play because it represented pure abstract reasoning rather than

## BOX 8.2   WASON'S PRIZE-WINNING GAMES 2

White: J. Bogason
Black: Peter C Wason
GB-Iceland match, 1946–1950
Opening: Nimzo-Indian defence

 1.  d4 Nf6
 2.  c4 e6
 3.  Nc3 Bb4
 4.  Qc2 d5
 5.  cxd5 Qxd5
 6.  e3 c5
 7.  a3 Bxc3+
 8.  bxc3 Nbd7
 9.  f3 cxd4
10.  cxd4 Nb6
11.  Ne2 Bd7
12.  Nf4 Qd6
13.  Bd2 Rc8
14.  Qb2 Nfd5
15.  Nxd5 exd5
16.  Bb4 Qe6
17.  Kf2

[diagram 4]

According to SF9, the game is even at this point with both players having played the opening accurately. It seems they have been following the moves of a world championship match as Wason (Black) comments here that Alekhin-Euwe, 1937, game 8 continued 17 ... Na4 18. Qd2 b6 19. Ba6 with White going on to win. Alekhin marked Na4 as an error in his post-match analysis and recommended instead the move that Wason actually played next. Note that correspondence players have unlimited and legitimate access to such information.

... Nc4

SF9 actually regards this as an inaccuracy and recommends f5 as better

18.  Bxc4 Rxc4
19.  Rac1 Rxc1
20.  Rxc1 Bc6
21.  Rc3 Kd7
22.  Qc2 f5
23.  a4 Re8
24.  g3 g5
25.  a5 a6
26.  Bc5 Rh8

27. Rb3 h5
28. Qb2 Kc8
29. Qe2?
[diagram 5]
White's first clear mistake according to SF9
... g4
It is around here that Wason demonstrates masterly positional and strategic play that differs from that typical of a chess engine. SF9 thinks this reply was also a mistake, missing Bb5. But Wason has a deep strategic plan as the next few moves reveal.
30. fxg4 hxg4
31. Kg1 f4!
32. gxf4 g3!
33. hxg3
[diagram 6]
A most unusual double positional pawn sacrifice which makes this game extremely memorable. Wason comments that the key to this position is White's astonishing weakness (and Black's strength) on the white squares. The sacrifice works because only Black has a light square bishop. SF9 agrees that Black holds an advantage here despite being two pawns down.
... Qh3
34. Qg2 Qg4
35. Rb1?
The rook moves to avoid being lost to Qd1+. Correct, according to SF9, was Rd3
... Rh3
36. Kf2 Bb5!
[diagram 7]
So dangerous now is the light square bishop that White is obliged to give up his rook for it on the next move. White cannot otherwise defend the twin threats of Qe2+ and B – d3 – e4 as Wason notes. We see now why 35 Rd3 was needed, to allow the defence Rd2 following Bb5
37. Rxb5 axb5
38. Be7 Qh5?!
Here Wason criticises his own move as a serious loss of tempo. Both he and SF9 say that 38 ...Qf5 was correct. The instructive point here is that despite almost unlimited time for analysis before making the move, the correspondence player often finds something better afterwards!
39. Bh4 Qf5
40. e4 dxe4
41. Ke3 Kd7?
42. Qxe4?
Black gets away with a lazy move 41 (correct was b4) according to SF9, which evaluates the position as even after 42 d5. However, White immediately

handed the advantage back

... Qxe4+

43. Kxe4 Rh1
44. f5 b4
45. Kd3 Rc1
46. Kd2 Rc8
47. Bf6 b3
48. d5 Rc2+
49. Kd1 Rf2
50. Kc1 Rxf5
51. Bc3 Rxd5
52. Kb2 Rb5
53. g4 Kc6
54. g5 Kd5
55. g6 Kc4
56. g7 Rg5

0-1

[diagram 8]

At this point, White throws in the towel. Play might continue for quite a few more moves, but it is a straightforward win for Black with good endgame technique.

Diagram 4

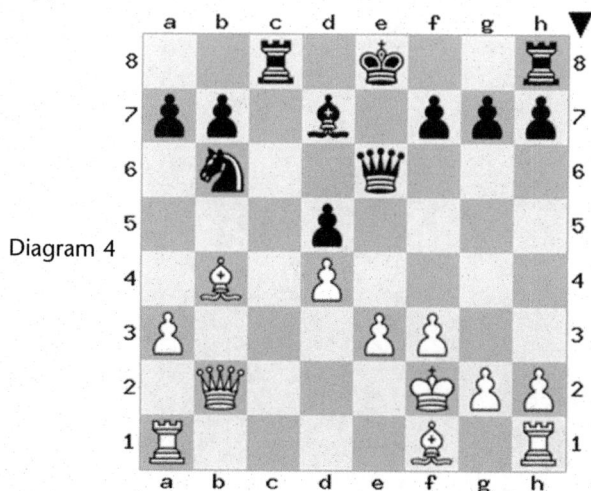

Diagram 5

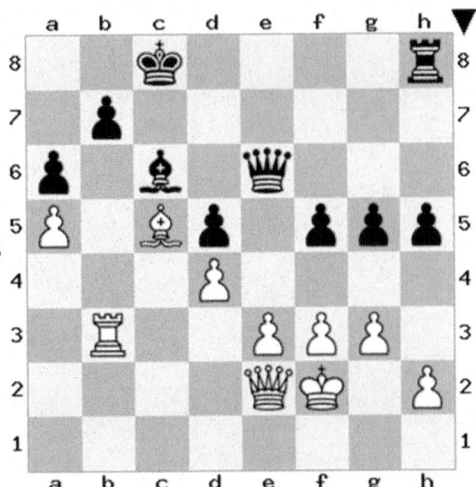

Diagram 6

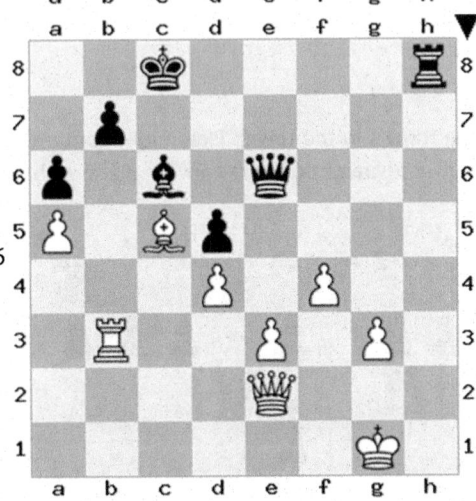

Diagram 7

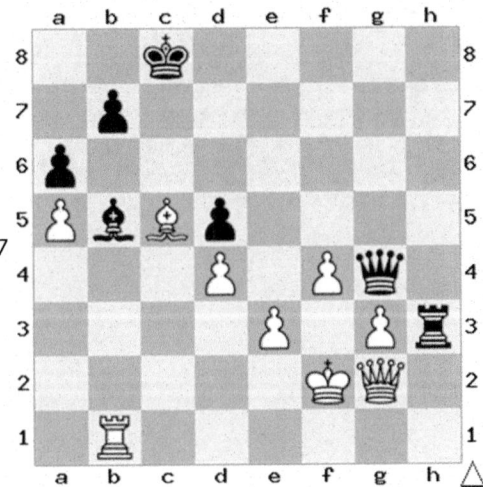

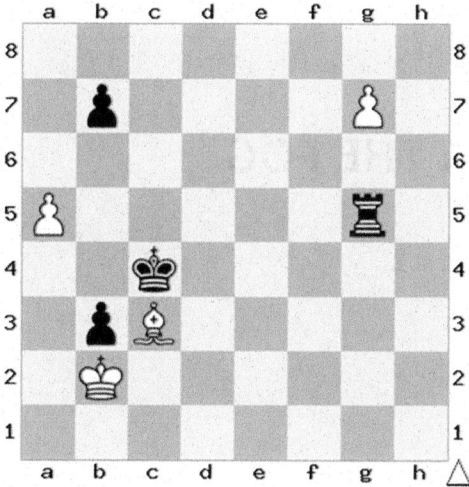

Diagram 8

gladiatorial combat. Others have also thought that it was the 'music' of the game that entranced him, as mentioned above. That being so, his switch to it in his late 20s was an early indicator of what would, within a short time after the high-intensity period of his life in the late 1950s, come to dominate his thinking: the nature of reasoning. He would not have realised it at that time, but he was not only about to open new doors in studying it, but construct a whole house of them.

# 9

# CLEARING THE FOG

## Trees and lists

Wason's PhD was awarded in 1957. Its title was *The effect of compressing information on its retention*, and it is an interesting piece of work in a number of ways. Firstly because, despite Wason's creativity in research, it was a topic that came not from his own interests or imagination but from his allotted supervisor, John Whitfield. Allotted: at the time, if you applied to undertake PhD study, you were given someone to supervise you. You may have had some say in the matter, but in the end, the decision was not yours. These days, you are just as likely to apply for a particular project, and the supervisor comes with it; it is one of a number of ways in which you can obtain a PhD studentship.

The second way in which this work was interesting is that it is clearly a piece of cognitive psychology, in that it involves experiments using a behavioural measure (in this case, how much of a prose passage can be reproduced after a period of time) in the investigation of a mental process, memory. Bear in mind that Wason would have started working on it in 1953–1954; if you pick up a textbook today, you will find the origins of modern cognitive psychology located at or just after this period, with the appearance of texts such as Jerome Bruner, Jacqueline Goodnow and George Austin's *A study of thinking* (1956), Donald Broadbent's *Perception and communication* (1958) and Noam Chomsky's destruction of the behaviourist approach to language in his famous review – it is one of the most celebrated and influential book reviews in the history of science – of B.F. Skinner's *Verbal behavior* (that's what language is to a behaviourist) in 1959. Chomsky himself had published, at the age of 28, his paradigm-shifting work in theoretical linguistics, *Syntactic structures*, in 1957. Although not a psychological work, it became for many years the pre-eminent influence on psycholinguistics, the psychological study of language.

So to be studying memory for prose passages in 1954–1957 was to be in at the very start of a scientific revolution. Or, to look at it from a different angle, Wason's work gives the lie to the idea that Psychology was all behaviourism until 1956; and Whitfield, after all, had published his two best-known and most inventive papers, both on cognitive topics, in 1950–1951. That is another way in which Wason's PhD work is interesting. Dating the start of the cognitive revolution in Psychology is a bit like dating the start of rock & roll music – at very much the same time – or tracing the source of the Nile: you can always find early trickles before the main stream. There is a fourth source of interest, if you find educational practice in the UK interesting, that is. Wason's thesis, produced on a manual typewriter from his longhand draft, and with hand-drawn graphs and tables, is about 30,000 words long and contains just one main experiment, plus a couple of pilot studies. That is about one-third as many words and one-eighth as many experiments as you would see in a cognitive psychology thesis these days. And people say the youth of today have it easier.

The research itself is also interesting: Wason found that the originals of passages (he gave people extracts from the writings of Bertrand Russell, another thing that would surprise the modern student) led to better recall of the passages' main points than did summaries which preserved all these points but were a quarter of the length. The reason this is interesting is that these summaries strongly resembled the versions produced by people when they tried to re-member the originals. There is thus a lot of apparently redundant extra in-formation in the originals which is lost when people try to recall the passages, but this information clearly helps us to remember these main points, and Wason spent several pages hypothesising what this help consisted of. And here is the last point of interest: this research was a blind alley as far as Wason was concerned; he would never again study memory, and only wrote up this work for publication in a research journal five years later. For researchers, obtaining a PhD is rather like passing the driving test: once you have it, you can set off by yourself and do some real driving. Wason promptly headed down another road. Little did he know, but a new assignment from the Medical Research Council (MRC) would define this road for him, and ensure he never had to contemplate following up his doctoral work.

This assignment concerned the understanding of official documents and regulations. Everyone knows the problem: they vary between hard to follow and completely incomprehensible. Wason set out to find out why, and what could be done about it. He did this in concert with the other significant University College London (UCL) figure introduced in Chapter 7: A.R. Jonckheere. Wason had come across Jonckheere before, as far back as his un-dergraduate days, and went to him for help with statistical analysis when he was doing his PhD work; the thesis contains an acknowledgement of this. He could hardly have gone to anyone better, although his supervisor, John Whitfield, was also an expert statistician, who not only taught on the subject but published original research on it. Perhaps he could not understand Whitfield, or just wanted a second opinion.

A.R. Jonckheere has, to this day, near legendary status among Psychology staff and students at UCL, past and present. The initials stand for Aimable Robert, the latter being the name of his French-Belgian father, a notable astronomer (he discovered double stars), who split up from his English mother when Jonckheere was seven, whereupon mother and son moved to Enfield, now in North London. No one ever used these names: everyone called him Jonck. He died with his boots on, as the saying goes – he was working in the department up to the day before and was intending to come back in the following Monday – in 2005 at the age of 85, after being at UCL since the immediate post-war years, initially as an undergraduate (he obtained a first in psychology and statistics), then as a lecturer, appointed in 1951. In the mid-1950s, he spent some time in the Geneva laboratory of one of the towering figures of 20th century Psychology, the great developmental psychologist Jean Piaget, going on to publish a book with him and Benoit Mandelbrot (Jonckheere was bilingual in French and English).

In London, he provided statistical assistance to the likes of Sir Cyril Burt, professor at UCL at the time, and Hans Eysenck, and later also to Jerome Bruner, and became the fount of all methodological and statistical knowledge in the Psychology department: contemporaries all tell of a semi-permanent queue outside his office door, as people, both staff and students, waited to discuss the design of their studies or the analysis of their data with him. He was very adept at critical analysis, having studied under the logical positivist philosopher A.J. Ayer as an undergraduate, and used this facility to unpick published papers; it was said that he could not only pick a paper to pieces, but pick the pieces to pieces. This stance could be double-edged as far as students were concerned: having your ideas subjected to this kind of critical sandblasting could prove either exhilarating or intimidating, depending on your temperament. Either way, it was done without ego on Jonckheere's part. Intellectual macho jousting was not his way.

He took this lack of ego to what would now be considered an extreme, becoming almost allergic to having his name on research papers published by people whose ideas he had influenced, even when his contribution to the research – not just to data analysis but to its design and conceptual underpinnings – was very substantial. This happened a lot. A former colleague, the eminent cognitive neuropsychologist Prof. Tim Shallice, writing in an obituary, reckoned that he had influenced hundreds of publications in this way, invisibly to all but those who knew. He tended to be hyper-critical, and was not happy to have his name associated with anything he considered less than perfect. As a result, his stature was largely local, and his contribution undervalued by the university powers-that-be. This was illustrated clearly when a deputation of young academic colleagues, which included Shallice and Phil Johnson-Laird, petitioned the head of department in the 1960s to have him promoted to a professorship. The petition failed; Jonckheere was never a professor. Was he bothered? Not so that anyone noticed. It was ideas, not status, that were important to him, ideas not only in Psychology but in other areas too, such as philosophy and art (he sometimes gave classes at the nearby Slade School of Art, part of UCL, having worked with Sir Ernst Gombrich and another great figure in British Psychology, Richard Gregory, on the psychology of perception).

It is worth making this point again: as with Wason, someone like Jonckheere would, even with all his qualities, struggle to survive in the modern university system, with its metrics, audits and league tables. He certainly would have had to operate differently. He would have had to cast off his allergy to author credits, for instance: academics are assessed on the papers that have their names on them, they have to produce a criterial number of them, and attain a criterial quality in each one; departments are then assessed on their academics' 'performance', and universities on that of their departments. They are also assessed on their success in attracting research funding, which is strange, since funding is an input, not an output. A department which produces 50 first-rate papers and brings in £10 million will be more highly rated than one that produces the same but brings in £1 million, and yet the latter is more efficient. As Shallice laments in his obituary of Jonckheere, "The modern British university is a production line for advanced training and the creation of new technical knowledge", more than it is the kind of "community of scholars" that it may have been 50 years earlier. Perhaps that is a romantic view, and there was a need to be more vigilant about the use of public money in the university sector, especially as it was so greatly expanded in that time. But the idea that someone like Jonckheere might today be considered a burden rather than an adornment to a university department is a sad one.

Jonckheere and Wason could hardly have had two more contrasting intellectual styles: Jonckheere quick-witted, especially when confronting and dissecting the ideas of others, Wason slow and ruminative. Both were highly creative, but in very different ways; both were interested in ideas, although Wason was much the more liberal of the two, Jonckheere the more critical. Perhaps because of these contrasts, though probably mainly because they just liked each other, they became friends as well as colleagues. Jonckheere would remain Wason's statistical guru for years to come; Wason himself, while not a complete statistical dullard, nevertheless found the activity of analysing data less than fun, and was happy to delegate it to someone else. He would later discourage one of his daughters from studying Psychology because of its mathematical content.

Jonckheere's creativity came to the fore when Wason set about his assignment of trying to clear the fog from official regulations. To give you an idea of what the researchers, and the general population, were up against, here is a short passage that has appeared in several of Wason's accounts of this research. You are wondering about National Insurance contributions, which go towards determining your eventual pension entitlement, among other things. You come across this sentence (it is from a Ministry leaflet of the late 1950s):

> A Class 1 contribution is not payable for employment by any one employer for not more than eight hours in any week – but if you normally work for more than eight hours in any week for any one employer, a Class 1 contribution is payable except for any week when you do not do more than four hours work for that employer.

When did your mind begin to cloud over? At the second 'not', probably: Wason was quick to identify negation as one of the problems with these rules. There are two types of negation on display here, technically known as explicit, which is when 'no' or 'not' is used, and implicit, where a word is used which implies a 'not'. 'But' and 'except' are examples of implicit negation in this sentence. So in this one sentence, the poor reader encounters five negatives; 'normally' also has implicitly negative connotations, i.e. that something sometimes may not happen. This is legalistic language, designed to rule out ambiguity so that everyone knows exactly where they stand. Except that the language itself puts up a barrier to understanding. Your task is to find out which parts of the rules apply to you, as well as to decode them, and with the rules set out as plain prose this is difficult to do. It is not the words that are the problem – there is no arcane jargon here – but the way the sentence is structured. The solution that Wason and Jonckheere came up with was simple but radical: don't use prose. Use a means of structuring the words that helps readers rather than hinders them in their quest for relevance.

Here is another example to show you what they did. Imagine you are a woman, approaching retirement (the ages given no longer apply since the women's minimum pension age was raised from 60 to 65 by the Pensions Act of 2011, in a move which caused much anger). You want to find out when you can claim the state pension. The official leaflet tries to guide you (these are its exact words):

> The earliest age at which a woman can draw a retirement pension is 60. On her own insurance she can get a pension when she reaches that age, if she has then retired from regular employment. Otherwise she has to wait until she is retired or reaches age 65. At age 65 pension can be paid irrespective of retirement. On her husband's insurance, however, she cannot get a pension, even though she is over 60, until he has reached age 65 and retired from regular employment, or until he is 70 if he does not retire before reaching that age.

I trust I make myself clear, you can almost imagine the stern-looking counter assistant at the social security office saying. It is not clear, of course. Once again she, the citizen wanting to know her rights, has to hack her way through the syntactic brambles before she finds out. And it's a painful business. Jonckheere suggested an alternative, which he and Wason called 'logical trees'. Here is the women's pension regulation reformulated in this way:

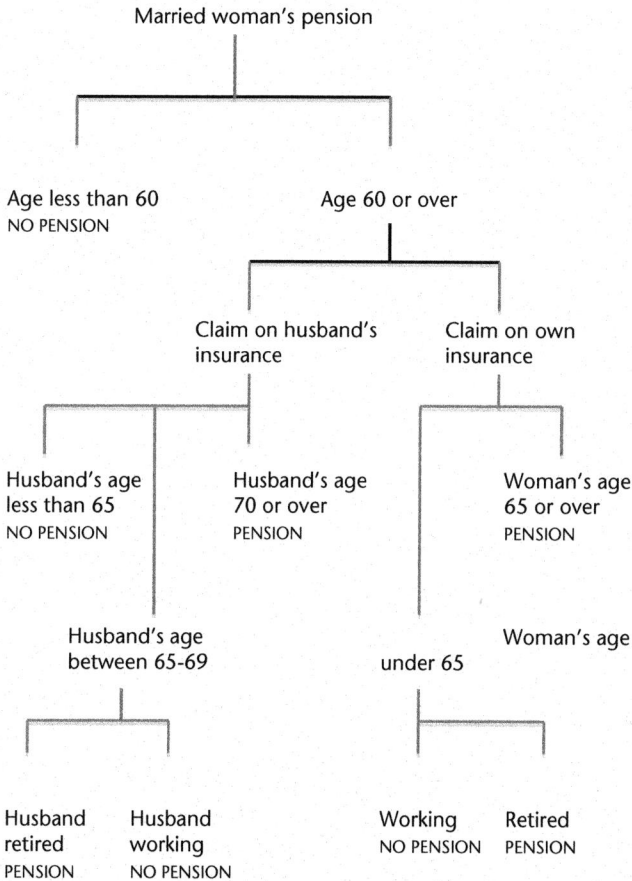

Married woman's pension

Age less than 60
NO PENSION

Age 60 or over

Claim on husband's insurance

Claim on own insurance

Husband's age less than 65
NO PENSION

Husband's age 70 or over
PENSION

Woman's age 65 or over
PENSION

Husband's age between 65-69

Woman's age under 65

Husband retired
PENSION

Husband working
NO PENSION

Working
NO PENSION

Retired
PENSION

Now, you do not have to read all the passage, trying to work out which bits apply to you; just follow the tracks dictated by the yes/no items, and the ones about age, and you arrive at the right decision (assuming you don't make a mistake). The tree turns each proposition in the regulation into a yes/no dichotomy, and proceeds downwards from the most general to the most particular, removing all redundant information from the reader's view as it does so. You have a lot less reading to do, and next to no thinking.

It is possible to achieve the same result without using the tree structure, and in fact this second format is the one that appears most often in official forms, occasionally aided by colour-coded panels, arrows and other graphic devices. Wason called it 'list structure' form, and this is how the pension regulation appears when it is used (I have slightly adapted it from Wason's original):

Married woman's retirement pension

| 1. | I am under 60 | yes.....................................................NO PENSION |
| | | no....................................................go to Question 2 |

| 2. | I am claiming | (a) on my own insurance.............go to Question 3 |
| | | (b) on my husband's insurance...go to Question 5 |

| 3. | I am under 65 | yes.....................................................go to Question 4 |
| | | no....................................................PENSION |

| 4. | I am working | yes.....................................................NO PENSION |
| | | no....................................................PENSION |

| 5. | My husband's | (a) less than 65.............................NO PENSION |
| | age is | (b) between 65 and 69.................go to Question 6 |
| | | (c) 70 or more.............................PENSION |

| 6. | My husband | yes.....................................................PENSION |
| | has retired | no....................................................NO PENSION |

Although this work was done in the late 1950s/early 1960s, it took a while for it to filter into the thinking of government and the wider world, even though it was commissioned by government. There is inevitably some inertia in such 'knowledge transfer', to use the modern term, and sometimes there is a suspicion that this inertia is motivated. When the new Labour government took power in 1964, the incoming minister, Richard Crossman, visiting the UCL department and enquiring about this work, was heard to remark that it may sometimes be useful for social security regulations to be a little opaque, otherwise everyone would claim what they were entitled to and it would cost the government money. It was perhaps said in jest; no-one was quite sure.

A second reason, besides this purely practical one, for the continuing interest in Wason's work on de-fogging official regulations was that he did not stop there, but carried on to research the psychology behind the difficulties he had identified. Other researchers also started work on this topic, and references to these other research efforts, confirming that Wason was the true pioneer, can be found in an official publication from Her Majesty's Stationery Office, published in 1967. Wason's work was by then sufficiently well-known for a national newspaper, The Observer, to devote a feature to it in its new year's day Review section of that year; the second appearance of his work in the national press. It reproduces the prose, logical tree and list-structure versions of the pension regulation we have just been looking at. The paper even sent a photographer, and there sits Wason in his study in Blackheath, tweed-jacketed, pipe in mouth, shelves of books in the background, accompanied by Marjorie, with her hand on his shoulder, and the two girls, ten and eight years old. He was then aged 42, but looked older; she was 45, but looked younger (Figure 9.1).

## Threads

Just what was it that made negatives cause difficulties in the understanding of language? Wason embarked on a series of studies on this question with another person who became a very significant figure in his story: Sheila Jones. She was also employed in the Industrial Psychology Research Group and is mentioned in the Observer feature as his co-worker; he likes clear writing, she likes logic, she says in it. She definitely fell into Wason's class of interesting people. This was because she had a rich hinterland outside her work in Psychology. She was married to a professor of physics, and was centrally involved in the Campaign for Nuclear Disarmament (CND), which was established in 1958: she was in fact one of its founder-members.

As Peggy Duff, one of CND's early movers along with Jones, recounts, it may seem strange that co-ordinated opposition to nuclear weapons should have begun 13 years after their first use in anger, at Hiroshima and Nagasaki. There were a few local oppositional groups in various places in the UK before then. What motivated them to coalesce into a national organisation were firstly the British H-bomb tests at Christmas Island, beginning in 1957, where weapons hundreds of times more powerful than those used against Japan were exploded. Then, in October, the same year, came the massive defeat at the Labour Party conference of a motion in favour of British unilateral nuclear disarmament. This was brought about largely by Aneurin Bevan, who was Shadow Foreign Secretary at the time, supported by trade union block votes. Bevan was perhaps the greatest orator the party ever had, and his speech is still remembered today for its plea not to send Britain's Foreign Secretary, a position he coveted, "naked into the conference chamber", a ringing phrase that earned itself a place in the Oxford Dictionary of Quotations. This outcome dismayed those on the Left who wanted to push a unilateralist policy, but it also spurred them to action outside conventional party politics.

Sheila Jones lived in Hampstead, north London, a self-contained hilltop suburb that even today retains the feel of the village it once was, and a prosperous village at that. The chairman of the precursor to CND, the National Council for the Abolition of Nuclear Weapons Tests, which had been set up in 1955, was Arthur Goss, a pacifist Quaker who owned the local newspaper, the Hampstead and Highgate Express, the 'Ham & High' to its friends. Jones became the Council's secretary, and for a while the NCANWT operated from her house. Realising that to raise its profile the campaign needed not just snappier initials but some nationally known figureheads, in 1958 the committee running it, which included Jones, recruited some, among them Bertrand Russell (by now a Lord), the writer

*DAVID NEWELL SMITH*

Dr Peter Wason with his wife, Marjorie, and his daughters, Sarah and Armorer.

they include Gillian Freeman on under-the-counter literature, Bernadine Bishop on nuns, David Kunzle on fashion and fetishism, Dr Charlotte Banks on hooliganism, and Martin Seymour-Smith on fallen women.

## Knowing the form

*' The earliest age at which a woman can draw a retirement pension is 60. On her own insurance she can get a pension when she reaches that age, if she has then retired from regular employment. Otherwise she has to wait until she retires or reaches age 65. At age 65 pension can be paid irrespective of retirement. On her husband's insurance, however, she cannot get a pension, even though she is over 60, until he has reached age 65 and retired from regular employment, or until he is 70 if he does not retire before reaching that age.'*

THIS DAUNTING passage is a fine example of the tortuous prose of Government pamphlets and leaflets. But, according to two psychologists in the Medical Research Council, it's not the fault of the people who write the leaflets: it's simply that English doesn't adapt itself to explaining complex regulations.

Dr Peter Wason and Dr Sheila Jones have just written a report on the subject. It took a year's research, working with the co-operation of the Treasury. They say continuous prose should be abandoned and replaced by diagrams or by a simplified question/answer form. Both are based on

read only what is relevant. He just has to decide yes or no at each stage. Presented as a diagram, it looks just like a family tree.

It is a practical application of purely theoretical work Dr Wason and Dr Jones have been doing for about eight years.

' An affirmative statement,' says Dr Wason, ' is much easier to understand than a negative. You simplify by doing away with all those " unlesses " and " if nots ".'

' Dr Wason,' says Dr Jones, ' can't bear to see things badly written, and I enjoy the logical breakdown.'

Dr Wason says he has a mental block about forms and that he never does his own income tax returns.

' Besides the cognitive difficulty,' he says, ' there is the image of the tax man, of us and them, which puts you in a punitive position. I'd like to do a test with a form dealing with something innocuous, like football pools, to see how important this factor is.'

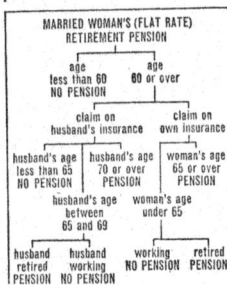

MARRIED WOMAN'S (FLAT RATE)
RETIREMENT PENSION

age less than 60 — NO PENSION
age 60 or over
claim on husband's insurance
claim on own insurance

husband's age less than 65 — NO PENSION
husband's age 70 or over — PENSION
woman's age 65 or over — PENSION

husband's age between 65 and 69
woman's age under 65

husband retired — PENSION
husband working — NO PENSION
working — NO PENSION
retired — PENSION

**FIGURE 9.1** The Observer Review feature, with Wason and family photographed in his study at Blackheath. By permission

J.B. Priestley, star journalist James Cameron, and Michael Foot, also a star journalist as well as a politician, whose career would culminate in leadership of the Labour Party and a rather ignominious election defeat, to the Conservatives under Margaret Thatcher, in 1983. Unilateral nuclear disarmament was part of the party's manifesto in that campaign, but the electorate, like the party conference 26 years earlier, was not persuaded: Labour recorded its lowest vote since 1918.

Russell was elected President of the newly constituted CND, the only time this title was ever used, and Sheila Jones remained on the committee. In time, she would occupy the post of official CND archivist, and would remain active in the movement for the rest of her life, as long as she was able. Her politics were in tune with those of Peter and Marjorie Wason, and the couple would go on ban-the-bomb demonstrations with her, such as the Aldermaston marches, which Peggy Duff had helped to instigate. Aldermaston, a village in Berkshire, was where the Atomic Energy Research Establishment was situated. It is unlikely that, with one and then two small children, besides Wason's leg injuries, they did the whole 53 miles (85 km) from Aldermaston to Trafalgar Square.

Wason's work on negation with Jones was the real start of his research career, and led directly to the later work which would secure his place in scientific history. It also led to immediate recognition on its own merits, and not just in government circles, as mentioned above. It had direct implications for a psychological account of language too, a field that had been given a huge boost, and was now dominated, by Chomsky's linguistic theory, set out in his groundbreaking book in 1957.

Initially, though, Wason's work was not conducted with these threads in mind. In his first reported investigation into negation, he took a leaf out of John Whitfield's book, and, just as Whitfield had done, began to devise his own methods to experiment on something which had, up to that point, been little explored by psychologists. The first such method became known as the 'verification task'; it would be reinvented, in a simpler and more direct form, by American psychologists in the early 1960s. It is simplicity itself in outline: take a non-linguistic situation such as a picture, and a sentence purporting to describe it. Are the sentence and picture consistent or inconsistent with each other? You can be right or wrong about this, of course, but since the task is usually so easy, it is the time taken to give the response that is the preferred behavioural measure. From such small seeds do great forests of research findings grow.

Wason published his first paper using this technique in 1959. This, his second published research paper, appeared five years after *Soap wrappers' "jig"*. This is not particularly unusual with recent PhDs: the doctoral programme and the resultant thesis take up a lot of time and effort (and Wason was conducting his alongside his full-time employment at the MRC Industrial Psychology Research Group as well at the time). Some people get it out of the way before they start writing papers, some write papers while they are doing their PhD, finding that it helps with the writing of the thesis and gives their research career some early propulsion into the bargain. It is a matter of style.

The 'pictures' in the experiment reported in this paper were squares divided into four numbered sectors. Each was accompanied by a sentence that the subject had to adjust to make sure that it either agreed or disagreed with the picture, as instructed. ('Subjects', by the way, was the word that was then used for the people who took part in experiments. It fell out of use in the late 20th century, to be replaced by the less oppressive-sounding 'participants'.) The sentences could be either affirmative or negative. Wason found that there was an interaction between truth and 'polarity' (i.e. affirmative v. negative). True affirmatives were predictably easiest to process, as measured by time taken to adjust the sentence, but affirmative sentences that were false turned out to be easier than negative sentences that were true: affirmation trumped truth in terms of ease of mental processing in this experiment.

This pattern caused quite a buzz among psycholinguists (psychologists who study how the mind processes language), and established Wason as an important figure in the field. This was because he had discovered that truth acts in opposite directions depending on polarity: with affirmative sentences, a true one is easier to process, but negative sentences are easier when they are false. This was a very surprising finding, and Wason, his students, and several other researchers set out to try to explain it.

It was sufficiently exciting for Wason to be invited to spend a year at the Center for Cognitive Studies at Harvard University in 1963, to conduct research. The invitation had been issued by George Miller, another of the advance guard in the cognitive revolution in Psychology: he was the co-author, with Eugene Galanter and Karl Pribram, of the highly influential *Plans and the structure of behavior* in 1960. Miller had fallen under the influence of Noam Chomsky, and was conducting a research programme asking, does the mind really work in the way that Chomsky's theory implies? The initial findings of experimental work on this question were promising for the disciples of Chomsky: a negated sentence takes longer to process than does an affirmative, a passive sentence takes longer than an active sentence, and a passive negative takes longer still; the two 'transformations' each add a separate component of difficulty that the mind has to process, as Chomsky's theory predicts.

Wason's work complicated the picture for Chomskyan psycholinguists. The complication comes from the surprising reversal of the role of truth in affirmative and negative sentences, particularly with negatives, where, as we saw above, false negatives were easier to process than true negatives. On the face of it, this is surprising because 'false negative' sounds like double negation, which should demand more processing than single negation. But it is not a double negative, as Wason attempted to clarify by giving the four sentences these tags:

| | |
|---|---|
| True affirmative: | a fact |
| False affirmative: | a falsehood |
| False negative: | denial of a fact |
| True negative: | denial of a falsehood |

Thinking about the problem in these terms activated the noticing part of Wason's brain, always ready to pounce. He realised that 'not' does not work in these experiments, or in official regulations, in the way that it does in everyday language. After all, it causes little difficulty when we speak and read about ordinary things; why then should it cause difficulty here? Inspired by his reading of books on logic, he proposed that, as he later put it in a paper that summed up all this work, "negation functions in an affirmative context". Suppose, at work on Monday morning, a colleague announces out of the blue "I didn't spend the weekend in Paris". You would say, "I didn't know you were going to!" Her comment only makes sense if you had believed she would be doing so; that belief is the affirmative context.

This is an example of what linguists call pragmatics: factors outside language that affect how the language is understood. Meaning can even be reversed in this way, something with which we are all familiar. I once heard a TV commentator say, over film of some rather lamentable 'folk dancing', "That was damn good". He meant the exact opposite, of course: he was being ironic. And funny. The context supplied by the film and his tone of voice made sure of that.

The everyday function of negation is, then, to deny a plausible preconception. It is hard to make sense of a person's denial unless you already know that what they are denying might have been true; a denial without such a context invites you to fill in the blank. In a later book, Wason drew on his Freudian sympathies in pointing out that Freud himself had treated negation in this way; indeed, Freud wrote a whole paper on the subject. An out-of-context negation should direct the therapist's attention, says Freud, to the thing being denied, since the negation reveals the preconception that was in the patient's mind. Wason quotes this exchange from Freud's paper:

PATIENT: You ask who this person in the dream can have been. It was *not* my mother.
FREUD: We amend this: so it was his mother.

As the psycholinguists, Herb and Eve Clark (and others) have pointed out, this was also one of the ways in which the disgraced US president Richard Nixon brought about his own downfall, when he stated on TV "I am not a crook". Ah – so we're right to think you might be!

Wason, along with Jones, conducted a series of experiments that systematically tested and confirmed this pragmatic influence on the understanding of negation. Their work showed that language use cannot be understood without psychology: you have to know something about what is going on in the minds of speakers and listeners, their beliefs, goals and expectations, beyond the syntax and semantics of the phrases they are using.

Miller's invitation to Wason to go to Harvard for a sabbatical year in 1963 and immerse himself in research was received enthusiastically. Instead of worrying about how his young family would cope in his absence, and how he would cope without them (he would be bound to miss them terribly, as well as depending on Marjorie for practical matters), he took them with him. He never thought of doing anything else. His daughters, who were only five and seven years old at the time, still vividly remember their time in the US. Marjorie charmed all the researchers as well as their wives (the researchers were all men) and came into her own when it came to entertaining, which was just as well, given Wason's aversion to small talk. There were some high-powered people at these gatherings: one of Wason's daughters remembers sitting on Noam Chomsky's knee, a recollection unfortunately not shared by Chomsky himself. Her memory is a probably a true one: the episode no doubt made more of an impression on her than it did on him. Especially in retrospect.

# 10

## AS EASY AS 2-4-6

### Second strand

Remarkably, given the importance and influence of Wason's work on official regulations and their psycholinguistic difficulties, both among scientists and in the wider world, his work on negation was not the only strand of research that he inaugurated in the late 1950s. More remarkable still is the fact that this other strand of work would go on to generate a huge amount of interest both within and beyond Psychology, interest that continues to the present day, six decades and more after the work began. And even this work was to be surpassed in the 1960s by the research that would really make his name.

To stay with the pre-60s work for the moment: in 1958, Wason had taken on his first PhD student, Jonathan Penrose. Supervising doctoral students would become something that Wason would not only enjoy, in stark contrast to his scalding experience at stand-up lecturing, but excel at. With Penrose, he developed a project on a particular kind of problem-solving known as 'concept attainment'. The basic idea is related to the old games of 20 Questions or animal-vegetable-mineral: there is an object or concept that is hidden from you, and your task is to find it by asking a series of questions that gradually eliminate possibilities until you arrive at the concept in question, if indeed you do. Penrose's project, which unlike Wason's own PhD involved three main experiments rather than just the one, was concerned with the kinds of questions people asked, how they responded to the experimenter's feedback (yes or no as to whether the proposed instance was or was not an instance of the hidden concept) and how efficiently they arrived at the correct concept.

In his third experiment, Penrose found something interesting: that people who received more disconfirming feedback, i.e. when they were told that the idea they volunteered was not an example of the concept, were quicker and more accurate at coming up with the right one. Wason seized on this, and began to wonder about the psychology of scientific thinking: how do people go about generating hypotheses, and how do they deal with evidence for and against them? Apart from his work with Penrose, there were two other major impulses behind this particular object of his curiosity, and with these two bits of knowledge in his mind, together with his work with Penrose, Wason was primed to embark on his new line of research. One was the pioneering work of Bruner and colleagues, published a couple of years earlier in *A study of thinking*. Although regarded as revolutionary work by many psychologists, there are clear connections with John Whitfield's earlier research on problem solving, reported in his 1950–1951 papers; Whitfield was offended not to have been given, as he saw it, proper acknowledgement in this famous book. Bruner and colleagues opened the way for, as its title promised, the study of thinking using experimental methods, and influenced a lot of people. Wason was one of the first.

The second impulse was the work of Sir Karl Popper, still the best known of all philosophers of science. His impact on Wason's thinking was profound. Karl Popper was an exile from Vienna. He had emigrated to New Zealand in 1937, well in time to avoid the Second World War, but also well into the Nazi hegemony in the German-speaking world. The writing was already on the wall for German Jews, with anti-Semitic legislation enacted and persecutory violence commonplace both before and following Hitler's accession to the Chancellorship in 1933. After the War, already a well-known philosopher, Popper moved to Britain, and took up an academic post at the London School of Economics ( LSE); he was made Professor there in 1949, and stayed so for the next 20 years, until his retirement. He gave regular lectures at the LSE and also held a weekly research seminar, at which visiting speakers and members of LSE staff presented their work. Like A.R. Jonckheere, Popper was notorious for his unrestrained criticism; presenting a paper at one of these sessions, with the great man in full cry, must have been a character-forming experience. Wason, who later admitted finding them "rather above my head as well as disputatious", attended these meetings, which were open to anyone from the University of London, of which the LSE, along with University College London (UCL), was a constituent part. It was partly at these sessions that he was exposed to Popper's doctrine of falsificationism.

This, briefly, was a principle put forward to save science from the age-old 'problem of induction', first set out systematically by the great Scottish philosopher, David Hume, in the 18th century. Induction is the form of reasoning where you volunteer a general rule – a hypothesis – to account for a set of instances; that is, you reason from the particular to the general. Suppose, to adapt a clichéd example, you encounter some swans. As you tot up observations of swans on your country walks, you notice that, unlike the ducks and geese, they never seem to make any noise. You conclude – by inductive reasoning – that all swans are mute. The 'problem' that Hume set out is that you can never be sure that this rule is true, because it is always possible that a calling swan may turn up. In fact, there are such swans: Whooper and Bewick's swans make a lot of noise. Sure, they are not the same kind of swans that you see in the park; those really are mute swans. But they are swans all the same, so the hypothesis that all swans are silent is false.

How, asked Popper, can science be built on induction, when induction can only lead to fragile hypotheses like this? He focussed on the possible-swan case: the one round the corner which might at any moment undermine your conclusion about them. One single honking Whooper is sufficient to falsify your claim about their universal muteness, while no amount of silent swans can prove it true. It is the possibility of falsification that distinguishes science from non-science, and from pseudosciences such as astrology, argued Popper. Or Freudianism: Popper's ideas have been used as a stick with which to beat psychoanalytic theory, since, the critics claim, it can explain anything you say or do, even saying or doing nothing. Therefore there is no way in which it could ever be shown to be false; it is on this score an unscientific theory.

Popper had published these ideas before he left Vienna, in a book written in his native German, called *Logik der Forschung* (*Logic of research*). Perhaps not surprisingly, they became better known, in fact widespread, once the book had appeared in English translation, which it did in revised form under the title *The logic of scientific discovery* in 1959. That was the year in which Wason latched on to Popper's philosophy in developing his new line of work. His timing was once again fortunate. He had been exposed to Popper before the book came out, not just at his LSE lectures and seminars but also by reading papers that had been published before *Discovery*. Wason recalled these later as "scintillating", less technical than the book, and so easier for the non-specialist to understand. So he was there with a psychological examination of the ideas the book contained about as early as he could have been. And once again, he had noticed something interesting in every day life: people did not seem to be natural Popperians. Although quite keen to shoot other people's ideas down, we are not keen on falsification where our own beliefs are concerned: we seem more favourably disposed to arguments and evidence that confirm them. Would it be possible to devise an experiment that would shed light on this behaviour?

Of course it would. This was where his knowledge of Bruner's work came in. Bruner, Goodnow and Austin had given people the task of discovering a hidden rule by presenting them with an array of items, consisting of coloured shapes. Wason devised a much simpler procedure. Instead of presenting his subjects with an array of instances from which to make selections, he had them produce their own, as happens in 20 questions. He did this by presenting them with a numbers game: they were given the sequence 2-4-6 and told that it was an exemplar of a rule he had in mind which they were to discover by generating further 'triples', as they were called. The subjects were told, for each triple, whether or not it was consistent with the rule, and that they should announce the rule once they were "highly confident" that they had got it. Ask yourself what you would give as the next triple, after 2-4-6, if you were doing this task.

Going by what has commonly been observed in dozens of experiments down the years, it is likely to be a sequence such as 8-10-12, or, if you're feeling especially bold, 3-5-7. You may already be incubating in your mind a hypothesis about the secret rule that links the numbers: 'ascending even numbers', perhaps, or, for the bold, 'numbers increasing by 2'. Both of these triples get 'yes' feedback, so you are now feeling more confident that you are on the threshold of discovery. Just to make sure, you advance another instance: 16-18-20, say, or 9-11-13. Yes and yes again. Now highly confident, as Wason demanded, you announce your rule: cautious you says 'ascending even numbers', bold you says 'numbers increasing by two'. No, says the experimenter.

This is where the really creative twist in the tale comes in, because Wason had deliberately designed the task to be deceptive: he wanted to see how people behaved when they encountered initial confirmations of their hypotheses. He had, therefore, engineered the task to ensure that this would happen. The start-off triple, 2-4-6, leads you down a garden path: to think in terms of a regular sequence, of even numbers or intervals of two, because it has both these properties. The twist is that the hidden rule is more general than this: it is simply 'ascending numbers'. Your embryo hypothesis was too narrow, but since the initial triple you produce yourself, such as 8-10-12 or 3-5-7, is consistent with both this and the hidden target rule, it gets a 'yes'. This shot of confirmation strengthens your belief in your hypothesis. The experimenter's 'no' if you announce it as the true one comes as a shock. What Wason was interested in was not just the initial confirming behaviour, which he expected, but what happens next.

There were big differences in what happened next. Of the 29 university students who took part in the experiment, eight never found the correct rule at all; after 45 minutes, Wason took pity on them and released them, and they were also allowed to give up earlier if they wished. The majority, 15, made at least one incorrect rule announcement before hitting on the right one (the record was five attempts). Just six announced the right rule first time.

Wason was able to trace his subjects' behaviour because he had them write down on a form the triple they were proposing, the reason they gave for proposing it and the experimenter's feedback (conforms/does not conform to the target rule). Thus, he was not only able to analyse their performance statistically (using a test developed by his old mentor, John Whitfield) but also qualitatively, an approach he adopted throughout his research career; not all experimental psychologists make use of qualitative data. The qualitative data in this case were the subjects' stated reasons. There was the side benefit for the participants that they did not have to remember what they had produced: it was recorded in front of them. Several of these records, known in the trade as 'protocols', were reproduced in the paper reporting this experiment, which Wason published in 1960, and in later ones, and enable us to see this for ourselves.

Characteristic of the successful six was that they varied the nature of their triples at an early stage, and so did not become blinkered in their reasoning. They also tended to produce more triples before making their (correct) rule announcement than the others did: 8, as against an average of just under 4 for the less successful. The latter jumped to conclusions, if you like. Recent researchers have discovered that this is a characteristic trait of delusional thinking, as is the failure to consider alternative possibilities, which the less successful subjects also showed to varying degrees. Indeed, in a later paper, Wason used psychoanalytic language in discussing these less successful attempts: he called it "fixated, obsessional behaviour". Thus, the one who took five attempts to find the rule began with four triples increasing by two, and first announced "two is added each time" as the rule. Wrong. She then produced two triples that broke with this pattern before announcing another incorrect rule; then two more and the third incorrect rule; one more and the fourth; then one more and finally the right rule. One of the completely un-successful subjects hit on the notion that the rule involves regular intervals be-tween the numbers after producing just three triples that are consistent with this idea, and never escaped from it: she announced three more hypotheses which are mere rephrasings of the initial one, with six more triples consistent with them along the way. Finally, after producing two descending triples but no more hy-potheses, she was put out of her agony and the session ended, after 45 minutes.

'Agony' may not be quite the right word. Wason reported that most of his subjects, even the unsuccessful ones, enjoyed doing the task. They said they did, and he also observed them while they took part in it. He concluded from his statistics and his qualitative observations that success depended on what he called "eliminative" behaviour: trying to rule out possibilities, as opposed to "enu-merative" behaviour, which the last example shows so clearly, where the parti-cipants merely stacked up confirming instances of their own ideas. This was just what Penrose's earlier study had revealed. Wason had designed his experiment so that confirmation cannot lead to rule discovery, because an item consistent with a narrow rule such as 'increasing by two' will always be consistent with the wider one of 'ascending numbers': you have to try to eliminate the narrow one. You have to try to falsify your own idea.

This paper, Wason's first on reasoning, contains the earliest psychological re-port of a flaw in thinking which has come to be known as 'confirmation bias'. This is a familiar phrase now, having passed out of Psychology and into common usage, especially in political discourse. Wason is widely credited with coining the ex-pression, as a web search will confirm, but it appears nowhere in his writings; the nearest to it is a section heading in his 1966 *New horizons* book chapter, 'Confirmation versus elimination in reasoning', where he summarises his 1960 2-4-6 paper. He did later write about 'verification bias' or 'verification strategy', and we shall come to that in later chapters.

I mentioned earlier that this paper set in motion a line of research that con-tinues to the present day. This bald statement hides a set of surprises. The first is that none of these further studies was reported by Wason. He did publish a second paper on the 2-4-6 experiment in 1968, with the subtitle "a second look": it was a chapter in a book he co-edited with Phil Johnson-Laird. But it contained no new detailed experimental studies, only passing references to follow-up studies done by research students, colleagues and himself. Wason reports, in just ten lines and without any data, that in one of his own studies, financial incentives served only to increase the number of triples generated; the rate of incorrect rule announcements was unaffected. This showed, he argued, that confirmation bias had its root in thought, not motivation. Jonathan Penrose, he tells us, conducted a verbal version of the task: the target rule was 'living things' and the initial instance 'a Siamese cat'. Only three of ten participants announced the correct rule first time, a proportion similar to Wason's 6 out of 29. There was a similar preponderance of confirmatory behaviour over attempts to challenge initial conclusions. Thus, the behaviour observed by Wason was not to do specifically with numbers.

This was a comfort, because when he took the experiment to the USA, during his sabbatical year at Harvard in 1963, a disturbing incident occurred. His assistant, Martin Katzman, came into Wason's room and told him that the participant he was testing was "behaving like a lunatic". The man was indeed experiencing a psychotic breakdown, refusing to quit the task and being unable to stand up. He was carried to an ambulance and taken to the Harvard Medical Center. A preoccupation with numbers is characteristic of certain forms of schizophrenia, and it seems likely that the task triggered an acute crisis in a person predisposed to this condition. Thankfully, nothing like it has appeared in the literature since.

Although this incident undoubtedly affected Wason – he gave separate accounts of it not just in the 1968 'second look' paper but also in his 1972 book with Johnson-Laird – it is unlikely to have been the reason for his reluctance to publish any more systematic follow-up studies. A far more likely candidate is the criticism that the 2-4-6 paper quickly ran into. This criticism was not widespread, but it was piercing, and its source was a factor in its effect. The critic was Norman Wetherick, and he and Wason had a history. It was a history that reached not only into the past, but would extend into the future too.

## Dissent

Wetherick was an undergraduate Psychology student at UCL at the time Wason was starting his 2-4-6 research. He already had a degree, in Philosophy, and had undertaken a second one, in Psychology; at the time, if you already held a British university degree, you could do a second one in two years instead of three. This he did. His undergraduate project was supervised by John Whitfield, whom Wetherick admired, as everyone did, for his originality, although by this time Whitfield's alcoholism was already severely limiting his ability to function. Upon graduating in 1960, Wetherick was seeking to go on to study for a PhD, on the relation between logic and psychology, and under the system described earlier, he was allotted Wason as supervisor. Wetherick was already 30 years old, just 6 years younger than Wason, and a Philosophy graduate; he probably therefore already knew more about logic than Wason did. Upon meeting him, this impression was reinforced. It is clear that, for one reason or another quite apart from this, they took a dislike to each other. Wetherick flatly refused to be supervised by Wason. Speaking over 50 years later, Wetherick was vituperative about Wason, and not only on this count. There would be consequences.

Thus, they were soon at daggers drawn, a situation that almost reached the proportions of a shooting war when, in 1962, Wetherick published a critique of Wason's 2-4-6 paper. There are several strands to it, including Wetherick's claim, later backed up by other researchers, that the 2-4-6 task is not representative of either everyday or scientific hypothesis testing. Wason had declared that it was. But the central point he makes is that Wason was not justified in talking about his less successful subjects' failure to find the rule as being due to their not engaging properly in 'eliminative' behaviour: attempting falsification. This, Wetherick argued, was because Wason had missed a vital distinction: between confirmation and positivity (and their complements, disconfirmation and negativity). Suppose, after being given 2-4-6, you begin to entertain the thought that the rule might be 'numbers increasing by two'. A positive test is one where you produce a triple that is consistent with your hypothesis and which you expect to get a 'yes', affirming that it also conforms to the experimenter's hidden rule. One like 3-5-7 would do this. A negative test is one which does not conform to your hypothesis and which you therefore expect to get a 'no', such as a descending sequence. However, as Wetherick pointed out, both such tests are in fact confirming tests: you expect the positive test to get 'yes' and the negative test to get 'no', and they do. Disconfirmation only happens when a positive test gets a surprising 'no', or when a negative test gets an equally surprising 'yes'. The latter would happen with a triple such as 4-8-10: this is a negative test of 'increasing by two'. It is not possible to give such an example of the former in the 2-4-6 task because positive testing can never result in disconfirmation – the 'yes' items always confirm hypotheses which are consistent with the target rule, because the target rule, ascending numbers, is always more general. Whatever triple is consistent with 'ascending by two' will be consistent with just 'ascending'.

As Jonathan Evans remarks in a recent article, in which he gives a retrospective review of the 2-4-6 paper and the extensive research it led to, Wetherick's critique "might have been expected to stop the 2-4-6 task in its tracks". Actually, it did just that, and for a very good reason: Wetherick was right. As we have heard, Wason never published another properly written-up account of his or his colleagues' research using the task. He had not discovered true confirmation bias after all. He had discovered, although he did not appreciate it, a positivity bias: people can more easily think of positive instances of an idea than negative ones. It looks like confirmatory behaviour only because of the way the 2-4-6 task was structured, with the target rule more general than the participant's initial hypothesis, prompted by the leading nature of the given triple 2-4-6. It is possible to order this relation differently, and if you do, positive testing can lead to effective and efficient discovery. Suppose the target was a narrower rule: 'even numbers increasing by two', say. A triple such as 3-5-7 or 4-8-12 would immediately get a 'no', and knock out initial hypotheses such as 'even numbers increasing' or 'numbers increasing by two' at a stroke. So the same behaviour, positive testing of your own idea, looks like confirming behaviour in one context, and falsifying behaviour in another.

Wetherick's paper was far from being the end of confirmation bias, however, or indeed the end of the 2-4-6 task for that matter. But there was to be a long pause in work on the latter: it would not be revived until the late 1970s, a decade and a half after its debut. Wetherick's critique would have to wait even longer for its resurrection: until the work of the American psychologists Joshua Klayman and Young-Won Ha in 1987, who are responsible for working out the relations between hypotheses and the target rule, and the role of positive testing within them, outlined in the previous paragraph.

Wetherick, looking back in 2015, thought that Wason was contemptuous of him and his work; Wason had published a rather dismissive rejoinder to his 1962 critique, failing to address its central point about the distinction between positivity and confirmation. Very late in his life, in one of his last pieces of academic writing, a foreword to a book written in 1996, Wason did obliquely acknowledge the force of Wetherick's critique. He managed to do so without mentioning either Wetherick's name, the experiment in question or the nature of the critique (and he put the word "criticisms" in scare-quotes), which is about as grudging, and as late, a concession as he could have managed.

However, others see things differently. Wason, with his slow, contemplative thinking style, never enjoyed the cut-and-thrust of academic conferences; he preferred giving papers at university seminars and research workshops, where he was more in control, and would later travel the world doing this. But he was not contemptuous of Wetherick so much as terrified of him: his pupil, Jonathan Evans, referred to Wetherick as Wason's Moriarty, a nice comparison given Wason's Sherlockian style and demeanour. They disliked each other in any case, and if he knew that Wetherick would be at a certain conference, Wason would not even attend it, let alone give a paper. He must have harboured the suspicion – the dread – that Wetherick had found a fatal flaw in the view of human reasoning that was starting to coalesce in his mind, and set about suppressing it. But in 1962, this was not going to hold Wason up. The force was with him now, and was about to lift him higher.

# 11
## HITS OF THE SIXTIES

### Cards on the table

When Wason decamped to Harvard for his sabbatical year in 1963, he took not only his young family, and the 2-4-6 task, but also something else. It was the thing that would secure his lasting reputation in, and later beyond, Psychology; the thing that he would write about in his 1966 *New horizons* chapter. It was another thinking task, the third he had devised in as many years, to go along with the verification task and the 2-4-6. As Wason tells it in a retrospective piece written to accompany a Festschrift devoted to him, he thought up this new task in 1960 or 1961; in an earlier review piece, he had located its invention in 1960. As always with acts of invention, it is possible to identify several lines of thought that led to its creation.

The first was his work on those appalling official regulations, which the Medical Research Council (MRC) had commissioned him to investigate in the late 1950s. In the early 1960s, he was still involved in this project, and more especially in his follow-up investigations into the psychology of a major source of difficulty in understanding them: negation. This work was largely in collaboration with Sheila Jones, as we saw earlier. Negatives are not the only bit of language that scrambles the mind when you try to make sense of official rules and legal injunctions. There is also the word which, for its size, has some claim to be the most pregnant with meaning, and difficulty, in the dictionary: *If*. Wason's noticing faculty had already registered this nugget, and you can see the little beast in the two examples of regulations given in Chapter 9. *If* always asks you to do some thinking, so the more *If*s there are, the more thinking you have to do, and the greater the effort that will be needed for understanding. *If* is going to occupy us more and more in the coming pages.

The second line was Wason's reading outside his psychological studies (he always read more outside Psychology than inside it, with consequences that would give him problems later on, as well as benefits now). In particular, he was currently interested in logic. He was already conversant with Karl Popper's work, both before and after the devising of the 2-4-6 experiment, as we have seen. The logic of *If* is central to Popper's doctrine of falsifiability in science. Take our well-worn example of the swan hypothesis, that they make no noise. 'All swans are silent' can be expressed as an *If* sentence: 'If it is a swan, then it is silent'. We saw that this claim, which is in effect a scientific statement, is false: there are examples of swans that are not silent. Indeed, the existence of just one thing which is both a swan and not silent decisively falsifies the hypothesis.

In addition to Popper, Wason had also read, been impressed by, but found difficulty in fully understanding, the philosophical work of W.V.O. Quine, who had developed a logical notation for deciding the validity of arguments involving conditionals, which is the technical name for *If*-sentences. Quine had set out the logical 'truth conditions' of *If*-sentences in a book called *Methods of logic*, published in 1952, a few years before Popper's English-language *Logic of scientific discovery* and like the latter, just in time for Wason to start to make use of it. (An interesting but completely irrelevant factoid about Quine: his nephew, the late Robert Quine, was a noted rock guitarist, especially for his work as a sideman to Lou Reed.)

In traditional logic, there are only two truth values: true and false; there is nothing in between, the so-called law of excluded middle. With just these two values, it is possible to state the conditions under which an argument is logically valid or invalid, or a claim is true or false. Heading out into the park again, we can begin to set out a 'truth-table' for the relation between swans and silence. Logically, there are four possible values, two for each term: a bird can be either a swan or not a swan, and it can be either mute or not mute. Or to put it another way, it can be either true or false that a bird is a swan, and true or false that it is mute. These were the intricacies that were causing Wason difficulty, as you are no doubt appreciating right now.

Here are the four logical cases, which may help to make things clearer:

| This bird is: | and it is: |
| --- | --- |
| A swan | silent |
| A swan | not silent |
| Not a swan | silent |
| Not a swan | not silent |

You can see that the Popperian case, the one that decisively falsifies the claim that all swans are silent, is the second one. It is the only one that does so, and given the two truth values, the other three cases must make the claim true – because they do not make it false. So a squawking parrot – it is not a swan, and is not silent – makes the claim about swans logically true.

Confusion on such points is understandable, since this logical use of *If* seems so unlike its usage in everyday language; Wason was perplexed as to how its two-valued logic could fit with common usage. It is a perplexity that occupies researchers and theorists still. To try to clarify in his own mind the truth functions of conditional sentences, Wason set out cases like the ones above on cards with the various permutations of values on them. The 'swan' card could have 'silent' or 'not silent' on its other side, ditto for the 'not-swan' card; and you could have a 'silent' card with 'swan' or 'not swan' on the other side, ditto for the 'not-silent' card. Those are all the possible combinations. Setting out the cards in front of him, Wason wondered about the implications of each one for the truth or falsity of a conditional claim such as the one about swans. It would depend on what was on the other side. What could be on the other side of a card that said swan, or not swan, or silent, or not silent? And what would it mean?

It struck him immediately that this aid to his own thinking could be turned into what he would later refer to as "an amusing puzzle", and from there it was a short step to turning it into an experiment on how people judged the truth or otherwise of an *If* sentence. He, therefore, distilled the task into what he regarded as a purer form, taking out any meaningful content. There is a tradition of doing this in psychological research: the assumption is that if you take out meaning, you have stripped the process you are trying to study bare and can observe it unhindered.

To take out the meaning, Wason replaced words by symbols, both on the cards and in the claim to be tested. The claim went like this:

> If a card has a vowel on one side, then it has an even number on the other side.

The cards showed the four cases outlined above, except that now they were just letters and numbers, like this – these are the ones given as an example in Wason's 1972 book with Johnson-Laird:

| E | K | 4 | 7 |
|---|---|---|---|

The E card is equivalent to swan, K to not-swan, 4 to silent and 7 to not-silent. These are just the showing sides of the cards, remember: the possible values that go with each symbol are on the reverse, out of sight, so the letter cards have numbers that could be odd or even on their backs, while the number cards could have a vowel or consonant on theirs, just as Wason's own self-teaching aids did.

He gave this setup to two friends; one was surely A.R. Jonckheere. The experimental task was to determine which of the cards you would need to turn over to determine whether the stated claim was true or false. You, dear reader, now have a choice: you can either pause and try to figure this out for yourself, or just carry on reading and let me tell you.

The answer, as Wason saw it, is as follows. To test a conditional claim, or any other, you have to test it to destruction: find the conditions under which it might fail. As we saw above, in the case of the silent swan hypothesis a single non-silent swan serves this purpose. With the vowel–even claim, the answer is logically the same: find a card which has a vowel on one side but does not have an even number on the other. That's your first step: to realise that this is what you have to do. The second step is to ask yourself which cards could carry such a combination of values: a vowel with an odd number. The third step is to find them, and it is very easy to trip at this one, even if you have made it this far. It is obvious – the vast majority of people who have attempted the task manage this bit – that you need to turn over the E card, in case it has an odd number on the back. Any others? It is equally obvious that the K card can be left alone, because the claim is not about consonants; again, almost everyone does this. As for the number cards: you need to turn over the 7 card, since it may have a vowel on the back, in which case the claim would fail. The 4 card can, like the K, be left alone, since neither kind of letter, vowel or consonant, on its reverse could show that the claim was false. So you need to select the E and 7 cards, just them.

Incidentally, Wason was adamant that this new task was not developed as a psychological test of Popper, and irritated with those authors subsequently reviewing his work who said it was; that, he said, was true of the 2-4-6, but this new one, which is now commonly known as the Wason Selection Task, was "founded simply on the truth functions of the conditional… Popper had nothing to do with it at all!" (Figure 11.1). Wason's two friends both arrived at the right answer, "after some thought", as he recalled. His assistant, who in 1960 would have been either Sheila Jones or Jonathan Penrose, thought the problem lacked potential. He put it to one side, but turned to it again at Harvard in 1963, where he tried using meaningful material, such as 'If I go to Chicago, I catch a train'. He found that his US subjects were more amused by such an idea than anything (Boston to Chicago by train? Are you serious?), and did not record any data.

There is one more current running in the evolution of Wason's new selection task. This was his work on the 2-4-6 task. It was not a factor in his development of the problem, but it came to determine his reaction to the results he got when he started to use it in experiments. Given the discouragement he had at first encountered, it is faintly astonishing that he did start to use it again, and he never, in retrospective reviews such as the ones mentioned at the start of this chapter, gave an account of why he did. Perhaps he was spurred to do so because the selection task was not his first pass at the psychological study of reasoning with *If* sentences. In May 1962, he had submitted a paper (subsequently published in 1964) using a different technique, known as the conditional inference task.

Take another sentence about swans:

If it is a swan then it is white.

You can take each component, swan or white, and affirm it (it is …) or deny it (it is not …), then ask what follows. If you affirm that it is a swan, it follows validly, and almost trivially, that it is white. The one other valid inference is harder to appreciate, and comes about when you deny the second part and say that it is not

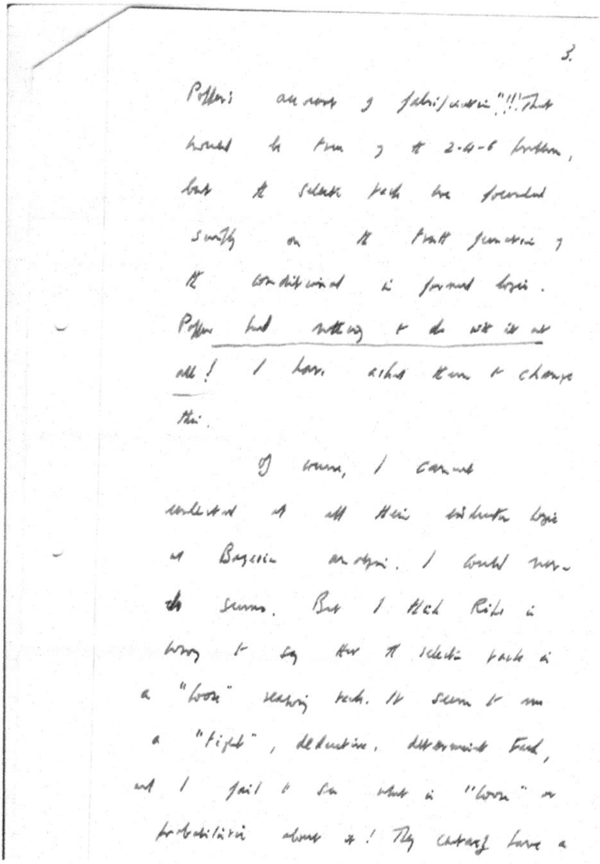

**FIGURE 11.1**    Extract from a letter from Wason to the author about the relation between the selection task, the 2-4-6 task and Karl Popper, December 1993.

white. The conclusion which must follow (that is what a valid inference is: when a conclusion must necessarily follow) is that the bird is not a swan. Whiteness is a necessary part of swanness: no white, no swan. Two invalid inferences, or fallacies as they are known, come from the mirror image of the two valid ones. It is not a swan? It is tempting to conclude that therefore it is not white, but of course we know there are many more white birds than just swans and so this does not necessarily follow: it might be a seagull or a snowy owl. It is white? OK, it may be a swan, but it isn't necessarily, for the same reason. In Wason's experiment, he induced people to commit the fallacies and then to perform the valid inferences, and found that doing the latter stopped them committing any more of the former. It is good to know that illogical reasoning can be corrected.

On his return from the USA, convinced on the back of this success that conditionals still held promise for a curious scientist, Wason looked to the selection task once more. His 1966 *New horizons* chapter was when he gave his first written account of the resulting experiment, calling it "a small study". As with his rather notional follow-up to the 1960 2-4-6 paper in his 'second look' eight years after, it was an informal report; a properly peer-reviewed scientific paper would appear two years later. In both these publications, he reports the essential result that occurs whenever the selection task where meaningless content is used is given to people – and this has happened a literally uncountable number of times since. Using the alphanumerical example above, most people select the E card, a smaller but still substantial proportion select the 4 card, but hardly anyone selects either the K card or the 7 card. It is the last of these which is the real killer observation, because logically, you should select the 7 card, not the 4 card: vowel+odd is the critical falsifier, remember, and E and 7 are the cards that could carry it. E may have a number on the back which is not even, while 7 may have a letter on the back which is a vowel. You need to check both and only these.

What Wason was convinced he had was something that resembled the behaviour of his subjects in the 2-4-6 task: a tendency to favour verification over falsification. In selecting the vowel and even cards, people seemed to be trying to prove the claim true, rather than seeing if it could be false, just as when they produce positive, confirming triples when they form a hypothesis about number sequences. It looked like another instance of the confirmation bias that Wason thought he had discovered a few years before, and confirmation bias looks like a major fault in human rationality. No wonder Wason was afraid of Wetherick. Whenever you think, as Wason did now, that you have made a major discovery, you get very excited – it could make your name, after all – and the last thing you want is for someone to pop up and say, or worse still, demonstrate, that you have done no such thing. And that is just what Wetherick had done with his critique of the 2-4-6 task. This fear of the 'emperor's new clothes', or impostor syndrome to give it its popular current tag, dogs a lot of people in science, and in other creative areas. Like the little whispering demon on the shoulder of a cartoon cat, there is always the lingering fear that someone, somewhere, is poised to show the world that all you have done is worth nothing.

In the mid-1960s, Wason was becoming a well-known figure, both within and outside Psychology, as we have seen. His work on official regulations, with Sheila Jones, was sufficiently significant to attract the attention of government ministers and the national press, and in 1965, he published a paper on work on the psychology of negation, conducted at Harvard, whose title contained another Wason coinage that has entered the general language: 'The contexts of plausible denial'. This was not even the half of what he had done, though. There was the 2-4-6 experiment, the 1964 study of conditional inferences and the 1966 report of the selection task. These three studies formed the basis of a whole new field of research: the psychology of reasoning. There had been psychological studies of reasoning before, almost all on Aristotelian syllogisms (All A are B, All B are C, therefore …), named after the philosopher who first specified them, nearly 2500 years ago, but these were relatively isolated studies scattered over a long stretch of time, from the 1920s to the 1950s. No one had studied reasoning with *If* before. Now, in the shape of the inference task and the selection task, psychologists had not only something worth studying, but the means – the experimental methods devised by Wason – by which to carry out this research.

## Making moves

In his retrospective chapter for his own Festschrift, published in 1995, Wason gave credit to a number of people who had helped him over the years: Johnson-Laird, Evans, Jones, Bruner, Miller and Jonckheere. Alongside them was a nod to the director of the MRC during Wason's time on its staff, Sir Harold Himsworth. He was thanked "for generous moral and financial support". And with good reason, because following his return from Harvard after his sabbatical year, Wason's position at University College London (UCL), despite his increasingly exalted reputation, was not as secure as it might have been. In 1965, the MRC decided to disband its Industrial Psychology Research Unit (IPR U) at UCL. Wason, Jones and the others were not to be thrown out on to the street, but transferred to UCL. Initially, the idea, expressed in a letter from Himsworth to the Provost of UCL, Sir Ifor Evans, in September, was that the MRC would fund them, but that UCL would then take them over, paying them at rates close to their MRC stipends. It did not quite work out that way.

A week after the Himsworth-Evans letter, the Provost wrote to the head of the Psychology Department, George Drew, who confirmed that most of the IPRU staff had moved to the National Institute of Industrial Psychology. One other, Anna Zajaczkowska, was taken on by Psychology, and it was anticipated that Wason and Jones would join her. They didn't. Drew had them in his office to discuss their futures, and Wason made it clear that he, for one, would like to stay on the external staff of the MRC, because he preferred to do research without other duties. For a university academic, these other duties largely consist of teaching and administration: student admissions, open days, examinations, committee work, that sort of thing. Admin for most academics is drudgery pure and simple, but acknowledged as necessary and done with a greater or lesser degree of good grace.

Not for Wason. He was now convinced, and the evidence was stacking up to support him, that he was doing important work in his research and took the view that he should be supported to do it, unencumbered by donkey-work. He may also have been sufficiently self-aware to realise that he would be no good at admin in any case, as he was notoriously impractical. His attitude to teaching undergraduates was more basic: he had a visceral aversion to it, stemming from his experience 15 years before at Aberdeen. "I refuse to teach!" he proclaimed to Jonathan Evans toward the end of the decade, and assumed that the university would bend to his will on this. Evans regarded this attitude as evidence of a sense of entitlement; perhaps it was a product of his social background, in addition to his idea of the importance of his research.

He certainly was unsuited to undergraduate teaching. His reading within Psychology was narrow to the point of tunnel vision: as with his attitude to people, he would only read about what he was interested in, and mostly that meant outside the subject (with the exception of psychoanalysis: he was always sympathetic to Freud's insights, though not uncritically so). Inside the subject, he read only that which was necessary for his research, and then usually only after he had run an experiment. This is contrary to most people's practice. For instance, although he had done important work on psycholinguistics, in the shape of his experiments on the pragmatics of negation, he knew next to nothing about wider research in the area, and did not care to find out about it. He could not have taught a course, even on this: to teach undergraduates you have to read about a lot of things that may have nothing to do with your own interests. He would urge his research students not to read very much before devising experiments, only after collecting the data, but it would simply not be possible to function in this way in academic research now. It was obviously more possible in a new research area, where there was little previous literature that could interfere with one's creativity.

He could be bloody-minded in other ways too. Once, given some exam papers to mark, he was found to have deducted grades for answers that included diagrams, a prohibition he had conjured for himself. The whole lot had to be re-marked by a colleague.

Himsworth, replying to Drew, was resistant to Wason's argument. He felt in the first place that the turn taken by Wason's research, towards reasoning and away from language, made it no longer a good fit for the MRC's specialised research units. He also did not want to create external staff appointments, lest they form a privileged class who were allowed to cherry-pick the work they did, with a private line to external finance. Nevertheless, he left the door slightly ajar: his opposition to such appointments was "unless there is very good reason for doing it". He must have been swayed, because the MRC did then agree to continue funding Wason and Jones up to the summer of 1967 (the decision was made in December 1965). Wason was designated an honorary research associate in the Department of Psychology, honorary since his funding was from an external source.

'Research associate' was not quite the status that Wason had in mind, nor felt that his efforts and output in research merited (he was quite right about this), and in mid-1966, he sought a transfer out of Psychology into the newly formed Psycholinguistics Research Unit, in the department of Phonetics and Linguistics, under the directorship of Prof. Frieda Goldman Eisler. This came as a relief to Drew, who by now was wondering what to do with him, given his lack of engagement with other aspects of the work of the Psychology department, and the muttering this was causing among his colleagues. And so it came to pass: from August 1967, he joined this unit, with the title of Senior Lecturer Grade 1 in Phonetics and five years' worth of external funding, to the end of September 1972. A skilfully devious political animal, which Wason was not known to be (Johnson-Laird thought he didn't even know what office politics were), could not have played the system any better. As for Sheila Jones, she finally joined the Psychology department. Their scientific collaboration was at an end.

In transferring to Phonetics, a subject he knew nothing about despite his job title, Wason became detached from the Psychology department physically, as well as in terms of membership. This was because the Psycholinguistics Research Group, which consisted of little more than Wason, Goldman Eisler and some postgraduate students, was re-housed in 1968 some way away from the Bloomsbury base of the main part of UCL, across the thundering artery that is Euston Road, in a not terribly attractive building down a side road, Stephenson Way. You have to know it's there: it is not one you pass through on your way around London. Some of the PhD students from the Psychology department also found themselves there in time; the department had expanded beyond the capacity of its original home, so the drab Wolfson House became an overspill area, as well as home to Goldman Eisler's unit. In due course Psychology would in turn be re-housed, along with the Institute of Education, in a new building rather shamefully put up at the cost of the demolition of a Georgian terrace. The University has other reasons for environmental shame apart from this one: it also brought about the destruction of most of nearby Woburn Square, including the tower of the early 19th century Christ Church, at around the same time.

Goldman Eisler and Wason got on well together, part of the reason that Wason wanted to move to her research unit, and this surprised some people, since she had quite a ferocious reputation. She was what you might call a no-nonsense operator. Once, a new PhD student, who had been assigned her as a supervisor, turned up for a preliminary meeting. "You will arrive at ... and you will work on ..." barked Frieda. The student was not prepared to have her research topic dictated to her like this, turned on her heel and left. She ended up being supervised by Wason.

Frieda Goldman Eisler was an interesting person quite apart from her interpersonal skills. Interestingness was part of what made her attractive as a colleague for Wason, of course, but another was that she, like him, was a Freudian. In fact, that is a decided understatement: she had actually studied under Sigmund Freud in her home city of Vienna, and published research on psychoanalysis during her time there. Some of this work was on the topic, still live today, of therapist-patient interaction: she found that therapists' speech pauses varied according to which patient they were seeing; the patients' did not vary according to the therapist they were talking to. This led her into work on psycholinguistics, and in the year Wason joined her unit she published a whole book on spontaneous speech, the core of which was her study of pauses. At this point, she was the only female professor of psycholinguistics in the country. She had fled to Britain following the fascist putsch against Jews in Austria in the early 1930s, as had her husband, Paul, whom she met and married after their separate arrival in the country. Paul Eisler can be said to have changed the world: he invented the printed circuit board, alone in a flat in Hampstead before the outbreak of the Second World War. Taken up and exploited by American companies – the British were not interested – it became fundamental to military applications such as anti-aircraft missiles and later to the development of computers. Paul naively and inadvertently signed away the rights to his invention and never benefited financially from it. He and Frieda did not live in poverty, though: besides her academic eminence, his inventiveness never waned (the car rear-window demister is one of his) and he went on to a successful business career, founding his own company.

If, as many thought, Frieda could be 'difficult', she had surely earned the right through her life experiences. But you can understand why that beginning PhD student turned tail: not everyone could take her directness. She tolerated Wason's foibles and Wason found her interesting; he tended to be drawn to Jewish intellectuals, especially those from Central and Eastern Europe, this reflecting his contempt for parochial Englishness. He perhaps also saw something of himself in her being regarded as a somewhat 'difficult' person. In any event, he was now in a position of some stability, whereby he could push on with his research.

# 12
## MOVING ON

### Team work

Wason may have had a gut aversion, turning into a flat refusal, to teaching classes of undergraduates, but the same could not be said of his dealing with postgraduate PhD students. On the contrary, he positively revelled in this, and he was good at it. Apart from Norman Wetherick, who never allowed Wason near him again after their first encounter, former students have over the years been generous in their praise of his skills as a supervisor. This was not just to do with his approach to one-to-one sessions with individuals, either: he also during this time started running a postgraduate seminar programme, still recalled in awed terms by those who were there.

In the normal run of things, a seminar programme in a university department features researchers, from within and outside one's institution, talking about their work, giving an account of their results and their theoretical ideas, and so on, and fielding vigorous, even hostile, questions at the end. Popper's seminars at the London School of Economics (LSE) were certainly like this, and so was the one run alongside Wason's by Jonckheere. Not in Wason's seminar, however. The ground rules, outlined in general terms by Wason at the start of the series and never challenged by anyone, were that its purpose was to help people develop their ideas: speakers would talk about what they were interested in, how they proposed to study it, and where they thought it might lead, and the other attenders chipped in with their thoughts. Criticism was only ever to be constructive. This was in line with Wason's personal practice: he liked to ruminate by himself when generating ideas for research, collaborating with people only once he had something. The seminar was a way of formalising this procedure: a student was to come up with an idea and then talk about it with others. It was also open to people other than Wason's students: Sheila Jones was a regular participant, as were other members of academic staff, and it sometimes included external speakers, occasionally from outside Psychology altogether (Popper's almost equally celebrated successor at the LSE, the philosopher of science Imre Lakatos, was one). They were invited by Wason purely on the grounds that they or their ideas were, his guiding principle, interesting.

Praise for Wason's approach as a supervisor was not without reservation, it should be said; one, Liz Valentine (Elizabeth Cornish, as she then was) spoke for many in recalling how Wason was no use at all when it came to analysing research data. He himself relied on Whitfield and Jonckheere for statistical advice; John Valentine, her future husband, filled this role for her. She had George Drew as a nominal main supervisor; Wason was not allowed to fill this role as he was not a payroll member of University College London (UCL) staff, being externally funded. This or a similar arrangement must have applied to all those he supervised while he was still funded by the MRC.

She also ran into problems with Wason's fixation on correct and elegant English: he was punctilious about usage to the point of pedantry. As he recalled himself, this fixation could be traced to his student work with David Cecil at Oxford: every sentence was read by him or to him, and was open to criticism, so Wason took great pains over each one, and continued to do so for ever after. Valentine had to produce three drafts of her PhD thesis before he was satisfied that it was fit for submission. Not that he was immune to lapses: the 1964 paper on self-contradiction, for instance, contains an unfortunate occurrence of the 'yob's comma': "The aim of the present investigation, is to make the individual aware ..." (p. 30). And he was not above using 'less' instead of 'fewer', ironically in a piece entitled 'How to write an essay' ("a group of high self-monitors ... produced *less* new ideas", original emphasis, p. 18). It is reassuring to know that perfection eludes even the best.

Cornish received her PhD in 1968, as did another of Wason's protégées, Judith Greene; the latter, daughter of a cabinet minister in the Labour government of the time, would go on to an eminent career as, ultimately, a professor of psycholinguistics (at the Open University). An echo of Frieda Goldman Eisler. Liz Valentine also had an outstanding academic career, with a best-seller, *Conceptual issues in psychology*, among her credits. These two women were in fact Wason's fifth and sixth PhD graduates. To produce so many successful doctorates so early and in such a short time is exceptional (his avoidance of other duties surely helped). The first we have met already: Jonathan Penrose, receiving his award in 1962. The second was Athol Hughes (in 1966), who, despite producing a thesis on hypothesis testing, would become a celebrated psychoanalyst and clinical psychiatrist. She used the selection task in her research, the first person other than Wason to do so. The third was Kate Jackson (later Lowenthal), the student who had defied Goldman Eisler and been reassigned to Wason. She received her PhD in 1967. The fourth, though, who also graduated in 1967, was one of the most important people that Wason ever met: Phil Johnson-Laird (Figure 12.1).

Johnson-Laird was, like Wason, a latecomer to Psychology; indeed, he was a latecomer to academic life (Wason had had his false start at Aberdeen University and

**FIGURE 12.1** Phil Johnson-Laird. Thanks to Alchetron

his earlier degree in English at Oxford). Born in Leeds, Yorkshire, he left school at the age of 15, in 1951, without formal qualifications. He found a job as a surveyor, hated it, but stuck at it for five years, until leaving and then drifting from job to job, from baker to librarian. He was a talented musician as well, and earned money as a jazz pianist; music, and the psychology of music, continue to engage him to this day. At that time, in the late 1950s, he was becoming politically aware and increasingly active. He joined the nascent Campaign for Nuclear Disarmament, one of whose founder-members, as we heard in Chapter 10, was Wason's then major collaborator, Sheila Jones, and it is likely that Johnson-Laird and Wason took part in the same anti-war demonstrations, before they knew each other. Johnson-Laird embraced pacifism, which Wason never did, and refused national (military) service, which was soon to be abolished in any case. He was allowed to work as a hospital porter instead.

Discontented with his chequered and directionless employment history, Johnson-Laird resolved, in the early 1960s, to find an interesting job, perhaps a career, one which would mesh with his existing interest in science. He would need to go to university to go any further, but without qualifications, he was restricted in what he could do there. Taking and passing the necessary A-levels as a part-time student, he opted for Psychology; it was then just as likely to be found in an Arts faculty as in Science, which means that many psychologists' first degrees from that time are BAs rather than the now almost universal BScs. He was accepted on to the BA Psychology degree at University College London. He already knew he was also interested in logic, and so opted for Logic as his subsidiary; at that time, the Philosophy department, in which logic was studied, adjoined Psychology, then still in its old premises in Gordon Square, which made life easier. Never having previously considered himself an academic, and with no such tradition in his family, Johnson-Laird found that he liked the student life, and student life in London in the early 1960s, a lot. He was 25 when he started, seven years older than the standard post-school undergraduate, and already with a whole volume of life experience behind him. Again, the parallels with Wason are clear.

Johnson-Laird's interests in psychology and logic, and the proximity of the Psychology and Philosophy departments, kindled in him an interest in the topic of reasoning, and the possibility of a psychological study of it. At that time, not only was there very little research literature to bolster such an interest, there was not even an undergraduate course on thinking that he could take. But there was Peter Wason, and in his first year as an undergraduate, he found himself participating in Wason's experiment on self-contradiction, the one that was written up as the 1964 paper. That was how they met, and the experience made a vivid impression on him. He also took part in a selection task experiment, selecting the E and 4 cards (or their equivalent), as most people did. What piqued his interest was not only the fact that he seemed to be falling prey to common logical errors – committing the fallacies in the self-contradiction experiment, and selecting the 'verifying' cards in the selection task – but also Wason's practice of asking his subjects, through a fug of pipe-smoke, for their views and judgements after the experiment. With Wason, it was never a case of come in, do the task, thank you and goodbye. He wanted to know what you *thought*. So his experimental method was an intriguing, and fruitful, combination of behavioural and clinical techniques. He used to say that when you do an experiment, you should never be completely sure why you're doing it. This is bizarre advice for anyone else, but it worked for him: it was fully in tune with his exploratory approach to research.

With Johnson-Laird's resonant personal history and political stance, Wason could not help but slot him into his category of interesting people, and their mutual respect would carry them, despite very different working methods, through a decade of close collaboration. Wason could be cutting about people he did not find interesting, though never to their face. He was scrupulously polite when talking to people, but did once confess to Johnson-Laird that he had a coded signal for when he found himself bored by someone. He would wait on his moment, and then at some point say, "How *terribly* interesting". A few minutes later, in the course of this same conversation, Wason turned to Johnson-Laird and said, "how terribly interesting"!

Johnson-Laird now not only had an existence proof in front of him that it was possible to study reasoning psychologically – Wason was doing it, so it must be possible – and the means, devised by Wason, by which to do so, but he had also encountered in Wason a person whose approach and character were immediately appealing. He also had another piece of ammunition that would further his newly formed plan to become a psychologist. Despite his truncated education, lack of family precedents, and unfocussed occupational history, he turned out to be a student of rare brilliance, and took an outstanding first class degree. Wason was sufficiently moved to write him, in July 1964, a congratulatory note (Figure 12.2). It read:

Dear Phil,

I have just heard from Valerie that you got the best first in the University. I am absolutely delighted but of course not surprised!
Your happiest moment will be waking up to-morrow morning and wondering if it has all been a dream. Nothing will ever taste quite so sweet again.

Many congratulations on your magnificent performance, and warmest regards,

Peter Wason.

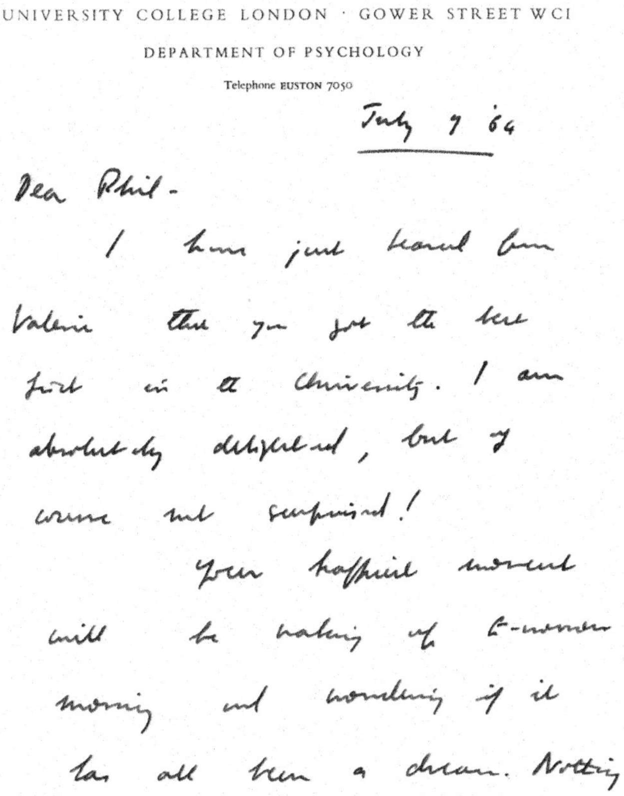

UNIVERSITY COLLEGE LONDON · GOWER STREET WCI

DEPARTMENT OF PSYCHOLOGY

Telephone EUSTON 7050

*[handwritten letter]*

July 7 64

Dear Phil –

  I have just heard from Valerie that you got the best first in the University. I am absolutely delighted, but I were not surprised!

    Your happiest moment will be waking up t-morrow morning and wondering if it has all been a dream. Nothing

**FIGURE 12.2**  Wason's first letter to Johnson-Laird in July 1964. Courtesy of Prof. P.N. Johnson-Laird

Johnson-Laird was moved too. He kept that letter, and practically everything else that Wason would write to him over a 37-year period, until 2016.

Coming from someone else, Wason's pat on Johnson-Laird's head might have looked like a fairly shameless attempt to snaffle the best prospect for himself in the next round of PhD studentships. Such guile was not part of his modus operandi, however, and it seems to have been sincerely meant, with no ulterior motive: there is no "do come and see me if you want to discuss your future" there. But, as with his success at maintaining his external funding source and thereby his pure research post, Wason ended up getting his wish, if wish it was, anyway. George Drew, the head of Psychology, remarked to Johnson-Laird: "Of course, you'll be staying on to do a PhD". There had been no 'of course' about it in Johnson-Laird's mind up to that point. He was taken aback by the casualness with which such opportunities could open up (it would certainly not happen like that today, now there are equal opportunities procedures written into academic law), but was not going to refuse it. Apart from anything else, he now had a young family and needed the income that a studentship would bring, along with the doors that it would surely open up.

He was duly assigned Wason as a supervisor. Surprisingly, given his emergent interest in reasoning, that was not the topic of his PhD. Rather, and following another of Wason's then current interests, he studied an aspect of the pragmatics of language. Wason had studied negation, and had just returned from his year at Harvard, the invitation coming from George Miller largely on the back of this work, so he was primed to study pragmatics some more. For his PhD, Johnson-Laird studied the passive voice, and discovered that, while an active and passive version of the same proposition should, linguistically, mean the same thing, psychologically there is a difference. Politicians are particularly adept at exploiting this difference, as when they offer 'regret' for mistakes that have been made, or offence that may have been caused, rather than apologies for mistakes they made or offence they caused. It is a way of dodging blame. That Johnson-Laird found himself researching this topic for his PhD was largely down to Wason. He was not a martinet when it came to determining what his students would study; not for him the Goldman Eisler "you will do this" approach. Johnson-Laird called him a "nudger": he had a way of making it clear to the student whether something was or was not – yes – interesting, and steering them away from topics which, to him, were not.

Johnson-Laird's academic brilliance served him well again, and he produced an equally brilliant PhD thesis, well inside the three years that is usually allowed for it. Undergraduate and postgraduate brilliance do not always go together: the mental activities needed are not the same, after all. To succeed as an undergraduate, you need to assimilate vast quantities of knowledge from a wide range of topics, and reproduce and adapt it on demand, under pressure, among a group of people all (their tutors hope) working to the same end. There is some scope for individual initiative in project work, and in essay assignments. A research degree is almost the mirror image of this. You work in a fairly circumscribed area, largely on your own, mainly on project work, writing a book-length account of it in whatever time it takes to do so. The only exam you take, and it is the last one you ever do, is the defence of your thesis (the *viva voce* examination) in front of, usually, two examiners, one from your own university, one from outside. That is the practice in Britain; in other countries, there are different traditions, e.g. allowing observers to sit in on the *viva*, or even holding it in public.

The two forms of brilliance did go together in this case, and before he had even finished his doctoral work, Johnson-Laird was approached by Drew again, and asked if he would like to join the academic staff. And of course he did; he swears that until then, even as a PhD student, he had not contemplated an academic career, but had assumed he would go out into the world as, perhaps, an applied psychologist. On hearing the news, Wason came to see him. They were both intrigued by the selection task, an apparently simple problem, easy to explain, that nonetheless most people, Johnson-Laird among them, failed at. It was far from clear what was the source of this difficulty. "Why don't we write a grant application to study the selection task?" Wason suggested. They did, and submitted it to a research council. It succeeded: three years of funding to research the Wason selection task. Thus began not only the most active period of Wason's academic career, but the only part of it that ever resembled a research programme, as we normally understand it: a series of experiments and follow-up studies, testing hypotheses and refining explanations, ultimately synthesised into a theory, published in a series of scientific articles and, all being well, a monograph.

## Moves and losses

Wason's experiences at work, where one after another things had fallen into place seemingly by themselves, were not mirrored by his home life. In December 1966, The Observer, a national Sunday newspaper, had, as we saw, sent a photographer round to his home in Blackheath, for an illustration of its feature in the following month's Review section of his and Jones's work on official regulations. Wason afterwards remarked on how glum he had looked in this picture, and gave an explanation: his father, Monier, had just died. While they were never close, there had been something of a rapprochement in recent years, as Wason had found his path as a psychologist, and had provided him, as his older brothers Eugene and Jim had done, with grandchildren. So the loss of the old man was a blow.

This blow was amplified when his mother decided straight away to sell the family home, Grafton Lodge in Bath. It is easy to understand why she did this: now in her 80s, it would have been hard for her to manage such a large property, even with the housekeeper that she had retained. She stayed in Bath and moved to a large flat; she kept the housekeeper, who would stay with her, reaching her 80s herself, until the Hon. Kathleen's death at the age of 96, in 1980. Everyone holds memories of the house they grew up in, especially if it was the only one they lived in as a child. For Wason, it had also been, along with Ballykilty, a refuge in times of trouble in his young adulthood too; he had gone there in the early stages of his recovery from his war injuries, after the months spent in a Nottingham hospital. He had gone there after his breakdown in Aberdeen. Now that too was gone. It must have felt like another kind of bereavement.

His injuries, however, had not gone away; they never would heal completely. It was a problem he would have to live with forever. Indeed, the pain and discomfort they caused would get steadily worse as the years advanced, despite his constant intake of analgesics. Mobility was becoming a problem. While he enjoyed walking at weekends, at his own pace, from the house into the village part of Blackheath, where there were, and still are, a rich variety of shops and eateries and some green space beyond, it was a different matter when it came to the daily commute into UCL. At this time, the mid-1960s, before his transfer to Goldman Eisler's group in Linguistics, Wason was still based in the Psychology department in Gordon Square. It is close to the tube stations at Russell Square and Goodge Street. But this fact is of little use to someone living in Blackheath, which is in south-east London, a quadrant which then was practically devoid of connections to the Underground (it is still not well provided for in this respect, though better than it was, thanks to the Docklands Light Railway). He had to walk to the station, take the train, and make several changes on the journey, before the final, and considerable, walk to the department.

The Blackheath house, in Foxes Dale, was modern and fairly large and the family was happy there, but all was not well. The children were not happy at their schools and consequently not progressing as well as they might have, and the strain on Wason through his commute to Bloomsbury was too much. For both these reasons, it was decided that the family should move to North London, where there would be better schooling and easier travel. Marjorie spent weeks poring over estate agents' details of possible properties, before they found one, in 1968, and moved to Frognal, a part of Hampstead. Hampstead's hilltop village section, which is similar to Blackheath's but includes a tube station, is a short walk away. The last house that Sigmund Freud lived in, in Maresfield Gardens (it is now the Freud Museum), is nearby too. But the move was not a success. The house they bought was a Queen Anne house, over 200 years old and, though picturesque and quirky, which made it interesting, it was dilapidated. "What's the matter, mate", said a removal man, in a remark that amused Wason; "you fallen on hard times, moving into this tiny house?" It had no spare room that Wason could turn into his *sanctum sanctorum*, and retreat to his chess, his pipe and his ruminations; indeed, the ground floor had been modified to an open-plan layout.

Wason and Marjorie did not at first realise just what a sacrifice this would turn out to be. In his study in the Blackheath house, he had a big chessboard set up, and an array of his uncle Rigby's puzzles, alongside his books and his pipes; just as in his office at UCL, there was always pipe-smoke in the air. Besides the large chessboard, he had a number of smaller, portable chess sets, some of which were kept in the capacious pockets of his typically academic corduroy jacket. He would retreat from family busyness there and ponder his correspondence chess games – he would have several on the go at any one time, the state of play of each recorded on one of the little sets – and incubate his ideas for experiments to study any intriguing observations he had made.

The move from Blackheath was a sacrifice for Marjorie too. She taught on a voluntary basis in a nearby school in the less salubrious area of Deptford, and was active in the local Labour Party, to the extent once of organising a major fundraising event in aid of victims of the Biafran secessionist war in Nigeria. This event even featured an appearance by the first British celebrity TV chef, Fanny Cradock. While she tried to maintain these connections after the move, they inevitably lapsed, and she was never quite so politically active again. She gave up a lot in the move across the river, and she did it for him and for their daughters.

The loss of his private study was counterbalanced, at least for a while, by the advantages of living in Hampstead: the journey to work was shorter and easier, and at the time, the area had a rather bohemian, intellectual atmosphere, which suited the Wasons much more than the milieu they had been used to, despite the loss of Marjorie's social network. No academic could afford to buy a house in Hampstead now. Sheila Jones also lived there, in the house which at one time had been the base for CND when it started, and she and the Wason family saw a lot of each other outside the work context. The Jones' daughters would babysit the Wasons', and Sheila would clip items from papers and magazines that she thought would interest the girls.

Marjorie now devoted herself full-time to the support of Wason and their two daughters; she was determined that they should not become 'latch-key kids': children who have to let themselves into an empty house when they come home from school. The girls were now aged 12 and 10. They had very different experiences of their parents, and their parenting. Nothing unusual about that, of course: most siblings will report experiences that, to an outsider, make it sound as if they come from different families, and it is equally common for them to identify and bond more with one parent than the other. There was an additional factor in the Wasons' case that is worth bearing in mind: neither Peter nor Marjorie had had any real experience of parenting themselves. Monier Wason was distant to his youngest son, and despaired of his hopeless impracticality, a permanent feature of his character, as Marjorie had duly discovered and as they both laughed about. Kathleen, his mother, caused him a great deal of ambivalence. Wason respected as much as loved her, and there was a lot to respect about her, but she could be haughty, imperious and also, like his father, distant. The rest of the time he was looked after by nannies, not all of whom could be described as cuddly.

Even this was more parental contact than Marjorie had had. A child of the Raj, she scarcely knew her parents at all during her childhood, losing her mother while in her teens. It was only when her father retired and she helped him move back to England that she really got to know him. Then, of course, he was very helpful to her and her new husband, especially when it came to setting up a home for them and, later, their children. They simply could not have done this without him, or at least, would not have found such agreeable places to live in.

Thus, when the children came along, the couple had nothing to go on, even more so than most new parents. They were, the daughters now recall, very unstrict: there were few petty rules in the Wason household. Both parents were liberal and unconventional, dismissive of polite middle-class English mores, generally accepting of people no matter what their generation or background, casual about their dress sense: Wason never wore a suit, and Marjorie would even, in her 50s, adopt the then fashionably radical dungarees. This liberality made the household an attractive proposition for school-friends, who regularly came around, something also aided by Marjorie's habit of having cakes and biscuits in the oven. Wason and his elder daughter, Armorer, formed a strong bond. When they were living in Blackheath, he would walk with her, just her, into its village part on Saturday mornings to buy his pipe tobacco and browse the bookshops; she would be parked in the stationer's while he did his rounds. Wason regarded her, more than her younger sister, as the 'intellectual' of the pair, and it became clear that he had higher expectations for her, enhanced by his and Marjorie's regular reminiscence about their time at Oxford in the late 1940s – sepia-tinged memories from 20 years ago, now. As is the way of these things, the younger daughter, Sarah, formed an equally strong bond with Marjorie who, in her turn, took a closer interest in her education than that of Armorer. Each can see elements of the closer parent's character in themselves, and in each other.

Wason and Marjorie were now living their lives on largely separate tracks, although there was a lot of talk and laughter in the house, and both daughters remember their father as a loving parent, who, despite his own early handicap in this regard, found that he was well suited to family life. He was not the going-out type in any case, so being at home suited his temperament. When they were small, Wason would compose bedtime stories for the girls, telling and re-telling family tales and make them laugh by imitating people's speech and behavioural tics; he would make up birthday cards with little drawings on them, stick figures and so on. His mimicry could occasionally descend into mockery, and he could also be disparaging of Marjorie and her family background, belittling them as arriviste, even though her father had been so helpful to them.

As the children grew older, dining-table discussions took on a more political hue, a reflection of their parents' allegiances and activities. 'Discussion' may not be quite the right word: Wason liked to lob in a point, and see what reaction it received, but he was rarely persuaded by anyone else's argument. He was not a great debater. This was especially true when the topic veered towards Ireland. The year 1968, when the family moved to Frognal, was the year in which the euphemistically-named 'Troubles', in reality murderous sectarian violence, broke out in Northern Ireland. So it was a topic that was bound to be aired frequently in a political household, being on the airwaves and in the papers constantly. When it came up in the Wason debating chamber, a row was all but guaranteed. Wason was a strong Irish republican, as a result of his earlier experience of, and love for, County Clare and the Irish people he came to know there. He had watched these local people being treated disdainfully by the elder members of his mother's family, who kept the house at Ballykilty, especially his Uncle Fitz. So strong was his sympathy, in fact, that he would voice support for the 'armed struggle' of the Irish Republican Army. "Your father's not normal when it comes to Ireland", Marjorie remarked to her children.

Marjorie herself was no mere housewife. She developed, or rather rekindled, the strong interest in art that had been planted in her by Sandy Wilson, and would take the children on regular trips to the London galleries and their special exhibitions. Very occasionally, Wason would accompany them; he was quite fond of the work of Mondriaan and Escher. But he was not really interested in the visual arts. He had his own cultural preoccupations: his literary tastes, from poetry through theology to psychoanalysis, and he had his chess. Surprisingly, for someone from his background, he was also not the least bit interested in classical music, and especially loathed opera. He did, however, listen to jazz and blues. As the 60s progressed, leather jackets began to replace corduroy in his wardrobe, in line with Lenny Bruce's comment about the attractions of jazz: the clothes and the attitude. Class-based cultural assumptions about Wason could be risky in other ways too. In the early 1970s, his then PhD student, Jonathan Evans, visited the Wasons, after they had moved from the Frognal house, with his wife Jane. "We thought he would be terribly sophisticated, and have a lot of classy stuff", Evans recalled; they assumed that someone like Wason was bound to have a stock of good wines in the house, and didn't want to blunder by taking the wrong kind. So as a light-hearted gesture, they took him some cider from Jane's home county, Somerset. But there was only a bottle and a half of wine in the house when they arrived. Embarrassment all round.

Marjorie was also a driver; Wason was proud of the fact that he could drive a motorbike and a tank, but not a car; his injuries would probably have precluded it in any case. When overseas academics came to visit, she would immediately become friendly with both them and their partners, ferry them around London in the car to see the sights, and put on dinner parties. She could keep the small-talk going too, when Wason ran out, which he did fairly quickly. One of these visiting academic couples was Jerome Bruner with his then wife Blanche; he left Harvard for a while to take up a professorship at Oxford. The Bruners and the Wasons became friendly and saw quite a lot of each other. Wason, however, was ambivalent about Bruner, as he was about so many people. Bruner was one of the most exalted names in 20th century American psychology, extraverted, and with an exuberant speaking style: his conference presentations, words delivered at machine-gun pace but every one worth hearing, made listeners wonder when he found the time to take a breath. Wason resented the fact that when both of them were in the room, it would be Bruner, and not he, who would dominate.

Wason had, throughout his life, very few close friends. As his former UCL colleague and later obituarist, Prof. Tim Shallice, put it, he was friendly, but it was hard to be his friend: he would not reach out to you, but would respond warmly if you reached out to him. At this point, as the 1960s made way for the 1970s, there was Sheila Jones, who remained a friend of the family despite the ending of her and Wason's professional collaboration, and the well-known psychoanalyst and theorist, Eric Rayner, another Hampstead neighbour. He was also still in contact with Claude Miéville, his one true friend from Oxford days, and his family; the Wasons would go and stay with them at their home, a converted rectory in Norfolk. This arrangement would not last much longer: the days of Claude's relationship with his Oxford sweetheart, Luki, were numbered, and there would be an acrimonious divorce.

There was also Phil Johnson-Laird.

# 13

# FRUITS OF THE FIELD

## Momentum

The year 1968 was pivotal for Wason. Not only did it see the family's misjudged move to the "tiny house", as the removal man had called it, in Hampstead, it was also when his research, and his consequent reputation, really gathered momentum. Indeed, the five years from 1968 to 1972 can be regarded as his *anni mirabiles*: so many good things happened, so much progress was made. The years 1969 and 1970 saw his peak production of refereed scientific papers: four in each year. This is a very good level of output, and would be regarded as such even today, where there is much more of a push from external agencies to maximise an individual's research productivity than there was in those rather more relaxed days. A scientist who could sustain this level of activity over an extended period would be destined for academic stardom. Wason could not; but he did attain stardom nonetheless, through his extraordinary creativity. Nevertheless, this five-year period delivered an impressive return. There were four more peer-reviewed papers, the gold standard of academic achievement, on top of the eight in 1969–1970, along with eight other kinds of articles (such as reviews, popular pieces and book chapters) and two books. Before the 12 'proper' papers in 1968–1972, he had published 11, in 14 years; afterwards, he only ever produced another 11.

He was nonchalant about the production-line aspect of an academic's work, but this did not stop him being status-conscious. He had chafed at his designation as a (mere) research associate, and was gratified to be appointed as a senior lecturer. But only for a while: he had ambitions for further recognition. This was going to have to depend on his research alone, since he had turned his back on the other essential elements of a lecturer's role, teaching and administration, in a way that no modern university academic would get away with. But during this time, his research output and the esteem that went with it were heading skywards, and this did not go unnoticed by his new department. Its head, Prof. Dennis Fry, discussing Wason's funding position in a letter to the Provost of University College London (UCL), Sir Noel Annan, in November 1968, described him as "a scholar of great distinction ... a most able and inspiring supervisor of postgraduates". No one would have argued with either of these epithets.

His work was becoming widely known. Once, he was stopped in the street by Imre Lakatos, Karl Popper's successor as professor of philosophy of science at the LSE. "We disagree with everything you say", said Lakatos; "you must come and give a seminar". Which he did. Wason treasured the memory of this incident, and told his family about it. He was no doubt glowing with the fact of recognition from an eminence such as Lakatos.

Wason was seeking promotion to Reader. This is a peculiarly British university role. It is a senior post, mainly, or purely, devoted to research; Readers are not expected to undertake all the teaching roles of a lecturer. It is one rung below, and usually regarded as a stepping-stone to, Professor. Wason's reluctance to hide his light under a bushel paid off: in 1970, little more than a year after Fry's paean to Annan, and despite Annan's misgivings about the cost implications, Wason was promoted to Reader in Psycholinguistics, the designation he would retain for the remainder of his career.

The pickup in Wason's research was down to two major factors: his own talents, especially his creativity, and his collaboration with Phil Johnson-Laird. Over the next couple of decades, 'Wason & Johnson-Laird' would become a label, almost a brand, like 'Lennon & McCartney'. As with John and Paul, they were very different people with very different working styles, but these styles, and their personalities, did not clash: they complemented each other. Wason was the inventor, the facilitator, the exploratory researcher who would run an experiment just to see if there was anything interesting there. Johnson-Laird was a voracious consumer, and limitless storer, of knowledge, which he would bring to bear on Wason's ideas; his approach was to run experiments to test hypotheses. There were no gaps in his expertise: he was an ingenious experimental designer, more than au fait with statistics, an inventive theorist and an enthusiastic early adopter of computational modelling, the expression of theories as computer programs. Together, they made a formidable team.

The late 1960s were the very early days of this approach, or rather, this new science: cognitive science. The term was not then in use, but would soon come to denote the interdisciplinary study of mental processes, with computer science alongside psychology at its centre, and a supporting cast of such subjects as philosophy and biology. Computer modelling is a rigorous mode of testing the integrity of theories: turning a theory into a program immediately reveals any missing components and any unsoundness in its structure. Either of these will stop it running. It can also lead to the revelation of surprising predictions, surprising in that they are often not made by the theorists themselves who write the program, but emerge from its functioning.

Johnson-Laird had been appointed to the academic staff of the Department of Psychology in 1967, straight after the completion of his PhD, a direct appointment at the behest of its head, George Drew. Just about the first thing that he and Wason did was apply for funding for a project to study the selection task. The project began in 1968, with the appointment of a research assistant, who was the person who would actually run the experiments, recruiting and collecting data from the participants. The second thing they did was to put together a proposal for a book. This was not to be an authored book, but a collection of classic and essential papers relevant to the new field of research that Wason had, almost single-handedly, done so much to establish: the psychology of reasoning. Edited volumes take a lot less time to compile than authored books do to write, especially if newly commissioned contributions can be kept to a minimum in favour of existing papers, and Wason and Johnson-Laird's book appeared in 1968, very early in their partnership. It was called *Thinking and reasoning*, the first appearance of this phrase, which would later become standard, in the academic literature.

*Thinking and reasoning* appeared as part of the Penguin Modern Psychology Readings series. It contains 29 papers arranged in 6 sections; their dates range from 1931 to 1968. The only one specially written for the book was Wason's own 'second look' at his 2-4-6 task; his 1964 paper on self-contradiction in the conditional inference task was also reprinted. Touchingly, they included John Whitfield's 'An experiment on problem solving', reflecting the respect they both felt for his inventiveness, and perhaps attempting to remind the world of it. There was no paper from Johnson-Laird, but his fingerprints can be most clearly seen on the inclusion of a section on computer simulation; its first paper was one by Kenneth Craik, one of Johnson-Laird's intellectual heroes, tragically cut down in a cycling accident at the age of 31. The final part, on cognitive development (i.e. children's thinking), contains two contributions from Wason's old associate, Jerome Bruner, and one from the giant of developmental psychology, Jean Piaget. This would not be the last time that Piaget would figure in Wason's thoughts and words. The book was a success: it was reprinted several times and sold in the tens of thousands, showing that the psychology of reasoning was attracting a serious amount of attention already.

The third thing they did was to begin their series of studies, enabled by the research grant, into the mysteries of the Wason selection task. The task was clearly, despite its less than auspicious debut in Wason's informal use of it with friends and at Harvard, full of promise as a research tool because it was paradoxical – something that Wason had spent a lifetime being attuned to. He would sum up the nature of this paradox in an elegant phrase, used in the title of an early review paper (actually the transcript of an address he gave to a conference): structural simplicity and psychological complexity. As we saw earlier, in its structure, the task really is quite simple: take a conditional *If*-sentence, such as *If a card has a vowel on one side, then it has an even number on the other side*, and four double-sided cards, showing E, K, 4 and 7: which should you turn over to test whether the sentence is true or false? The E card and the 7 card, because only these cards could contain a combination, a vowel with an odd number, that would decisively falsify it.

That's all there is to it. And yet the great majority of people who perform the task do not select this combination; Athol Hughes had found this in her doctoral research, completed in 1966, and Wason also had on his return from Harvard, as he reported in his *New horizons* chapter also in 1966, where the task was given its public debut. If their errors were random, that would probably be the end of it: the task could simply be dismissed as baffling, meaningless, and there is no psychological interest in giving people incomprehensible problems and watching them fail to comprehend them. But they are not random, and the task is not, and does not feel, incomprehensible. From its earliest days as a laboratory task to the present, most people – in excess of 90% – do not select the correct combination. And they err in characteristic ways. Most select the E and 4 cards, or the E card alone. It is this systematic pattern of performance that makes the task such a potent instrument for psychological research, and which has, as a consequence, ensured its longevity; somewhere in the world, someone will be looking at it right now.

Wason and Johnson-Laird, therefore, began to make changes to the task to find out what might be the source of the difficulty, a difficulty not experienced as such by all participants, it should be said. While it is quite common to watch some people wrestle with it, it is equally common for others to give their (incorrect) answer quickly and, in terms of effort, easily. That is a clue, as we shall see. Another early observation was that performance on the problem is not just to do with alphanumeric materials. I have kept to the E-K-4-7 example here to avoid introducing logical notation, which in my experience can cause people to run for the hills. We shall shortly see an alternative kind of abstract content that has been used quite often; several other forms have been tried besides these two. It makes no difference to the outcome of the experiment.

It is not, they also found, specifically to do with the presence of *If*, either: to use a Chomskyan distinction, a sentence can have the deep structure of a conditional without the surface structure of an *If*-sentence. It could read, 'Every card which has a vowel ...' or 'All cards which have a vowel ...'; again, it makes no difference to performance. They also wondered about the phrase 'the other side'. Was this confusing people? Other researchers – the task was beginning its spread through the discipline – had thought so. Wason and Johnson-Laird, therefore, devised a way of presenting all the information on the facing side, using a rule about the cards having a border round the outside and a certain shape in the middle. A system of masks was deployed which could hide either the outside or the middle of the cards. Same again: same pattern of performance.

Among all these abortive manipulations, they hit on a technique that did make a difference. It was one that arose from Wason's psychoanalytic interests, and had also been part of the armoury of pre-Behaviourist, introspectionist psychology.

## On reflection

Since his very earliest days as a researcher, studying soap wrappers in the early 1950s, Wason had never been content just to make behavioural observations, either in the field or in the lab. His preferred method was to collect not only quantitative (numerical) data, in the shape of errors, scores, or response times, but to collect qualitative data alongside them. By which I mean he would interview the people he was observing or testing, asking them to reflect on their experience, to say how they felt and what they had been thinking about. It is known as the 'clinical method'. Its great drawback is that it is very time-consuming and hence expensive: each session takes longer to do than a straightforward behavioural experiment would, and it also rules out testing people in groups. So it is rarely used, and when it is, the numbers of people tested tend to be relatively small, which weakens the power of any statistical findings. But it can be very fruitful, and it certainly was in this case. Ultimately, its use would lead to one of the most profound outcomes of research using the selection task, and it would do so in ways that Wason did not anticipate.

There is another paradox in play in the selection task. As we have seen, most people do not select both the cards that could potentially prove the target sentence false by having 'vowel + odd' on them; they select the E card but do not select the 7 card. However, if they are shown that a card with 7 showing turns out to have E on the other side, they will readily recognise that it is a falsifier, just as much as an E card with 7 on its other side is. What they don't do is select the card showing 7 in the first place. What would happen if they were given the selection task and then asked to talk about their choices as they saw each one turned over? What would they say about the 4 card they had chosen but should not have, and the 7 card they had not chosen but should have?

Rather revealingly, Wason would talk about the studies that tested this question as 'therapy' experiments; therapy for the error of, principally, failing to select the 7 card, that is. He would also use psychoanalytic language in interpreting their results. In the first of these published therapy studies, he used a different content from the letter–number one, and we shall now shift to it, because we shall need to refer to it in detail in a moment. The target sentence was:

> Every card which has a red triangle on one side has a blue circle on the other side.

Note that this is not an *If*-sentence but, as we have heard, it could be readily paraphrased into one, and the phrasing makes no difference to performance on the task in any case. The four cards, drawn from a set of eight that the participants were allowed to examine before doing the task, so that they would be in no doubt about their double-sidedness, showed on the sides facing upwards: a red triangle, a blue triangle, a blue circle and a red circle. These are equivalent to E, K, 4 and 7, respectively, in the letter–number version.

In Figure 13.1, you can see a photograph of these cards, the actual ones that were used in the experiment. They are similar in size to a credit card; slightly wider, slightly shorter. They were hand-drawn, of course (this was the 1960s – no computer drawing programs then), and bear little pencilled marks in their corners, presumably to tell the experimenter which ones were the four to be used in the experiment, and which way up they should be. In the picture, the critical four are

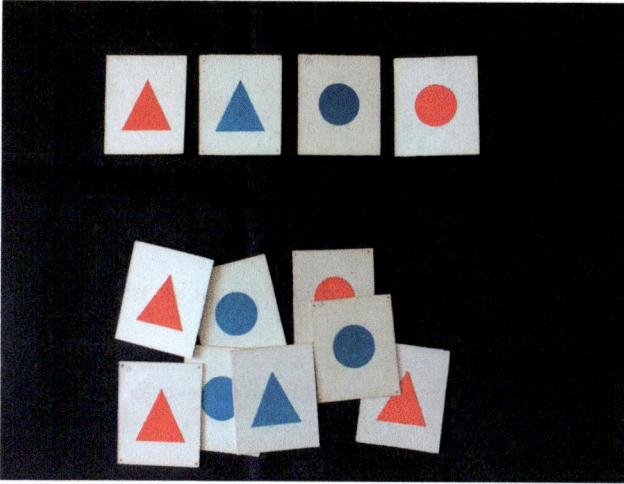

**FIGURE 13.1**    Selection task cards used in the 'Mensa protocol' experiment. The four at the top are the ones that were presented to the participants; the others are ones in the pack from which these four were drawn. Photo by K. Manktelow

shown, along with the others from the pile. They were arranged so that the red triangle card had a blue circle on the back, the blue triangle had a red circle, the blue circle had a red triangle and the red circle had a red triangle. The logical answer is to select the red triangle card, in case it has a *red*, not a blue, circle on the back, and the red circle card, in case it has a red triangle on its back. As indeed it did when the experiment was conducted.

The participants made their initial choice and then, presuming they did not correctly choose the red triangle and red circle cards first off (only 2 out of 32 did so, around 6%), they were taken through a series of scripted steps designed to confront them with an escalating sense of contradiction, a clear continuation of the idea behind Wason's 1964 paper. The aim was to induce them to see the error of their ways and arrive at the correct solution. The procedure was a success in that aim: in addition to the 2 subjects who were correct at the outset, a further 26 came to the correct solution at some stage. This leaves four who never did, and in his 1969 paper, Wason reproduced in full a record from one of these four: it was the process that people went through which interested Wason as much as the outcome of the 'therapy'. It gives a strong flavour of all the elements of the task: the stages of contradiction, the experimenter's script and the subject's part in the 'clinical' dialogue. It also delivers a nice punchline into the bargain. Here it is (the annotations in square brackets are mine).

EXPERIMENTER: Your task is to tell me which of the cards you need to turn over in order to find out whether the sentence in front of you is true or false.

SUBJECT: *A red triangle on one side... although there were some in which both sides were red... I don't know how many of them. At present we have two cards which could satisfy those conditions ... so you only have two cards to choose from: the red triangle and the blue circle.*

E: What could be on the other side of the red triangle?

S: *A red circle or a blue circle.*

E: If there were a red circle on the other side, could you say anything about the truth or falsity of the sentence?

S: *It would be untrue.*

E: And if there were a blue circle, could you say anything about the truth or falsity of the sentence?

S: *It would be true.*

E: By the way, what was your choice of cards to turn over in order to find out whether the sentence in front of you is true or false?

S: *The red triangle and the blue circle.*

E: Are you quite happy about this choice?

S: *Quite happy, as the other two do not agree with the statement made.*

E: What could be on the other side of the red circle?

S: *A red triangle or a blue triangle.*

E: If there was a red triangle on the other side, could you say anything about the truth or falsity of the sentence in front of you?

S: *The sentence would be meaningless because it doesn't apply.*

E: In fact it would be false.

S: *It could be but you are not doing it that way round. The statement would be untrue in any case, no matter what is on the other side.*

E: If there were a blue triangle on the other side, could you say anything about the truth or falsity of the sentence?

S: *No.*

E: Are you quite happy about needing to turn over just the red triangle and the blue circle in order to find out whether the sentence is true or false?

S: *Yes.*

E: Please turn over the red triangle and the blue circle and tell me whether the sentence is true or false.[The red triangle card has a blue circle on the other side, and the blue circle has a red triangle.]

S: *The sentence is true.*

E: I am now going to turn over the red circle, and I want you to tell me whether you still think the sentence is true.[The red circle is revealed to have a red triangle on its reverse.]

S: *Wait a minute. When it's put like that the sentence is not true. Either the sentence is true or it is not true. You have just proved one thing and then you have proved the other. You've proved a theorem and then its corollary, so you don't know where you are. Don't ask me about the blue triangle because it would be meaningless.*

E: Are you quite happy about needing to turn over just the red triangle and the blue circle in order to find out whether the sentence is true or false?

S: *There is only one card which needs to be turned over to prove the statement exactly: the red triangle. Strictly speaking, you don't need the blue circle. You must find every card with a red triangle on it and turn it over, but there is only one.*

E: But you just said when the red circle was turned over the sentence was false.

S: *That is doing it the other way round.*

E: The problem is very difficult. Very few people get it right. What we are interested in is why they don't get it right.

S: *I am a member of Mensa. I wasn't going to tell you that until afterwards.*

Mensa is a society for people who excel at IQ tests. This transcript has become known in the research community as the 'Mensa protocol'.

There is so much going on here that it would be possible to spend the rest of this chapter going through it, but the story needs to be kept within reasonable bounds, so we shall focus on the critical moment, as far as the development of the psychology of reasoning, and Wason's central role in it, are concerned.

This arrives when the experimenter, who in this case was almost certainly Wason himself, turns over the red circle card to reveal a red triangle. "Wait a minute ..." says the participant, and his confusion (he was a male chemistry undergraduate), as he is confronted by what Wason called concrete contradiction, is palpable. He is transfixed by his initial selection of red triangle/blue circle, confirmed in this by the revelation of their other sides by E, which are consistent with his belief ("You have just proved one thing ..."), and then wrong-footed by the further revelation of the red circle/red triangle combination, which is inconsistent with it. But he refuses to budge, and one can't help but feel a grudging respect for his doggedness. Wason used the Freudian term 'fixation' to describe this behaviour, and another one, 'regression', in the title of the paper in which he reports this study.

Regression means reverting to an earlier stage of psychological development. Wason in this paper does not refer to Freud but to Piaget, whose four-stage theory of intellectual development was then the predominant force in child psychology. Piaget's theory states that the final stage of cognitive development is that of 'formal operations' which, to put it crudely, means that people in adolescence acquire the ability to think abstractly and logically. Yet in this experiment, our Mensa man, and three other participants, signally denied the relevance of the critical red circle card; 12 others only accepted it when it was physically turned over, not when they were just asked to think about it (another fourteen did that).

Thus, it seemed that some of Wason's subjects were, when confronted by the evidence of their own deviation from the path of true logic, lapsing into earlier, childlike modes of thought: regressing. He compared the Mensa protocol to a typical dialogue with a young boy in a Piagetian experiment (Piaget also used the 'clinical method' in his research): Do you have a brother? Yes. What's his name? Jim. Does Jim have a brother? No. His interpretation of these protocols in Piagetian terms was influenced by Johnson-Laird, who, having recently had a new book by Piaget and the Belgian logician Evert Willem Beth to review, had talked to him about Piaget's ideas. Wason had hitherto been unfamiliar with Piaget, an outcome of his overly narrow reading habit, but would thereafter go on to quite a profitable sideline in setting out the awkward implications of his work for Piaget's theory. Perhaps Johnson-Laird should therefore have had an author credit on the Regression paper, rather than just a thank-you note at the end.

No matter; he did on a follow-up paper, published the next year, in which they explored further what they called the conflict between selecting and evaluating in the selection task. It was in this paper that they reported using the format where all the information was on the upward-facing sides of the cards, parts being obscured by masks. They found essentially the same things: firstly, that this format did not in itself lead to more selections of the correct cards, and secondly, that, while for some participants the two processes, selecting the cards and evaluating those selections, interacted, for others they seemed to "pass one another by", as they put it (p. 514). Selecting; evaluating. They sound like two different kinds of thought. The true implications of this distinction had not, yet, occurred to anybody. It would take the arrival on the scene of some new characters to take the selection task into new territories, and to grant it eternal life.

## Advancing characters

The first of these characters was someone whose work we have been dealing with, but to whom we have yet to put a name. She was Diana Belt, shortly to assume, on her marriage, the name by which she became well known in the psychology of reasoning, Diana Shapiro. Diana was the research assistant appointed by Wason and Johnson-Laird as part of the research grant awarded to them to study the selection task. She was the experimenter in many of the studies reported in the papers that emerged from this grant, though not, it seems, in the 1969 'regression' study we have just been looking at: Wason credits her with preparing the materials (so that is her handiwork on display in the photograph) and recruiting the participants, but not with collecting the data and being E in the dialogue.

How Diana Shapiro came to work with Wason and Johnson-Laird is a story in itself, and once again reveals much about the times, and how they have changed, and about the play of circumstance in deciding courses of events. She had done her undergraduate degree at Manchester University but had to delay her final year because of illness. By the time she graduated, her friends and contemporaries had moved away. Many of them had moved to London, and some had taken probationer posts in clinical psychology, a possible career that Diana was interested in. It was 1966 and London was beginning, dare I say it, to swing. She followed them down.

She was looking for postgraduate work and found herself on two short-term research contracts, the first of which was with the famous sociolinguist, Basil Bernstein. This involved being trained as an interviewer, which would come in handy later when she worked with Wason. When these posts ran out, she needed another job, and that was when she saw the advertisement for someone to assist two researchers studying the psychology of reasoning. Although interested in the idea of studying thinking, she knew nothing about the psychology of reasoning – few people did anywhere in 1968 – but she did have an interest in related constructs such as people's understanding of probability, a legacy of the research interests of her professor at Manchester. There was the additional attraction that she could enrol on a PhD programme while working as a research assistant. So she applied.

She was duly interviewed, and was impressed by the competition: it seemed like a strong field. When she was given the job, she was surprised. She was even more surprised when, some time later, she learned what one of the factors was that had apparently been taken account of by Wason. He had enquired during the interview whether she was married, and she had remarked that she was in a relationship and that her boyfriend, David Shapiro, was a graduate of New College, Oxford. That, of course, was Wason's alma mater, about which he was for ever nostalgic, and his delight at this revelation was clear to see, and a surprise to Diana. Whether he actually used it as a point in her favour, we cannot be sure; but he did take notice of it, enough to mention it to Johnson-Laird.

Although on the staff of the Psychology Department, Diana found herself, along with some other postgraduates, in the annex that housed Wason's research unit, at dingy Wolfson House, on the 'other' side of Euston Road. The accommodation was bleak; her office's only natural light came from a window that looked out on a dull open space towards a lot of other windows; there was no access to it. It was here that she was able to observe at close quarters Wason's typical working day, and the contrast between this and Johnson-Laird's routine.

Diana regarded Wason as everyone did: a gentleman scholar. He certainly played the role, typecast as he was. He liked to avoid the rush-hour, understandably in light of his mobility problems, and so would arrive just before 10:00 am. He was still making the arduous journey from Blackheath in the early days of her involvement with him. On arrival, he would light his pipe, and then settle down to his chess problems and correspondence games. This disposed of the next 90 minutes. He had a chessboard set up; a decade later, another PhD student, Phil Brooks, would recall his playing a game through the window with a passing schoolboy, who would indicate his moves through gestures, one move per day. He had not, therefore, withdrawn from over-the-board play entirely, although this was a rather detached version of it. Sometimes, Diana would be invited to discuss chess problems with him, even though she was not herself a player, and the talk would then often turn to the experimental problems he had been musing about.

At lunchtime, Wason would ring Diana up if she was in her own room, and they would troop off to Birkbeck College, some way away near the main part of UCL in Bloomsbury. Many people recall this regular lunch party, which could be quite large: it included not just postgraduate students, but colleagues such as Sheila Jones and other members of the Psychology academic staff. Johnson-Laird was among them, but not often; he was usually too busy. The attraction for Wason, and probably most of them, was the international cuisine in the Birkbeck refectory. Wason disliked traditional English fare. He would also sometimes lunch at the School of Oriental and African Studies, whose canteen served curries that Wason relished, and he liked to take visitors to the Indian restaurants in Drummond Street, just around the corner from Wolfson House. This area had become an enclave of Indian cuisine since the opening of the Shah, one of the first Indian restaurants in Britain, in 1952 (it is still there, now one among many), which had people queuing down the street. Wason liked his curries very hot.

There was another attraction to these lunchtimes at Birkbeck and SOAS: afterwards, he could repair to the huge corner bookshop nearby, then known as Dillons, and he would spend another hour browsing there. Not every day, of course, but often; at other times, he would instead spend an hour with Diana, other postgraduates, or Johnson-Laird, discussing research ideas, sketching out designs on the backs of envelopes. He would talk to her about his ongoing spat with Norman Wetherick; once, she was detailed to write a rejoinder to one of Wetherick's critiques of his work, a tactic that irritated Wetherick, perhaps as it was designed to. He also liked to reminisce with her about his difficult time at Aberdeen, or how he was happy to be away from the demands of the Psychology department, in his little out-of-the-way billet. He was well aware that his was a position of some privilege. As so often in his post-war life, he had been lucky: his situation suited his gentleman-scholar working style and his temperament, and it gave him time and scope for his eternal ruminations. It could easily not have been like that. In fact, it would not always be so.

Towards the end of her first year working with Wason and Johnson-Laird, Diana started to become disenchanted – with Wason, not with Johnson-Laird, for whom she had then, and retains now, a high regard. The episode at her interview had taken her aback: would a male applicant, she wondered, have been asked about his personal circumstances? She had a strongly applied-psychology focus: she was interested in the world outside the lab, where people love reading murder mysteries, where planes take off and campaigns are planned; people reason and solve problems, and enjoy doing so, all the time. She wanted to explore, for her PhD, the circumstances under which the Wason selection task, which so far had defeated practically everyone who attempted it, would be solvable. And at this point, she formed the view that Wason did not actually want it to be solved. In this, he was summoning the shade of his Uncle Rigby, who resented people solving one of his Victorian puzzles, and if they did so would promptly shove another one at them.

Wason did not encourage Diana's interests, and she felt that this was in part because she was a woman, trying to navigate her way through a man's world. One of her female fellow postgraduates felt the same. This was despite Wason's admirable record of successful supervision of female PhD candidates. They had good reason at the time to regard Psychology as a rather male science, with, at UCL, a hard experimental focus that Diana did not find conducive: in the year we are talking about, 1969, there were 44 professors of Psychology in the UK; just 4 were women. The imbalance is not as extreme now, but there is still an under-representation of women at senior levels, especially given that around 80% of Psychology undergraduates are female. So she and Wason would argue, and she felt that he was being dismissive, in a patronising way, towards her. In the end, after the project she worked on had finished, she followed her star towards clinical psychology, with the support of her husband, David, a clinical psychologist himself and, in time, an eminent one. After she had left her research assistant post and gone to the Institute of Psychiatry for her training, she had one further meeting with Wason, whom she still liked despite the difficulties in her professional relationship with him, to discuss how she might complete her doctorate. He showed not the slightest interest in it, and after thinking about it for some time, she let it go.

However, Diana Shapiro did leave her mark on the psychology of reasoning, and in early 1969, she did it in the way she had aimed to all along: by introducing the real world into the Wason selection task. She ditched the abstract contents, letters and numbers, coloured shapes and so on, that had been used up to that point, and devised a format that contained realistic materials. She gave participants the following claim, said to have been made about four journeys, mentioning a familiar destination for her:

Every time I go to Manchester I travel by car.

The four cards each had a city name on one side and a mode of transport on the other side. In front of them, the participant could see cards showing Manchester (equivalent to the E card in the original format), Leeds (K), Car (4) and Train (7). Which do you need to turn over to test whether this claim is true or false? The ones that could show you a journey to Manchester made by other means than by car: these are the Manchester card, which might not have Car on the back, and the Train card, which might say Manchester. Out of 16 participants, 10 made this choice, compared to 2 out of 16 given a letter–number version.

Diana was delighted but Wason was shocked and disheartened by this result; he really did not want to see the task made easy. But after a brief period of melancholy about it, he began to see that it was in fact an interesting finding. It was also a lucky one: the journeys version has since been found to be a 'weak facilitator', only producing enhanced performance in about 40% of the studies that have replicated it. If Shapiro's experiment had been one of the other 60%, the course of this research area would have been different. The paper that resulted from it was written by Wason and not in the form that Shapiro wanted: the 'journeys' experiment had been preceded in the paper by another in which people had to evaluate the cards before doing the task. In reality, this one had been conducted later, and Diana wanted to report the studies in their real order. It brought to a head her disaffection with him. However, the paper is one of the most important ever published in the area. It set off a whole series of studies, not just by the Wason group but by others that were beginning to spring up in various other universities, to try to pin down the nature of this 'content effect', as it became known.

Wason's shock at Shapiro's result was short-lived. He was sufficiently stimulated to write a long letter about it and his selection task studies more generally up to that time to Sir Cyril Burt. Burt was long retired from his headship of Psychology at UCL but still active. Wason included reprints of his published papers along with an account of Shapiro's result. Burt gave him the courtesy of an 8-page, typewritten reply. It contains a lot of technical discussion, none of which seems to have made any impact on Wason's thinking about reasoning, except perhaps his references to Piaget, whom he would invoke in discussing his findings such as the Mensa protocol. However, there was also a description of a realistic selection task experiment Burt had run himself; he does not say when he had run it. This task involved a murder story (Shapiro would have appreciated that, but Wason seems not to have told her about it), including the claim that 'All the men have an alibi', with cards showing man, woman, alibi and no alibi. He reports that 57% of his participants, who were 12-year-old children, selected the man and no-alibi cards to test the claim, as they should have done, compared to 12% with an abstract version. Burt never published this study, which is a pity, as not only would it have added to the stock of information about the effects of realism on reasoning, but it is also the earliest known case of the use of the selection task with children. It would be another 20 years before such a study was reported in the journals.

# 14

# WORKING WITH THE PROBLEM

## A sense of reality

During the time that Diana Shapiro was working with Wason and Johnson-Laird, the stream of new people coming to work with Wason continued to flow. Wason at this time in his career could rely on the University's support in recruiting postgraduate students, his supervisory talents having been, as we saw, recognised by the hierarchy. But there were other sources of collaboration too, and one of these collaborators would turn out to be especially significant in our story, for more than one reason.

His name was Paolo Legrenzi, and he was an Italian psychologist working at the University of Padova. As a young man, he knew he was interested in Psychology, but in the early 1960s, Psychology in Italy was embryonic; in some universities, it was not offered as a subject at all. However, there was a psychological tradition at Padova, and so Legrenzi enrolled there, in 1962. Initially, he studied philosophy, and became conversant with the work of Karl Popper, before gravitating to experimental psychology. His undergraduate thesis was on perception, but he really wanted to study thinking. The problem was that there was little experimental study of thinking going on anywhere at the time, certainly not in Italy. Bruner in the US, Wason in the UK: that was about it.

However, he was about to have a large stroke of luck. After his national service, which he spent as an army officer, he looked to resume his studies, and in 1968, his fiancée, Maria Sonino, also a psychologist, gave him a copy of a new book she had found. It was a life-changing moment. The book was *New horizons in Psychology 1*, the one that featured Wason's chapter entitled 'Reasoning', and which contained the first description of the selection task to appear in print. It had been translated into Italian in 1967, only a year after its British publication. Wason's chapter immediately piqued Legrenzi's interest through the section on the 2-4-6 task and its references to Popper. But what especially excited him was something new: the brief account of the selection task. Here, he thought, was a psychologist attempting to develop a whole new method of studying thinking. Just what he was looking for. With a grant to stay on at Padova for another year, he immediately started devising and running experiments using Wason's selection task.

Once again, as often with Wason himself and with Johnson-Laird, circumstance stepped in to play a part in shaping Legrenzi's future. One of his professors, Giovanni Flores D'Arcais, spent some time at Harvard conducting research in psycholinguistics, which was booming at the time in the US, under the influence of Chomsky and his psychological vicar, George Miller. There, he had become familiar with the psycholinguistic work of Phil Johnson-Laird. It so happened that there was a conference on psycholinguistics coming up in the northern Italian Alpine town of Bressanone, partly organised by Flores D'Arcais, in July 1969. Legrenzi submitted a paper on his experiments, and at the conference was introduced to Johnson-Laird. They became friends immediately, and discussed the prospects of bringing Paolo and Maria – they were now married – to London for an extended stay at the Psychology department, after the end of his contract at Padova. At the conference, Johnson-Laird helped Legrenzi with the presentation of his paper; they were to be given, and questions answered, in English, and Paolo's English was not fluent. When someone asked him a question that he could not understand, Johnson-Laird stepped in.

Legrenzi's paper was on the selection task, reporting experiments that he and Maria had conducted. Like Wason and Johnson-Laird themselves, he focussed on the wording of the target sentence, and on the relation between selection and evaluation. Johnson-Laird also presented a paper on the selection task, describing studies relating to a theory of the problem that he and Wason had devised, in which participants' behaviour in the 'therapy' experiments was attributed to differing levels in supposed states of insight into the logical relation between (for instance) the letters and numbers in the problem. Both would subsequently appear in a book of proceedings from the conference, accompanied by a commentary from Wason, published in 1970 and co-edited by Flores D'Arcais.

By then, the Legrenzis were in London, Paolo on sabbatical from his new post at the Higher Institute of Social Sciences in Trento, not far from Bressanone. Johnson-Laird had broached the topic of hosting them as visiting scholars with Wason, who was strongly positive about it: Paolo's work was the first time, as far as he knew, that the selection task had been used by an overseas researcher. Legrenzi managed to obtain funding from NATO in Brussels to support them at University College London (UCL), and he and Maria set off in their car, making for the Channel crossing to Dover. The short sea voyage behind them, they found themselves detained at customs, held in what Paolo would later describe as "cage", and with no clear idea of how to get out of it. The officers wanted to know the purpose of their visit. Paolo had Wason's number, and they put a call in to him. He was able to reassure them that the Legrenzis were bona fide, and so they were finally waved through.

They had never met Wason before arriving in London, and when they did, they found out about his unusual arrangement, tucked away in his ground-floor garret at Wolfson House, detached from the Psychology Department. George Drew had found them a berth in the main part of the Department, where they were in regular contact with Johnson-Laird, and undertook some psycholinguistic studies with him. Twice a week, they would make the trek across the Euston Road to Wason's office, where they would discuss research ideas; Maria would help out with the English. The selection task, not psycholinguistics, was Paolo's first love in Psychology, and when talking to Wason about it he encountered straight away Wason's preferred exploratory research strategy: run experiments, even if – especially if – you have no clear idea why you want to run them. It suited the Legrenzis down to the ground. Paolo devised them, discussed them with Wason, and Maria collected the data from students at Commonwealth Hall, a University of London hall of residence housing students from around the world.

The relationship between Wason and the Legrenzis became more than just professional. They were regular guests at the 'tiny house' in Frognal, and would pile into the Wasons' car, a spacious Peugeot estate, with them and be driven by Marjorie to the cinema. The friendship developed to the extent that, after the Legrenzis' year at UCL, they twice swapped houses with each other for holidays. There was a special attraction here for the Wason family: the Legrenzis are Venetians, part of the ever-diminishing proportion of the population of Venice who actually are Venetians, and had – still have – an apartment there. While Marjorie and the girls would tramp round the city's endless labyrinth of alleys, canals and bridges and see the sights, Wason, surrendering to the pain in his legs, would be content to be parked at a café with a coffee and his pipe, watching the world go by, or contemplating chess positions from correspondence games on his little portable sets. He could happily while away a couple of hours this way. Perhaps some of the ideas for his later work were conceived here.

The major outcome of the Legrenzis' stay in London was a study that, like Diana Shapiro's with the journeys content, was to become massively significant in the field; the paper reporting it has since been cited hundreds of times by others. Despite being on the Wason selection task, it was surprisingly co-authored by Johnson-Laird, not by Wason himself. In the experiment, the participants were concerned not with assessing the truth or otherwise of a claim about symbols, shapes or journeys, but with possible transgressions of a rule. The rule they were presented with was this:

If a letter is sealed then it has a 50p stamp on it.

And the participants were told to imagine they were post office workers sorting letters. The 'cards' this time were envelopes, showing one sealed (so this one is like the E card in the original task), one unsealed (K), one with a 50p stamp on it (4), and one with a 40p stamp (7). (I have updated the currency units.) Which ones should you turn over to discover whether or not they violate the rule? The fronts of the envelopes show the stamps, and the backs whether they are sealed or not. You may already have a feel for the right answer: it is to select the sealed letter, in case it does not have the dearer stamp on its front, and the 40p letter, it case it has been illicitly sealed on the cheap. Perhaps you find this much more obvious than the answer in the abstract tasks. The participants in the postal experiment certainly did: fully 21 out of 24 (88%) gave it, compared to two given a letter–number version (8%) – and they were the same people, as each did both tasks. Doing the postal task first, as half of them did, made no difference: this experience did not transfer to the abstract problem. When the use of realistic materials results in an improvement in selection task performance, it is called a 'facilitation effect.' This result is the all-time record facilitation effect.

Although it may not look like it, this was a fundamental departure from the usual ways of studying reasoning conducted up to this point. Quite how fundamental was something that would only truly become clear some time later. Johnson-Laird and the Legrenzis could offer only speculations as to what they considered was the participants' greater insight into the task's logical structure in the envelopes condition. They did point to one feature of this part of the experiment which marked out its difference from the abstract one: the solver's task was not to assess the truth of the rule, but to detect possible violations of it. It was later recognised that detecting rule-breaking is a categorically different mental activity from assessing the truth of claims: it is an aspect of thought known as deontic reasoning. This is a philosophical term with origins going back over two millennia to Aristotle, and concerns how we respond to rules such as those of permission (what you may do) or obligation (what you must do). It took the postal task, and especially its reassessment by subsequent researchers, to bring this basic and ancient distinction between two forms of reasoning, theoretical (the kind required by test-the-claim tasks) and practical (in rule-violation tasks) into focus in Psychology. It is a vivid example of how in science, asking a little question, such as which items are selected in a card-choosing task, can shed light on a big one, such as what is the nature of human reasoning.

## Matching ties

While Phil, Paolo and Maria were heading off in the deontic direction, sparking a line of research that would lead to profound insights into the way the mind works, Wason was heading off in another. It would itself lead to insights equally profound, perhaps even more so, although Wason did not yet appreciate the turn his work would take, and the seriousness of its implications.

He was still occupied with the difference between selection and evaluation, and what the precise nature was of the apparent irrationality revealed in findings such as the Mensa protocol. Something was happening here, but he was not quite sure what it was. He therefore dug further into the use of the 'clinical method' in his experiments. In 1970, he and Johnson-Laird had published a paper in which they offered an account of behaviour in the selection task, apparently revealed in the 'therapy' experiments, in terms of 'degrees of insight'.

Almost everyone, apart from the single-figure percentage that get it right first time, exhibits, they proposed, a state of no insight into the logic of the task, including into the necessity to find the potentially falsifying cases. As they are confronted by increasingly strong forms of contradiction between their selections and their evaluations of them, many subjects begin to see the light. Some acknowledge the need to select the 7 card, and include it in their revised choice, but still feel the need to select the 4 card alongside the E card. This, Johnson-Laird and Wason proposed, reflected a state of partial insight. The nirvana of complete insight was only attained when the subject chose just E and 7, which most, but not all, do in the end, as we saw in the account of the 'Mensa' experiment in the previous chapter.

Although embellished by a flow-chart model, arising from Johnson-Laird's computational modelling interests, the insight theory lacked something that it had to have to be a persuasive account: independent evidence, beyond the subjects' selections, of the states of insight that were proposed to underlie them. Without such evidence, it is a circular theory, a deadly scientific sin. Why do people not pick up the right cards? Because they lack insight. How do we know they lack insight? Because they don't pick up the right cards. And round and round we go. We need some other indication of insight.

You may already be thinking of one; Wason certainly did: why not ask them? Why not look for insight in the accounts they give of their thinking processes? Wason at this time was still wedded to the idea of a general verification bias, a continuation of the idea of confirmation bias that he thought he had discovered with the 2-4-6 task back in 1960. Surely, if a state of no insight arose from verification bias, then when asked to comment on their choices, people should talk in terms of proving the claim in the target sentence true. By the same token, as they were faced with escalating contradiction between selections and evaluations, there should be increasing talk of falsification. Those who select just E and 7, or their equivalents, should speak only of falsification.

The necessary experiment was conducted in association with another PhD student, Roger Goodwin, and reported in a co-authored paper in 1972. In it, they explicitly draw a parallel with the "verification set" (p.206) seen in the 2-4-6 task, so Wetherick's objection that Wason had found no such thing was sidestepped, or perhaps, to turn a Freudian expression back on Wason, repressed. 'Set' in this psychological context means something like habit, or tendency. Goodwin ran the experiment, which used a shape + colour content with items all on one side of the cards, partly masked. Translating that into the familiar letters and numbers, to make it easier to follow, 6 out of 32 participants (18%) selected the equivalent to the correct E and 7 cards, a higher than usual proportion, but not much higher. The authors attribute this slight facilitation effect to the use of one-sided cards, rather than to the participants' knowing that they were going to have to explain their choices; they had to write down, for each selection they made, their reasons for making it.

Typically for a Wason paper, there is an extensive report of these qualitative results, not surprisingly here as they were one of the main reasons for running the experiment. They confirmed that the levels of insight they indicated were closely related to the cards selected: if a participant, languishing with no insight, selected verifying cards, they wrote down verifying comments; if, in a state of apparently complete insight, they selected the falsifying combination, equivalent to E and 7, they wrote of falsification. We therefore have some nice confirmatory results for the insight theory.

It did not take long for a large bucket of cold water to be poured all over this happy scene. The hand doing the pouring belonged to the second of Wason's two starriest pupils, one whose name has already cropped up: Jonathan Evans. Along with Johnson-Laird, he was to become one of the leading figures in the field. To trace how he got to the position of undermining Wason's conception of his own problem, we need to take a step back, to the late 1960s again.

Evans enrolled on the BA Psychology course at UCL in 1966. Just like with others in this story, there was no academic tradition in his family, and he was the first to go into higher education. This is a historical artefact as much as anything, since far fewer young adults went to university in those days compared to now. London in 1966–1967: it was an exciting place to be for a young man from a small town in Devon, and Evans admits that he did little more than cruise through his first year. That was to change in his second year. The trigger was a talk that Wason had been invited to give to students, at the University of London Union. It was on his work on negation. Evans went to this talk, found it interesting, and the following day made his way to Wason's door, knocked and asked him a question about it. Within minutes, in a clear echo of Johnson-Laird's experience from only a short time before, Wason asked him whether he had thought about doing a PhD, saying that he would be interested in having Evans as a student. Evans scarcely knew what a PhD was, and had certainly never thought about one, nor about the possibility of an academic career. But it lit the fire, and he became at once highly motivated. Hedonism was replaced by hard work, and he emerged in 1969 with a first class degree.

With this triumph under his belt, he applied to work with Wason and was taken on. He was given some office space in Wolfson House, along with the other postgraduates, including Diana Shapiro. This led to some friction with Sheila Jones, who regarded the space allocated to the postgraduates as her research space. She complained; she lost. It was an awkward start. His second supervisor was Phil Johnson-Laird, but he took a distant back seat in this role, being at this time fully occupied in a number of different projects, whose success would before long take him away from UCL and, ultimately, from the UK.

For his doctoral research, Evans brought together two elements of Wason's work: reasoning and negation. Looking back, Evans was at a loss to explain what led him to combine *If* and *not*, but doing this produced a discovery that led directly to the cold water that would shortly be poured on Wason's view of the selection task as a reflector of people's irrational adherence to confirmation. It was called matching bias. To give the result before the game, matching bias is a tendency for people to focus on the items named in the sentence, irrespective of the logical status of these items. Think back to the E-K-4-7 example of the Wason selection task, with a target sentence of (for brevity), 'If a card has an E on one side then it has a 4 on the other side'. The common pattern of selections is of the E and 4 cards, or just E. Wason attributed this tendency to a bias to verify the sentence. But it is also the case that E and 4 are simply the items named in it.

Could it be that people are doing something even more basic than verifying – they are just selecting the named items because they are named? We need a way to distinguish verification from matching. Negation is it, and Evans was the person who thought of this. It is an example of the kind of flash of inspiration you need in science to make progress, and it is as easy to understand such moves after the fact as it is hard to summon them up beforehand. Take the sentence we have just re-visited, and put a negative in it, so that it now reads, 'If a card has an E on one side then it *does not have* a 4 on the other side'. Now we can see whether people are verifying or just matching. If they are verifying, they will select E and 7 with this sentence, since these are the ones that are logically consistent with it: the 7 card is plainly one that does not have 4 on it. What will they do? Evans ran the experiment, and the results were unequivocal: people overwhelmingly chose the E and 4 cards with both sentences (and with ones where the E part was also negated). They were just matching.

Evans showed these results to Wason, and he immediately, and, as Evans tells it, graciously accepted their significance. He seemed a lot less bothered by this finding than he had been by Shapiro's journeys experiment. The next move was clear. In the Goodwin and Wason paper, participants had talked about verification when selecting verifying cards and about falsification when selecting falsifying cards. What would they do when confronted with their responses to the two sentences we have just been looking at, 'If E then 4' and 'If E then not 4', and asked to explain themselves? Wason and Evans decided to work together to find out.

# 15

# TWO MINDS

## Setting out

Wason and Johnson-Laird had been quick off the mark when they started working together in 1967, producing in short order a successful research grant application and an edited book, both of which were in place the following year. The book helped to ground the new field of the psychology of reasoning, while the grant provided fuel for their own research effort, which did so much to energise it. The result, as we have seen, was Wason's wonder years of 1968–1972, his peak period of activity as a scientist. Johnson-Laird, in his turn, continued his work in psycholinguistics alongside his collaboration with Wason on the study of reasoning.

During this period, they once again did not let time slip though their fingers. Well aware of the pioneering nature of the work they were doing, they decided to set it down in the form of a monograph: a book describing their research programme. It would appear in 1972 as *Psychology of reasoning; structure and content*. Writing it was a shrewd and profitable move. Profitable in two senses: it immediately secured their wider reputations, and it sold in large (for an academic book) quantities. It attained a US publication and was translated into other European languages. Almost all of the research that has been outlined in the current pages so far is described in *Psychology of reasoning*, from Wason's work on official regulations and their syntactic mind-fogging properties to the experiments with Diana Shapiro and the Legrenzis on realistic versions of the Wason selection task.

Although it is not difficult for an aficionado to tell which parts are more Wason and which parts are more Johnson-Laird, they did not write separate sections or chapters, and in the preface to the Italian translation of the book, written in 1973, Wason tells us how the two authors collaborated. Each would rough out an initial draft of a chapter and give it straight away to the other, who would offer criticisms and amendments. They would then prepare a second draft and repeat the process.

Most of the time, any issues were settled after this stage; they acknowledged each other's different takes on the matters in hand, and the need to arrive at an integrated view. The introduction and conclusion chapters were different: "hammered out orally", as Wason put it, before being written. The original preface thanked Shapiro "for conducting our experiments with enthusiasm and devotion". This irritated her: she thought 'devotion' made her sound like a servant, rather than an assistant.

Much of this communication was done by post, partly out of necessity, as Johnson-Laird was in the US for some of the time the book was in preparation. But not just for such sound reasons: Wason was a compulsive letter-writer, always in longhand, always using a favourite fountain pen. He would write to someone even when he knew he was going to see them the next day, and would sometimes append a second letter to one already written. His writing was difficult to read if you were not used to it, but the more you saw it, the easier it became. In Figure 15.1, you can see one of his supporting letters to Johnson-Laird, concerning his first draft of Chapter 16, on the 2-4-6 task. That this topic was dealt

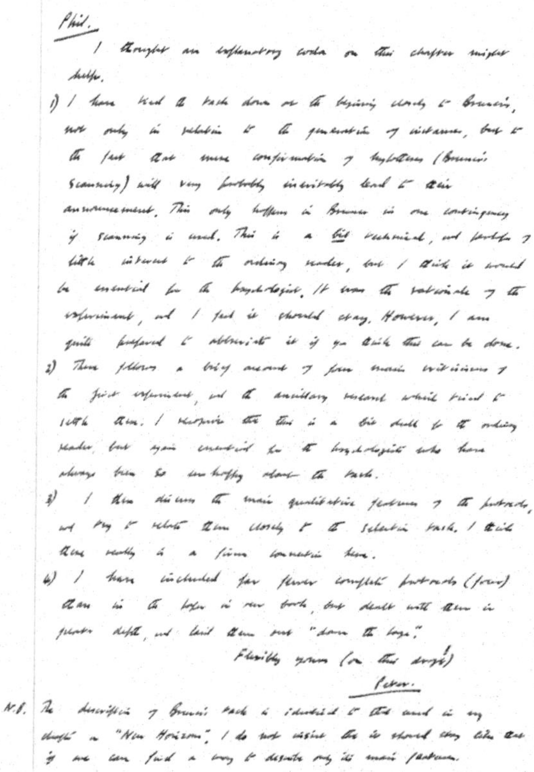

Phil.

I thought an explanatory note on this chapter might help.

1) I have tied the task down at the beginning closely to Bruner's, not only in relation to the generation of instances, but to the fact that mere confirmation of hypotheses (Bruner's scanning) will very probably inevitably lead to this announcement. This only happens in Bruner in one contingency if scanning is used. This is a bit technical, and perhaps of little interest to the ordinary reader, but I think it would be essential for the psychologist. It was the rationale of the experiment, and I feel it should stay. However, I am quite prepared to abbreviate it if you think this can be done.

2) There follows a brief account of four main criticisms of the first experiment, and the ancillary variant which tried to settle them. I suppose this is a bit dull for the ordinary reader, but again essential for the psychologists who have always been so unhappy about the task.

3) I then discuss the main qualitative features of the protocols, and try to relate them closely to the Selection task. I think there really is a firm connection here.

4) I have included far fewer complete protocols (four) than in the paper in our book, but dealt with them in greater depth, and laid them out "down the page."

Flexibly yours (on this draft!)

Peter.

N.B. The description of Bruner's task is identical to that used in my draft on "New Horizons". I do not insist that it should stay like that if we can find a way to describe only its main features.

**FIGURE 15.1** Letter to Johnson-Laird during their collaboration on *Psychology of Reasoning*. Courtesy of Prof. P.N. Johnson-Laird with so late in the book, although it was his earliest real study of reasoning, shows that the book was not a chronological record of their work. His research on official regulations, the first that he conducted after his early excursion with the jigging soap wrappers, appears in it even later. As Wason explains in the Italian preface, their concern was to present a themed account, and this meant putting the material into a conceptual rather than a temporal order.

Wason's particular interests are visible in the book in the inclusion of material from Freud, while Johnson-Laird's can be seen in the inclusion of research on syllogisms (All A are B, etc.). Although they were used in the earlier, pre-Wason psychological studies of reasoning, Wason never studied, nor had any interest in, these problems. But they would soon form the bedrock of Johnson-Laird's initial moves in formulating his grand theory, the theory of mental models. Wason's hand can also be detected in the choice of publisher: Batsford. This is an imprint best known for its stock of books on chess, so it is not surprising that Wason knew about it, although it is more surprising that he should choose it as the outlet for his research in Psychology. It was not, though, the only psychology book on its lists at the time: the flyleaf lists three others. It would publish another one 11 years later: Wason's book on the psychology of chess, the one he co-wrote with the well-known journalist and former English champion, William Hartston.

Wason was also responsible for the absence of an initial 'The' in the title. It was an active decision on his part. He did not want to claim that all that was known about human reasoning was what was known by him, although the methods set out in *Psychology of reasoning* would come to be the preferred techniques of the great majority of future researchers, and go a long way to defining the shape of their research and the theories that would emerge in the future. Perhaps he was simply aware that his tunnel vision in reading the psychological literature – he only ever read what he felt he had to read as far as Psychology was concerned – would undermine any such claim. No one was ever again as inventive in devising ways to study how people reason, so it is little wonder that his techniques came to play such a dominant role. Not only that, but they – the verification task, the 2-4-6 task and the selection task – were robust and reliable, and thus a godsend to researchers: a robust paradigm can be turned to any number of uses in research. And he was not finished yet, as we shall see in the next chapters.

Still in the golden period of 1968–1972, Wason's work was becoming sufficiently well-known that it was starting to attract attention from psychologists outside Britain. Partly, this was down to the influence of Paolo and Maria Legrenzi after the year they spent at University College London (UCL). Paolo would encourage the formation of an Italian school of reasoning researchers thereafter, based at a number of different institutions. But he was not the only person who had been stimulated by Wason's chapter in the *New horizons* book in 1966, and he was not the only one to realise that here was a new way of studying a new area of thinking, an area that had not been subjected to systematic psychological research before. It is worth bearing in mind that Psychology at this time was found by many students to be a rather arid discipline, not at all what they had anticipated it should be.

John Watson's inveighing against 'medieval conceptions', by which he meant mental processes, was still influential; the first book with the words 'cognitive psychology' in its title appeared only in 1967 – after Wason's *New Horizons* chapter – and there was almost nothing about actual *thinking* in it. Wason's work was part of the cognitive revolution, concerned as it was with re-establishing Psychology as a science of the mind, not just of behaviour. His innovation was to pick out an area of mentality that had hitherto lain largely undisturbed by experimentalists, and to devise the methods by which it could be studied. To do either would have been impressive; to do both was an enormous achievement.

On his return to Italy, Paolo Legrenzi began to plan a meeting of all those people he knew about who were conducting research using the Wason selection task. As he was now working in the northern city of Trento, he set about finding funding to support a conference there. His powers of persuasion were such that his new university agreed to stump up £600 of the £1,000 needed to support travel and accommodation for the delegates (that's about £12,000 in today's value). Wason himself managed to extract some more money from the British Council, and the conference was given the go-ahead. Arranging the date became something of an issue between Wason and Johnson-Laird. For Wason, it was a given that Johnson-Laird would be there, principally to act as a discussant (someone who would take a kind of panoramic view of the proceedings and offer a summing-up, like a high court judge). Johnson-Laird's commitments were now such that it was hard for him to allot time for travel (from the US) and attendance very far in advance. There were some testy exchanges between the two before the dates were finalised; Wason had had to take other people's preferences, and the start of the summer term at UCL, into account as well. In the end, Johnson-Laird had to surrender to the pressure of his other commitments: he did not make it to Trento.

So it was that a mere eight years after its first appearance in a vague description in a book chapter, and just six after its debut in a published scientific paper, the Trento Conference on the Selection Task eventually took place, on April 17–19, 1974. There were some 30 delegates present, the greatest number from the UK, but they also came from Italy (of course), Holland, Spain, Canada and the USA. Some of the North Americans had to pay for their own travel: the conference funds could not run to supporting all of them. As for Wason himself, he refused to fly, and so travelled to Italy by train: the Orient Express, no less. He was accompanied by Evans, and they shared a first-class sleeping cabin. Wason took one of his portable chess sets with him and while they spent a lot of time analysing games and discussing chess problems, they did not play each other; Wason's aversion to over-the-board play was not even slackened by these circumstances. Having a travelling companion was useful to Wason because he could not, quite literally, find his way from one side of a railway station to the other without guidance. Whenever he travelled to another university to give a paper, home or abroad, it was "I must be met".

The conference came at some cost to Wason, quite apart from the effort needed to set it up. He had been invited to Chicago to talk about his research, his first invitation to the US since the one from George Miller that had taken him to Harvard in 1963. He had to turn it down. But only temporarily: in late May of that year, he would at last return to the USA and give a series of lectures at various university departments. Closer to home, he had learned that his eldest brother, Jim, in some respects a Mycroft to his Sherlock but who had not had the good fortune in his career that Wason had had, was terminally ill with cancer in hospital in Liverpool, where he lived. He was only 61. It was a foretaste of even greater tragedy to come.

After the conference, which everyone agreed had been a success, Wason was fired with the enthusiasm to have the papers compiled in another edited book. He was not convinced by all of them, and was pretty frank about this in his communications with Johnson-Laird, but recoiled from the latter's suggestion that they should select the best and reject the rest, on the half-joking grounds that this would cause "immense offence, paranoia and potential assault on the person". A colleague of Paolo Legrenzi's, Valentina D'Urso, came to UCL in the August of that year to help with the editing. It was in vain. Wason put a lot of energy into negotiations with publishers, one in particular, but in the end they balked, and no such book ever appeared; the publishers thought that such a book would just be too specialised, and that the papers would be better located between the covers of academic journals. Several peer-reviewed papers based on those given at the conference would indeed eventually see the light of day in the scientific press.

The publisher he had been most closely involved with had an alternative proposal for him. Presumably impressed by the clear-as-a-bell writing that was one of the qualities of *Psychology of reasoning*, they wanted him to write a textbook of cognitive psychology. They didn't know him at all: it would be hard to imagine any academic less well equipped, given the narrowness of his reading, his lack of interest in things that did not interest him and flat-out refusal to teach, to write a general book for students. He floated the idea of a joint book to Johnson-Laird; with Phil's encyclopaedic knowledge and limitless energy, he would be well placed to do it. But when would he get the time? Johnson-Laird was fast on his way to becoming a world-leading research psychologist, active in several areas, collaborating with people in different countries, on different continents, collecting data, writing papers, working on a large-scale monograph with George Miller. It was the same set of commitments that had kept him from Trento. He gently declined.

## Two processes

When Wason and Evans decided to collaborate in studying the interplay between Evans' discovery, matching bias, and Wason's, the conflict between selection and evaluation in the selection task, neither they nor anyone else could have imagined the impact that this work would have. Particularly on Evans, as it turned out:

although he has been a prolific experimentalist, theorist and writer, his follow-up work to this brief collaboration with Wason, which has continued for over 40 years since, is the work for which he is now best known. In recent times, he has integrated it into a large-scale theory of human thinking, called hypothetical thinking theory.

As for Wason, his own work on the selection task was, surprisingly, coming to an end. After this work with Evans, he had one more move left in him: together with a former PhD student of Johnson-Laird's, David Green, he developed a version that he called the reduced array selection task (RAST). A forerunner of this adaptation of the task had appeared in an early paper with Johnson-Laird. Reduced in the sense of leaving out the letter items in an 'If vowel then even number' version: the participant would only see cards showing, for example, 4 and 7. Would removing the 'letter' cards make the problem easier? Yes, was the answer, especially when, in a particularly creative move, Wason and Green allowed repeated plays by offering two boxes of the items equivalent to the number cards.

Wason urged other researchers to explore the RAST further, but it never excited the interest that the standard four-card task did. In a letter to the author in 1999, he was still urging, talking, in a direct echo of his mentor John Whitfield, of conducting 'The imaginary RAST', where "it can be done walking along with your subject on a warm Sunday afternoon!" The paper in which he published his findings with Green, which appeared in 1984, was the last peer-reviewed scientific publication that Wason ever produced.

Others would take up his baton, and the selection task in its four-card form would become one of the most popular experimental problems ever devised by a psychologist: Evans recently found that there was still a steady stream of scientific papers on it in the 21st century, with 2004 being one of the all-time peak years in its citation count. While Wason would watch from the sidelines and politely applaud the efforts of his successors, he would revert to his curiosity-driven explorations of the quirks and paradoxes of human experience. Not for him the set-piece research programme with its systematic drilling-down into ever-deeper points of method and theory. He was at heart a breadth-first, rather than depth-first, researcher, a turner-over of rocks, wherever they might lie.

As so often in science, and in the scientific story told here, the experiment Wason and Evans devised was really quite simple, as simple as the impact of its outcome would prove to be immense. They used the abstract, letter–number version of the task, the 'If E then 4' type, with or without a negative in the number part, as described at the end of the last chapter. In addition, the participants were asked to write down the reasons for their selections, as in the Goodwin and Wason experiment. Evans had found that, whether or not there was a negative in the target sentence, the participants had a strong tendency to 'match': they selected the cards that were named in the sentence, no matter what form the sentence took. This matching response coincides with the 'verifying' response when the sentence reads 'If E then 4', but when the sentence reads 'If E then *not* 4' it coincides with the logically warranted, falsifying response. The word 'coincides' is used deliberately here: could it really be that with the negated sentence people were finding the right answer purely by accident, through matching? Goodwin and Wason had found that people talked of verification when verifying, and of falsification when they falsified; this was taken as evidence for no insight into the logic of the task in the former case, and complete insight in the latter. What would they say when confronted with a task with a negated sentence that they just happened to get right through matching?

When the data were collected, the results of the Wason and Evans experiment could not have been clearer. First, absolutely no one selected the E and 7 cards (keeping to these familiar examples; other letters and numbers were used in the experiment). This meant that with the affirmative, unnegated sentence, no one got it right; 12 of the 24 participants chose E and 4 and another 4 chose just E with this sentence, the majority choices as always. Second, 15 of the participants – they were from the same 24 people, as all did both tasks – also chose E and 4 with the negated sentence. This is now the logically correct answer: E and 4 falsifies the claim that If there is an E, then there is not a 4, because 4 is not not-4. So these people really did seem to be matching rather than verifying, and getting the right answer with the negated sentence by accident. In total, 15 correct with the negated sentence, none with the unnegated one, all through simply choosing the items named in the sentence.

Now for the crucial part of this study, their explanations. Again the results were clear. When the participants chose the matching cards in the affirmative version, they usually said they were selecting these cards in order to prove the sentence true. When they chose the matching cards in the negated version, they usually said they were assessing its possible falsity. This happened no matter which version of the task they did first: half the participants did the 'If E then 4' task first followed by the 'If E then not 4' task, half did them the other way round. This is a necessary move to control for any possible effects of doing things in a particular order, but here it revealed something extra. If the talk of falsification among the negative-first group really did indicate a state of complete insight into the logical relation expressed in the task, that insight would be expected to continue into the second task, which had no negative in it. After all, as Wason had found years before, removing a negative should make a sentence easier to understand. But nothing of the kind happened. When participants matched first with a negative sentence and then with an unnegated sentence, they spoke of falsification in the former case and verification in the latter. The insight apparently shown in the participants' accounts was an illusion.

So what were these accounts showing then? The answer that Wason and Evans put forward would in time turn into one of the most important, influential and widely known theoretical ideas to emerge from modern psychology. Wason set down his initial thoughts about the outcome of this experiment in a letter to Johnson-Laird in February 1974. He writes in terms that tell us the experiment has only just been done. He focuses on the finding just mentioned: the apparent complete insight shown in the reasons given by the subjects who did the negated task first, which then seemed to disappear in a puff of smoke when they did what should have been the easier affirmative task second. He considers three possible explanations for this state of affairs. The second is the one that we need to concentrate on; in any case, he is himself fairly dismissive of the other two. As he writes:

> The response is correct because the sentence is about [E and 4]; hence these are selected. But the S [subject] then brings his reasons (rationalizations?) into line with his response. This is consistent with both Freud and Watson (!) and implies a sort of 'parallel processing'. I am inclined to favour this.

The items in square brackets are added annotations; those in round brackets appear in the letter.

"I think this is quite exciting". he continues, "& reminds me of some of my 2 4 6 data". It was a parallel that has struck other people, and continues to do so: Evans himself maintains it in a retrospective paper from 2016. We can pick out other cherries from Wason's brief comments too. Firstly, he offers a psychological hypothesis about the matching bias that Evans had discovered: "the sentence is about [E and 4]". 'Matching bias' baldly stated is simply a description of a behavioural tendency: to choose the named items irrespective of their logical implications. It conveys no information as to *why* people match. Wason here is reaching for a distinction made by linguists between 'topic' and 'comment': the sentence may say not 4, but it is still about 4: 4 is the topic, not is the comment. It is a recall of his work on negation: if you say you didn't go to Paris, going to Paris is the topic, that you didn't is the comment.

The second and most important point is contained in the second and third sentences. Wason is distinguishing between "his response", in other words, the subject's selection of E and 4, and what he tellingly but hesitatingly calls "rationalizations", a psychoanalytic term; he makes the Freudian connection himself, as we can see. These, he thinks, imply "parallel processing". Although he does not state it in this letter, he must have had in mind findings such as the Mensa protocol and his earlier paper with Johnson-Laird, in which they talked about a conflict between selection and evaluation, processes which sometimes seem to pass one another by. Two distinct sorts of thinking are going on here, he realises: the one that guides selections, and the one that is supplying the subjects' reasons for their choices.

Despite using the word 'parallel', which implies that the two processes are occurring simultaneously, in speaking of rationalisation he seems to be saying something else: that when asked to give reasons for their choices, people look at what they have already done and ask themselves why they have done it. That is certainly closer to the line that Wason and Evans took when publishing their report of this study in 1975. In this paper, they introduce the term for this view of thinking which is still being used: the paper's title is 'Dual processes in reasoning?' The phrase 'dual processes' was coined by Wason; in the present day, the term 'dual systems' is often used in its stead, for theoretical reasons that do not need to concern us here. In this 1975 paper, they are cautious, as evidenced by the question mark in its title, in theorising about these dual processes. They favour a 'weak' dual-process theory, that there is a kind of continuous, dialectical, to-and-fro feedback relation between choosing and explaining. A strong form of the dual process hypothesis would be that choices are determined by an unconscious process, and it is choice once made that determines the reasons we then give for having made it.

In true Darwinian style, it is the strong form of the theory that has proved the better survivor. It is the polar opposite of the common-sense view of thinking, that we know why we do things before we do them, and that the reasons we give are a true account of the factors that cause us to choose what we do. If that were the case, then in this task people really would have been trying to falsify the negated sentence and verify the affirmative. All the evidence shows that they are doing no such thing. They are matching, and then justifying their matching responses once they have been made. One thing that participants in this kind of experiment never say is 'I selected the E and 4 cards because they were named in the sentence'. They never say this because they don't know that that is what they are doing. When it comes to figuring out how the mind works, common sense is sometimes no sense at all.

There is something else about these two processes that Wason and Evans themselves remark on. It is that the accounts that their participants gave of their reasons for their selections – to prove the affirmative sentence true and the negated sentence false – are in fact themselves logically sound. E and 4 really do just that. This is further evidence that selection and evaluation depend on fundamentally different thought processes: a basic bias when selecting, and something that looks more like actual reasoning when it comes to evaluating one's choices.

Further confirmation came from a follow-up study that Evans and Wason published a year later, a study that has given Evans pangs of guilt ever since. This is because they deceived their participants by giving them negated and unnegated versions of the task with the 'solution', E and 4, supplied, and asking them to explain why it was correct. Evans is uncomfortable with the use of deception in experiments, since it contravenes a basic ethical principle, that of informed consent to participate. There are big deceptions and little deceptions; the big ones matter and the little ones, not so much. Stanley Milgram had his participants believe that they had tortured somebody, sometimes to death, for no good reason, purely on the say-so of someone in a lab coat telling them to carry on. Although this may be the greatest lesson ever learned in a psychology laboratory, no present-day ethics committee would allow it to proceed: the deception was just too great, the risks to the participants' welfare from the resulting self-knowledge too serious. Gulling people into thinking a wrong answer was a right one in a reasoning task is not of the same order.

The participants' explanations in this second experiment were as Evans and Wason had predicted: they duly said, with an affirmative task, that E and 4 were the correct selections because these items prove the sentence true; because E and 4 prove it false, they said with a negated task. Thus, these participants behaved with a pre-packaged solution just as others had done with solutions they themselves had produced. It is almost as if, when asked to account for a choice you have made, you have a kind of out-of-body experience, asking yourself why this person, who just happens to be you, must have done what they/you did. You don't actually know: the process that determined your choice is not available to your conscious mind. But you can give a logically sound explanation, and because the explanation is sound, you think it must be real.

Dual-process theories of thought now abound in Psychology, the idea being one of those rare ones that has spread out from a scientific field into general discourse, and it is well on the way to becoming common sense itself, despite some dissenting voices. Perhaps the greatest boost to its percolation into 'folk psychology' (the untutored intuitions that ordinary people have about the way the mind works) was provided by Daniel Kahneman's account of it in his hugely successful *Thinking, fast and slow*. There is nothing like an endorsement from a Nobel Prize-winner to get an idea noticed. It should be borne in mind that dual processing was an idea whose time had come independently to a number of theorists in many different areas of the discipline, such as personality and social psychology, not just in cognitive psychology, the part that Wason and Evans were operating in. And the core notion of dual forms of thinking can be traced back even further, for instance to Wason's psychological guru, Freud. But it appears that, as far as the modern idea of dual processes in thinking is concerned, the idea came to Wason and Evans – and before them to Wason and Johnson-Laird – first. And Wason did invent the term, after all. Evans himself has become one of the foremost advocates of the dual-process theory, having produced, like Kahneman, detailed and wide-ranging accounts for both scientific and non-specialist audiences.

# 16

## READING AND WRITING

### Read the obscure

For any normal research scientist, the invention of an astonishingly fruitful experimental paradigm like the selection task, and the rapid worldwide attention it garnered, would have drawn its inventor into a lifetime's worth of work on it. Not to mention the theoretical advances made on the back of researching people's performance. These two achievements would make that inventor famous, at least within the research community, and set them on the path to greater rewards. Indeed, such was the excitement surrounding Wason's selection task in the 1970s that it featured independently at that time in exhibitions at two of London's major museums, the Science Museum and the Natural History Museum. For the former, where it was part of a psychology exhibition curated by Bob Audley, Professor at University College London (UCL), a version using shapes and masks was used, and set up so that responses could be recorded electronically. No account of the resulting data has ever appeared, but Wason gives a description of the version of the task used in the exhibition in his chapter on self-contradiction in the Johnson-Laird and Wason *Thinking* book. A contemporary tells of watching Wason lurking in the shadows behind the exhibit, waiting to pounce on unwitting customers as they inevitably picked the equivalents to E or E and 4 and put them right, like some kind of academic trap-door spider. It must have made for a memorable visit for such people.

At the Natural History Museum, it was part of the Human Biology display, and featured the 'journeys' content from the experiment reported in the 1971 paper with Diana Shapiro. Wason found that the task had been credited to Johnson-Laird in an internal memo, no doubt as a result of the designer reading about it in their 1972 book. The perpetrator called it "a simplified version of Johnson-Laird's four-cards trick". Wason seemed more amused than put out by this. It was not, incidentally, the only such misattribution: Paolo Legrenzi's colleague Vittorio Girotto found two instances where it was apparently credited to the evolutionary psychologist Leda Cosmides, who had used the selection task in an extraordinary series of experiments, reported in a paper in 1989, and whose writing Wason admired. Which is strange, since the phrase 'the Wason selection task' appears in the title of this paper!

But Wason was not, as we have already seen, any normal research scientist. He was a curious mixture of the amateur and the careerist, hampered in the latter case by naivety about how such a career was to be furthered. He was not streetwise. He thought that recognition should, and would, come to him by right. His good fortune lay in his work situation, which allowed him to stay true to his explorer temperament: he was allowed to get away with refusing to teach, or to make a mess of such admin as he was backed into, so that he was backed straight out of it again. His qualities as a researcher and supervisor were taken as sufficient compensation, at least by the university hierarchy, if not by all of his colleagues.

There was also not then the apparatus of accountability and evaluation that is now the lot of the modern academic, where there is a more or less constant round of research and teaching evaluations, process audits and performance appraisals. In a research-focussed university of today, one doubts that someone like the young Peter Wason would survive this environment. Being the progenitor of a whole new research area would not have been enough, unless it were accompanied by a stream of papers in prestigious outlets, supported by handsome chunks of grant money. As it was, it would dawn on Wason himself before too long, even without such externalities, that his days as a salaried gentleman scholar were in fact numbered.

The mid-1970s were the hour before this dawning, however. In September 1974, the director of the Psycholinguistics Research Unit, Frieda Goldman Eisler, retired, and the head of Linguistics and Phonetics, Dennis Fry, suggested that Wason take over the position. Frieda had been a professor; was a professorship therefore in the offing for Wason? No. It never would be. The Unit was not a large concern in any case, and it now reduced to being little more than Wason and his students. Funding for a postdoctoral research associate – something that Wason himself had been only a few years earlier – came with the post, but rather than advertising it openly, he wrote to Johnson-Laird asking whether he knew of anyone who might be suitable. It was still an era where the latter was possible without the former; not so these days, where public advertisement is mandatory. He continued to take on PhD students, notably, in this period, Evelyn Golding, who was interested in brain processes as well as mental processes (she had worked with the doyenne of British cognitive neuroscience, Elizabeth Warrington), and developed a project on neural processes in reasoning. Wason almost despaired, not of her scientific work, but of her writing, and in the lead-up to her examination, all but invited Johnson-Laird, recruited as her examiner, to fail her thesis. He did not: she passed.

Writing had long been a passion for Wason, and all his students had to get used to this obsession. He would either demand repeated re-drafts or, when it came to writing jointly authored scientific papers, insist on writing them himself. That was what happened with, for instance, Wason's two papers with Evans: when their 1975 dual-processes paper was reprinted in a collection of Evans' canonical publications, Evans had to add a note explaining why its style was so different from all the others, which had been written by him. Wason had his pet bugbears, as all writers do: not just the usual pendant's bêtes noires such as split infinitives and dangling prepositions (he was liberal when it came to beginning sentences with a conjunction, a reliable generator of disapproving tut-tuts from some English teachers), but also Americanisms and inflated terms such as 'simplistic'. He was irritated by other writers describing the selection task as 'deceptively difficult'. No, he said: deceptively simple. He was surely wrong about this: the task is more difficult than it looks and is therefore deceptively difficult, in the same way that a house that is more roomy than it looks from the outside will be described by an estate agent as deceptively spacious. Its apparent simplicity is deceptive, so the task is deceptively difficult.

Characteristically, Wason turned his interest in writing, and in the vagaries of language, into an object of scientific curiosity. He devised ways of assessing not only people's understanding of written material, but also the generative process of writing. In the former case, he kept an archive, dating back to 1957, of what he called 'golden sentences'. In a letter to Johnson-Laird about them ("for your private eye" he notes at the top) in April 1975, he says that the criterion for inclusion was incomprehensibility, with a sub-class of those he found "merely irritating". They were harvested from student work and from reviewing assignments. One example will give you the idea:

> The studies below cover various aspects of this considered necessary in the previous section to any systematic attempt to analyse the knowledge of the universe aspects of communication breakdown.

The last two words in this extract must have amused him. He intended to study such sentences by ranking them in order of difficulty and asking people to 'translate' them into meaningful terms, recording how long it took them to do so. But it seems that the study was never done. It is interesting to note that he started collecting these offences against clarity back in 1957, just before he was commissioned to study the sources of difficulty in official regulations. Given his predisposition to noticing bad English, he must have fallen on this commission like a kestrel on a vole.

Wason did not leave this matter to lie. In further correspondence to Johnson-Laird, he also told him about a study he was conducting, this time on something that clearly irritated him: jargon-ridden academic prose. He had come across an issue of the *Times Literary Supplement (TLS)* devoted to semiotics (the study of signs and symbols and their role in communication). Once again, he was struck by the paradox of a study of communication where its practitioners seemed not to be able to communicate clearly. He focussed on an article in the *TLS* by the French semiotician, Julia Kristeva, passed to him by a friend from the linguistics department at nearby Birkbeck College, part of the University of London, Ormond Uren.

If there was ever someone who slotted smoothly into Wason's category of interesting people, it was Ormond Uren. He had fetched up at Birkbeck after a personal history coloured by one significant event: he had been jailed for espionage while serving in the military during the Second World War. He was fluent in Hungarian, having conducted a love affair with a Hungarian countess before the War, while still in his teens, living with her for a year. This linguistic skill led to his recruitment into the Special Operations Executive (SOE) during the War, and while serving, he was accused of passing information to a man called Douglas Springhall. Springhall was national organiser of the Communist Party. He was also a Soviet agent; Uren denied knowing this, his story being that he contacted Springhall with a view to joining the Party covertly because of his position in the SOE. He was at best naïve. After prison, his name on a government blacklist closed most of the doors that might have been open to him; he had to content himself with bit-part teaching jobs and work as an interpreter and translator, exploiting his fluency in several languages. That was until he found his place at Birkbeck, where his linguistic skills and dazzling intellect at last found a home. And in Wason, he found a kindred spirit. Uren was five years older, and a sharper-focussed version of Wason: war service, intellectual, left-wing sympathies, a nose for the intrigues of life.

Their study of Kristeva's text, a translation into English from the original French, was conducted over the Christmas holidays of 1973. They sent out 49 requests to UCL people for them to paraphrase the passage into meaningful, everyday English as best they could, and 28 of the recipients did so. The original passage was 101 words in length; the paraphrases averaged 105 words, indicating that some found the task difficult. Wason and Uren also collected, following Wason's habitual practice, the participants' commentaries about the passage and the task of 'translating' it, and these form a large part of the article reporting it that finally appeared. When it did so, a year later in December 1974, it was in an unlikely outlet: the now defunct journal *New Society*, effectively the social scientist's house magazine. It is to its editor's credit that this fairly blatant piece of academic mickey-taking was published there; it would have tickled and offended different parts of its readership in roughly equal measure. The article itself comes to no firm conclusion, beyond what Basil Fawlty might have described as the bleedin' obvious: that "the lack of an adequate basis of shared assumptions is a formidable barrier to communications" (p. 814). There were no positive suggestions as to what might have been the serious point of the exercise: how such barriers could be overcome. It was not Wason's finest authorial hour.

## Thinking and writing

The same could, happily, not be said of Wason's explorations of the process of writing, which were more careful, considered and substantial. He had begun to write about writing smack in the middle of his golden period for publication, when invited to contribute his thoughts on the subject to the *Physics Bulletin* in 1970. In this two-page article, he starts by mentioning his cache of 'golden sentences', declining to quote any on ethical grounds and then, in tune with his lifelong approach to curiosity, reports an interesting observation about them. When confronting a culprit and asking them to explain themselves, he reports that often they would come up with a perfectly clear version of what it seems they were trying to say but had conveyed badly. This leads him straight into his prescription for good practice in writing: the dialectical, or generative, approach. This means setting down, in one sitting if possible, a complete first draft of a paper, keeping self-censoring to a minimum.

The great benefit of doing this, he tells us, is that writing has the effect of externalising thought. Only when this has been done can these thoughts be worked on, and this is what you do when writing a second draft, which is in effect a critique of the first draft. This critical process is itself another creative act, generating fresh ideas not only in themselves, but also about the connections that can be made between the propositions expressed in the text. The cycle can be repeated until the author judges that a complete draft has been written. Wason would repeat his take on writing in further studies and reports over the next 15 or so years, and to everyone who worked with him. He was adamant that writing was not a process of transmuting thoughts already had into words not yet spoken, but was itself a form of thought. As he put it in this early paper: "If you want to think, then write" (p. 407). It is a good curative for writer's block. Write something. Anything. This advice would be even more useful in the present day, where we use word-processor software and writers no longer have to overcome the inhibition of making the first mark on a virgin page.

This paper in the *Physics Bulletin* was an extension of one he had written the year before, for a student society. It was touchingly garnished with a drawing of him by his 10-year-old daughter, Sarah, alongside a photograph of him contemplating some experimental materials, not, apparently, his own (see the copy reproduced below, in Figure 16.1). He talks about his observation of 'golden sentence' writers readily clarifying themselves, and of the development of his generative approach to writing. He also attributes his own concern with clarity to his tutorial encounters at Oxford with Lord David Cecil, who, having gone through his curtain-pulling ritual, demanded after hearing a reading of his first essay: "What exactly do you mean by 'the *delicacy* of Spenser's poetry'?" Wason realised he did not know what he meant, and resolved from that moment on always to be clear in his writing. He repeated this anecdote in a published book chapter over ten years later. It was a written-up version of an invited paper he had given at a symposium on the psychology of writing at Carnegie-Mellon University, Pittsburgh, PA, USA in 1978. So here was another aspect of Wason's work that had attracted wider attention.

Not content with merely relating an interesting observation, Wason set about researching the topic further, again in collaboration with a colleague. This was the eminent historical geographer David Lowenthal, at that time Professor of

*Armorer with love Daddy.*

# ONE PROBLEM IN WRITING

by Dr. P. C. Wason

*

P. C. Wason:   Biographical notes

*Born 1924. Educated at Stowe, New College Oxford, and University College London. (Nick-name at prep school: feather-brain). Academic posts: Aberdeen University (Assistant Lecturer in English Litera- ture); Medical Research Council (Industrial Psychology Research Unit); Harvard University (Research Fellow in Cognitive Studies); University College London (Senior Lecturer in Psycholinguistics, Department of Phonetics). Co-editor with P. N. Johnson-Laird of Thinking and Reasoning (Penguin Books). Married with two daughters, Armorer (13) and Sarah (11), and lives in Hampstead.*

*Family background is very political. My great grandfather, Rigby Wason, was a Radical M.P. for Ipswich and a founder of the Reform Club. He sued the Times for libel - and lost, the case being a precedent in the law of libel. He published many tracts full of characteristic passionate outbursts, e.g.: "I shall now show you from acts which Mr Gladstone has done that it was most irrational to expect that he would cease to act upon Tory principles of the most offensive character when he was in power; and his conduct since has been far more in accordance with that usually exhibited by the chairman of a parish vestry, then what is expected from a leader in the House of Commons". My parental grandfather, the Rt. Hon. Eugene Wason, represented Clackmannan as a Liberal, while his brother, Cathcart, represented Orkney and Shetland. Both were distinguished by their enormous height, their radicalism and their eccentricity. My maternal grandfather was a Liberal Peer (Terrington).*

*Personal Likes: Foreigners (especially Americans, Jews and Czechs), doing research under pressure, writing and talking, seventeenth century literature, female company, jazz, chess, animals (especially cats), puzzles of all kinds.*

*Personal Dislikes: English reticence, sport, cars, wearing suits, being asked to mend things in the house, religious institutions, smart talk, the Kremlin, the Pentagon, Ronald Reagan, Enoch Powell, Ian Smith, Ian Paisley, etc. etc. etc.*

\*     \*     \*

      I used to wonder at the fact that some people, whom I knew to be highly intelli- gent, were unable to write with any fluency at all. In supervising half a dozen Ph.D. theses I frequently encountered sentences in which the expression clouded the thought. When I remarked on this the student would usually agree with me, and often proceed to re-formulate the sentence into one which was much clearer. This seemed to me a remarkable phenomenon. Why are so many people apparently content with a style which seems to do violence to their thought?

      At one time the exposition of rules concerned me, for it is here that we often find the greatest impediment to comprehension. Consider this passage from an official

\* Drawn by Sarah Wason, aged 10

78

**FIGURE 16.1**   The title page from *One problem in writing*, a publication for a student society. Courtesy of Armorer Wason

Geography at UCL (and no relation to Kate Lowenthal, featured in a previous chapter). They wondered about the experience of writing among their academic colleagues: although they themselves enjoyed writing, it was clear to them that this was not a universal feeling. So they sent a questionnaire to all 1,000 UCL academic staff, during the summer term of 1976. They received 170 replies, which seems low but is a fairly routine rate of return for surveys conducted in this way, and too small a sample size to permit systematic comparisons between groups on the basis of subject area, sex or seniority.

This was not much of a blow to Wason, of course, given his predilection for reporting qualitative findings, which he and Lowenthal duly spent much of the resulting paper doing. They do not tell us the proportions of their respondents who expressed positive or negative attitudes towards writing, except to say that for most of them, it was a combination of the two: they tended to find writing hard work but ultimately satisfying. Some of the negative comments were florid, such as when a psychologist described the process of writing as "worse than childbirth", while for a historian, it was enjoyable "about as much as being sick". One feels for these people, finding themselves in a profession for which such experiences will be unavoidable and never-ending. The most common negative experience was getting started, which one respondent likened to swimming in the sea: hard to get into, but nice once you are in.

The next most common complaint was frustration at the written words seeming to distort or get in the way of the argument that the author was trying to put over. As a political economist wrote, "I fight a losing battle in attempting to express on paper the subtleties and nuances which I clearly perceive in my own mind … my writing becomes stodgy and contorted". Wason had a remedy already to hand: his generative writing process, which he was only too keen to promote to others. Some of his respondents in this study had discovered it too: a librarian declared, elegantly, that "It's by writing that I move forward in my thinking. I know what I think when I see what I write". People expressing views such as this were the ones most likely to regard writing as a pleasure; some also revelled in the aesthetic process of choosing words and constructing sentences. They had, as the great American writer Tom Wolfe once put it, a musical facility with words: they were artists.

Lowenthal and Wason came to an emphatic conclusion: that the people who went in for a lot of planning before they wrote tended to be miserable. Those who thought as they wrote, or who, like Wason, acknowledged that writing was itself a form of thought, were happier, in part because they knew that writing was a thought-generating process that they could rely on.

A 12-page typescript of the report of this study was submitted to the premier scientific journal, *Science*, but rejected. It would appear in a shortened form in the *Times Literary Supplement* and four years later in an even briefer, one-page form in the cultural journal *Leonardo*.

Wason was not by any means yet finished with writing, neither as an activity for himself, nor as an object of study. In 1980, he was invited to edit a special issue of the journal *Visible Language*, under the heading 'The dynamics of writing'. He contributed an extensive review paper of his own; at 14 pages, it was one of the longest he ever produced, with an unusually large number of references indicating that he was sufficiently interested in its subject matter to read up extensively about it. It is also, I think, one of his best. In it, he takes as a starting-point the effect of conformity to established 'house styles', in mainly academic cultures, which is to stultify writing that, without these constraints, would be freed to display true engagement, what he calls commitment.

Drawing once again on his experience with the language of the French semioticians he had mocked in his paper with Uren, he zeroes in on a sin that afflicts, he maintains, the social sciences in particular, a category in which he includes Psychology, thus neatly sidestepping any possible accusation of inter-disciplinary point-scoring. This sin is something he calls obscurantism: the de-liberate use of convoluted syntax and difficult vocabulary with the aim not of enlightening readers, but impressing (or perhaps oppressing) them. Obscurantism is a greater offence than the difficulties that arise from unavoidable obscurity deriving from specialised knowledge, such as with technical terminology, or from plain straightforward error or clumsy wording. It can often, Wason contends, be used to cover up meaninglessness or vacuous thinking, and this was surely what he was getting at with his digs at semiotics.

There is a simple test, he tells us, which will enable us to tell necessary obscurity from unnecessary obscurantism: paraphrasing. Turning a specialised, obscure passage into plain English usually results in increasing the word-count, since technical terms have to be elucidated. A piece of befuddling obscurantist prose, on the contrary, will be reduced in length when made plain. Wason gives this passage, from the famous sociologist Talcott Parsons, as an example of obscurantism:

> An element of a shared symbolic system which serves as a criterion for selection among the alternatives of orientation which are intrinsically open in a situation may be called a value... But from this motivational orientation aspect of the totality of action it is, in view of the role of symbolic systems, necessary to establish a 'value-orientation' aspect.

"And so on for another 272 words," sighs Wason.

Another equally eminent sociologist, C. Wright Mills, paraphrased it as:

> People often share standards and expect one another to stick to them. In so far as they do, their society may be orderly.

Throw off the shackles of obscurantism and disciplinary house styles in favour of the generative process, urges Wason, and you can recover a committed voice with which you can find out what you think, say it, and then stop. These ideas were extended, with a greater emphasis on the emotional component of the writing process, in a later paper, co-authored with David Green. In this paper, they note that the generative method, or 'exteriorisation', an alternative term that Wason sometimes used, was independently promoted by Peter Elbow, in a book published in 1973, only a couple of years after Wason started proselitysing about it. Green and Wason urge its use to encourage 'happy writing'.

It sounds as if this method could, and perhaps should, possibly have uses in education. The same thought had occurred to Wason, and in 1977, he published a report, jointly written with an educational psychologist, of a game they had devised in order to encourage its use. Schoolchildren aged between 13 and 15 were given an initial starting-off sentence and asked to compose a story, either singly or in pairs. The latter was the game: each pair contributed alternate sentences to the story. The stories were then judged by a panel of teachers who were blind as to the experiment being conducted; the scripts were typed so that they could not tell which ones had been produced by individuals and which by pairs.

While there were no profound differences in the judged qualities of the singly and jointly authored stories, except for a slight tendency for the paired technique to improve standards for the less able group, there were significant effects on the quality of the writing experience: the pairing game greatly increased the fun aspect of writing, even when the exercise resulted in differences in style, as opposed to similarities, being highlighted. The main benefits of the game seemed to be to dissipate inhibition, particularly when starting the writing process, and to make it a happier experience than it might otherwise have been. Just as Wason prescribed with his generative technique for academic writing.

The research had actually been done two years earlier, in 1975, and Wason had originally submitted the paper on it to the *British journal of psychology*, a prestige outlet. But it was rejected, hence its appearance just in working-paper form in a US government series rather than in a refereed scientific journal. The educational psychologist who worked with Wason on this project was called Joan Williams. She was more than a mere collaborator. We shall find out how much more in the last chapter.

# 17

# NEW PROBLEMS

## Thinking and reading

The years 1968–1972, the intense period of collaboration with Johnson-Laird, may not have ever been matched again in terms of Wason's output of peer-reviewed scientific papers, but it would be a mistake to think that it also represented the peak of his activity generally. There were, in the immediate aftermath, no signs of laurels being rested on or feet being taken off pedals. There was, for instance, the research on writing, the ground-breaking dual-process work with Evans, and regular invitations to speak about his work at overseas universities and conferences. Sometimes he combined these trips with holidays with Marjorie; their daughters were now in their teens and perfectly capable of fending for themselves. In August 1975, for example, he was invited to the Aristotelian University in Salonika, Greece, to talk about the selection task and to a conference, on language, at Dubrovnik in the then Yugoslavia the following month; in May 1976, he went on a brief lecture tour of the USA, to St Louis and Delaware, and Marjorie went with him, as she had done to Greece. Her presence absolved him of the need to be met and guided around airports and stations.

Wason also went on family holidays, to the South of France, and particularly enjoyed the food and wine. It was in full 'Englishman abroad' mode: jacket and tie, shoes and socks on the beach, ever-present pipe, contemplating correspondence chess games. He was finally persuaded into swimming trucks, and enjoyed the sea-bathing, once he was in. He did, though, avoid a camping trip by car with Marjorie's brother Hugh to the Dordogne: besides the camping and the car journey, which would have been physically gruelling for him, he did not approve of Hugh, a colonel in the Army, and his strong Conservative views. The family also took occasional breaks with his old Oxford friend, Claude Miéville, and his family, at their converted rectory in Norfolk, and once went with them on a fondly remembered joint holiday in Connemara, Ireland. This time the two couples really did go together, unlike in 1948.

There had previously been the Trento conference on the selection task in April 1974, followed by the considerable effort, fruitless in itself, to find a publisher for a book of papers from it. This effort was not ultimately wasted, however. In rejecting the proposal for a Trento volume, the prospective publisher, Academic Press, held out another possibility: a more general edited book on reasoning, along the lines of Wason and Johnson-Laird's first one, *Thinking and reasoning*, which had appeared in 1968.

There was a good case for a new one: the 1968 book had been a compilation of 'classics' in the nascent field, with very little that could be considered a survey of contemporary work, largely because there was very little contemporary work to survey at that time. So Wason and Johnson-Laird started giving some serious thought to this prospect. They were given a nudge the year after the suggestion from Academic Press when the publisher of their 1968 book, Penguin, declined to approve a fourth reprint, on the rather amazing grounds that it was "only" selling about 3,000 copies a year at the time. They wanted at least 5,000. To that point, October 1975, it had sold a very healthy 46,700 copies worldwide. It had thus become a standard text for all those courses that were now including material on thinking and reasoning – there must have been many. It was doubly attractive to students because it was inexpensive: it retailed in Britain in 1972 at 75p; this was less than half the cost of a long-playing (LP) record at the time (12-inch vinyl albums were priced at around £2 in the mid 1970s). Its low price meant that Penguin had to sell large numbers to make it a viable concern; 3,000 was not large enough.

So now Wason and Johnson-Laird had this second reason to go for a new edited volume. The issue was firmly settled by an unexpected turn of events. Despite his antipathy to teaching, Wason accepted a commission to deliver part of a course for the Open University (OU); one of his former PhD students, Judith Greene, had an academic position there (she would end up as Professor of Psycholinguistics). The OU was a genuine educational innovation, the brainchild of the 1960s Labour government and a personal initiative of its Prime Minister, Harold Wilson, and Minister of Education, Jennie Lee. The incoming Conservative administration under Edward Heath carried it on, and it admitted its first students in 1971. It was designed for those who could not, or chose not to, attend a campus university. Whoever did the market research for it knew what they were doing, as it rapidly became the largest university, in terms of student numbers, in the country, a position it still holds today. Appropriately headquartered in the postwar new town of Milton Keynes, it was not a red-brick or any other coloured brick institution, as far as the students were concerned. Course materials were delivered by correspondence, and coursework went back by post the other way. Lectures were given on television, mainly on the relatively new 'highbrow' third channel, BBC2, late at night; the internet is a treasure trove of examples, particularly memorable for the male fashions of the early 1970s: luridly patterned shimmering jackets, kipper ties and Victorian sideburns.

Wason was consoled by the fact that the OU did not require any stand-up lecturing from him. He was charged with the task of preparing the printed course material, and his sections on *Hypothesis testing and reasoning* for Unit 25 of the Cognitive Psychology D303 course were, as expected, models of clarity. There were other Units on problem-solving and on computational modelling, and the whole 'block', in OU parlance, required a set text. It was clearly time for Wason and Johnson-Laird to compile one, and they set about the task with gusto. It was a ready-made opportunity to produce an updated volume of essential papers, this time with a more contemporary slant; the ones in the 1968 book went back as far as 1931.

Wason regarded his workload for the OU as "heavy", and the major part of the work on the new book began to transfer to Johnson-Laird. Dozens of letters made their way between them in 1976–1977, and at one point, Johnson-Laird pleaded for a "moratorium" on correspondence: Wason wrote to him about lots of other things, not just the task in hand. To no avail; the notes just kept on coming. Not much of this was idle chit-chat, though. In fact very little in their voluminous correspondence over 30 years and more could be dismissed as that; they were always businesslike as well as friendly in their dealings with each other. Wason had taken positions on the editorial boards of two major journals in the 1970s, and this itself generated a lot of work: specialist editors have to read articles submitted by scientists trying to get their research published, and send the papers to referees who advise them on whether they are worthy of publication; often there is a second or even a third round of this process, if revisions are to be considered. Johnson-Laird was an obvious choice as one of Wason's panel of referees, and there was traffic about this to add to the rest.

As far as the OU text was concerned, there were two parts to the project. The first was to select a set of readings, i.e. existing or commissioned works from a range of authors, to cover the span of topics on the course. This is quite a complicated business, with many aspects to it. For any topic, a suitable set of readings firstly has to exist, then they have to be of the appropriate length and style for a student readership, and they have to be available. This last aspect is sometimes the most troublesome of all, since there can be complications involving copyright, and fees to be paid. Several candidate articles ended up not being used simply because their publishers charged too much for them. Many of those that were used were edited down, sometimes quite heavily, to fit the brief. Papers that could not be edited in this way did not make it into the final edition.

The second task in compiling the text came about because they had to divide it into sections, to fit the course structure, and for each section had to write an introduction. These were substantial pieces of work, review papers in themselves, up to 15 pages long in the final printed book; longer than most of the papers they were introducing. These introductions were set readings for the course; the papers themselves were tagged in the course booklet as optional. Wason and Johnson-Laird departed from the method they had used in writing their 1972 book *Psychology of reasoning*, where they had closely collaborated on every part. This time, they divided up the introductions and wrote each one largely solo, showing them to the other for editorial comments and suggestions. In addition, they supplied either a wholly new chapter (Wason's on self-contradiction, where he integrated his older work with his new research) or substantial postscripts to their previously published papers. Johnson-Laird contributed a paper on syllogisms, adapted from a chapter written for another book, in which he deployed for the first time the notation he would use for his theory of mental models, a phrase not then in his lexicon.

In all, there were 7 sections, so 7 introductions, and 34 readings, 4 authored by them. The book was finally published (by Cambridge University Press), after a sometimes painful labour, in December 1977 under the title *Thinking: readings in cognitive science*. There it is: the term that had not existed just a few years before, now sufficiently well known to take its place in a book title. This was one of the first to have it. It was a much chunkier volume than the 1968 book, and its 600+ pages resulted in a retail price of £5.95, for the paperback; the hardback cost three times as much. Oddly, for a student text ('Open University set book' says the front cover), there was no index. The order of names on the cover reflected the burden of effort that had gone into its compilation: it was edited by Johnson-Laird and Wason, not Wason and Johnson-Laird.

Another boost to Wason's international standing, and to the impact of his research and thinking, came directly from his editorial work for the *Quarterly Journal of Experimental Psychology* (QJEP). In February 1976, he reported to Johnson-Laird that he had "accepted a paper from Ohio" for publication in it. He could not have known it then, but this act was about to blow open the doors that seemed to have shut on his first golden research egg, the 2-4-6 task. The paper in question had come from a team of researchers at Bowling Green State University, Jack Mynatt, Mike Doherty and Ryan Tweney.

The paper had been sent to the *QJEP* because the authors could not find an American journal that would publish it; the Bowling Green group were pioneers in their own country as far as this field of research was concerned, and journal editors there did not have much, if any, experience of relevant previous publications to go on. Tweney had written a positive review of *Psychology of reasoning* in a linguistics newsletter, which had resulted in a letter of thanks from Wason. He knew that Wason was on the editorial board of the *QJEP*, so sending his paper there was a shrewd move. It was not on the 2-4-6 task, but it was on the piece of psychology that the task had been designed to tap into: hypothesis testing. Tweney had brought Wason's work to the attention of his two colleagues, and they realised its relevance to their own. Astonishingly, bearing in mind that this was happening in the mid-1970s, the Bowling Green people had designed, constructed and employed a computer-based game resembling pinball (Mynatt did the programming, in Basic) in which the participants' task was to discover the rule governing the motion of 'particles' fired from the corner of the screen towards different shapes that varied in brightness. The shapes had invisible 'force fields' around them which stopped the particles' motion. As with the 2-4-6, there was an apparent but erroneous relation between the items, in this case, shapes and motion, and a hidden, true one: it looked as if it was the shape of the shapes that did it, but it was in fact their brightness. This could be discovered by calling up different displays from the computer, a similar process to the generation of triples in the 2-4-6 task.

Tweney and colleagues (although third author on the paper, it was Tweney who would go on to forge a close academic relationship with Wason) discovered some interesting things in this study, and in its follow-ups. Firstly, instructions to confirm, disconfirm, or just test their hypotheses made little difference to the participants' performance. This was because (the second interesting finding) they mostly adopted a characteristic pattern, for which the Bowling Green people composed, in a follow-up paper in 1978, a nice little jingle: confirm early–disconfirm late. That is, when you think you have discovered a scientific rule, don't discard it as soon as the first inconsistent finding comes along: keep calm, try to find the explanation for the inconsistency and carry on. Only when your hypothesis has been stood up should you subject it to more severe testing, possibly, as Karl Popper would have urged, to destruction.

Tweney and others have looked at the behaviour of real scientists to see whether this pattern of behaviour describes what they actually do in their labs. It does, as Tweney's archival research on the great 19th century physicist Michael Faraday confirms. It is easy to see why. Suppose you have conducted some experiments which have produced interesting findings and for which you think you have an explanation. But your next experiment throws up results that do not fit it. You will surely not go straight back down the snake to square one and abandon your idea completely. No, you will double-check the inconvenient experiment; perhaps there was something wrong with the method, or with the analysis of the data. This applies *a fortiori* with other people's claimed disconfirmations of your ideas, of course. Nothing fires up a scientist's critical faculties so much as a rival's claim that they are right and you are wrong. This dynamic sets up a harsh Darwinian environment for theories: you may not try too hard to disconfirm yours, but others surely will. Thus, the argument you sometimes hear that science cannot be objective because scientists themselves are not objective is wide of the mark. Only the fittest theories survive.

Following the acceptance of their paper for publication in the *QJEP*, Tweney and his colleagues began a series of studies using the 2-4-6 task, and he wrote to Wason to tell him so. Wason replied by return and then, before Tweney had a chance to respond, swiftly sent, on February 1, 1977, a further handwritten note on flimsy airmail paper. It contained a nugget of information that would ensure that the 2-4-6 task would attain only a slightly lesser degree of immortality than its upstart sibling, the selection task. Here is that nugget:

> Further to my last letter – during my writing it came to me that if, in the 2-4-6 task, the subjects were instructed to try to discover two principles, e.g. MED and DAX, then performance would be much improved. My idea is that (say) MED would apply to all number sequences which ascend monotonically, and DAX to all sequences that do not do so....

> The idea has only just come to me, but you may use it if you want to as a personal communication. At least I don't think it has been done before.

He was not quite right on the last point: Wetherick had put forward a similar idea in his critique of the 2-4-6 in 1962, a memory that Wason seems to have suppressed. But it had certainly not been "done" in the sense of being used in a published experiment before. So Tweney and colleagues immediately set about using it. They even kept the syllables that Wason had proposed, DAX and MED. The idea behind this methodological innovation is that there is no longer positive versus negative testing, because a negative test of MED would be a positive test of DAX, and vice-versa. As long as the two rules cover all possibilities, and they do in this case, all tests are positive in one direction or the other.

Wason was right in his proposal that this change in the task would produce improved performance, i.e. that people would discover the hidden 'numbers in ascending order' rule earlier than they otherwise would have. That is exactly what happened when it was tried at Bowling Green, and numerous researchers around the world have replicated the effect, in the course of running experiments to try to pin down what is behind it. At a stroke, this suggestion of Wason's, acted on by Tweney and his colleagues, gave rise to a revival in the use of the 2-4-6 task in research, a revival that is still going on, as evidenced by Evans' recent review. Mynatt, Doherty and Tweney's first paper on the computer-game task, which had so impressed Wason when he reviewed it for the *QJEP*, was subsequently included in the Johnson-Laird and Wason *Thinking* book.

Shortly after this exchange, in September 1977, Tweney visited the UK, on his way to a conference in Venice, and met Wason for the first time. Apart from his stay in London, Wason also recommended a brief trip to his home city, Bath, and lent Tweney a guidebook; Tweney duly made the visit, and expressed regret that he had not been able to stay there longer. Wason also urged him to contact the Legrenzis while in Venice, but Tweney did not manage to do so. As a result of these contacts, on paper and in person, Wason and Tweney struck up a friendship that continued for a decade. It was conducted largely through correspondence, rather in the way that Wason now conducted his chess. Wason would discuss his research ideas and more personal things in these letters; it was natural for him to do so with people he liked. It culminated in Tweney's arranging for Wason to visit Bowling Green, in the spring of 1982. Wason gave a couple of papers, to the specialists in the psychology department and in a public colloquium, and generally held court as an archetypal English gent abroad. Tweney was struck, as every host was, by his complete inability to find his way around without being met and guided. It only reinforced their fond impression of him as an exotic old-school creature.

From Bowling Green, he attended a conference in Virginia, near Washington DC, sponsored by the US military; the Army had paid for transatlantic travel to attend the conference, and the Bowling Green visit had been added to Wason's schedule to take advantage of his being in the USA. Wason told Tweney on his return that this trip had been "the time of a life time" and resolved to try to repeat it with a lecture tour to the USA the following year. This was destined never to happen, unfortunately.

## What is this thing called Thog?

During the early stages of getting the *Thinking* book together, Wason sent to Johnson-Laird, in May 1976, a hand-drawn coloured representation of yet another reasoning task he had devised. You can see the page in question below (Figure 17.1). It became known as the Thog problem, for reasons that will soon become apparent, and it was the last new reasoning problem he came up with. 'Thog' was not the name he initially gave it: the hand-drawn version he sent to Johnson-Laird was given the rather Sherlockian title 'The problem of the four figures'. In his chapter on self-contradiction in *Thinking*, Wason tells us he thought the problem up in 1976 – so around the time he was sending it to Johnson-Laird – because he was concerned that the selection task was becoming so well known that there was a danger that prospective participants would have seen it before and so would not be 'naïve', to use the technical term. Perhaps, he was worried about the exhibits including it at the two London museums; little did he know that the selection task still had decades of life left in it despite (or perhaps because of) its widespread use. Curiously, his memory was again deceiving him when he wrote his 1977 comment on Thog, because there is an earlier version in *Psychology of reasoning* (1972), in Chapter 5. Johnson-Laird, when asked about it in 2015, also had no recollection of this. They had even reported some data, from a pilot experiment conducted with Sheila Jones, and took three pages describing the study. It is strange how Thog's true debut ended up being overlooked by everyone, including its own inventor.

The Thog problem was a particularly impressive act of invention on Wason's part, because it is harder to trace its origins in his previous work and experience than it is for the selection task or the 2-4-6 problem; Wason himself cites the work of Bruner and colleagues in the 1950s as an influence, but that is the only clue he gives. For a start, it makes use not of *If*, the little linguistic connective that he had used predominantly up to this point, but of *Or*. This is technically known as a disjunctive, and comes in two basic logical forms, inclusive and exclusive. Inclusive disjunction is where you can have A or B or possibly both, as when a job advert asks for a degree or relevant experience: you would hardly be barred for having both, but you would be for having neither. Exclusive disjunction is where there is A or B but not both, as when a set lunch menu in a restaurant states you may either have a starter or a dessert with your main course. You could try to argue for both on the grounds that the menu does not make explicit that the exclusive rather than the inclusive reading of *Or* was intended, in the manner of the cartoon character Mr Logic from *Viz* magazine. But Mr Logic always comes off worse from such encounters, and so would you: the exclusive is clearly implicated. Wason and Johnson-Laird had published a paper on a disjunctive form of the selection task, i.e. where the target sentence read (for instance) 'Every card has a number which is even on one side, or it has a letter which is a vowel on the other side', but that was about as far as it went where Wason and *Or* were concerned. Until Thog came along.

The Problem of the Four Figures

1 am thinking about one of the colours (blue or red) and one of the shapes (diamond or circle) in the four figures below:

IF A FIGURE HAS EITHER THE COLOUR I AM THINKING ABOUT OR THE SHAPE I AM THINKING ABOUT (BUT NOT BOTH) THEN I LIKE IT AND OTHERWISE I DON'T LIKE IT.

I LIKE:

WHAT CAN YOU SAY ABOUT THE REMAINING FIGURES?

| ? | ? | ? |
|---|---|---|
| MUST LIKE | MUST LIKE | MUST LIKE |
| MUST DISLIKE | MUST DISLIKE | MUST DISLIKE |
| CAN'T TELL | CAN'T TELL | CAN'T TELL |

© P.C. Wason 1976

**FIGURE 17.1** Hand-drawn prototype of the Thog problem, from a letter to Johnson-Laird, May 1976. Courtesy of Prof. P.N. Johnson-Laird

The moment has come to set out the Thog problem and for you to have a go at it, should you feel inclined. The example coming up is closer to the version given in its formal debut in a peer-reviewed research paper published in 1979. Instead of talking about liking, as the hand-drawn version did, or accepting, as the 1972 version did, the task now is to identify which, if any, of the coloured shapes is a Thog, given that the blue diamond is one. The crucial information to turn it into a reasoning problem is (a) that the experimenter has written down a colour (blue or red) and a shape (diamond or circle) and (b) that a symbol is a Thog only if it has either the colour written down or the shape, but not both. The blue diamond is a Thog, remember, so it must qualify under rule (b). Do any of the other symbols qualify as Thogs? Definitely yes, definitely no, or insufficient information to decide?

I was present when Wason gave this problem to a conference audience – the place was packed – in December 1978. He gave us two minutes to try to solve it, and stood in silence while the clock ticked away. So I have first-hand experience of a first-time encounter with Thog. This is what that experience was like; see if it matches yours, if you have been brave enough to tackle the problem. Firstly, two minutes was quite long enough, because I could scarcely get started on solving the problem and felt the cold sensation of defeat within seconds. Hesitantly, I came to the following conclusion. Given that the blue diamond was a Thog, the red diamond and blue circle may or may not be (insufficient information), but the red circle definitely cannot be one. This turned out to be the solution that most people arrive at. We are completely wrong.

Here is the solution. Start with the blue diamond, which we already know is a Thog. The written-down properties could, therefore, not have been 'blue and diamond', since the rule is an exclusive disjunction and so the stated Thog cannot have both features; and they cannot be 'red and circle' either, since the stated Thog cannot, like the job applicant, have neither. So E must have written down either 'red + diamond' or 'blue + circle'. The first pair would exclude the red diamond as a candidate second Thog (because it has both properties) and the blue circle (because it has neither), vice-versa for the second pair. But neither of them excludes the red circle: it has one of the properties of the first pair and one of the second pair, just as the stated Thog does and just as the rules dictate. Whichever of the two possible pairs E has written down, the red circle must be a Thog.

Somehow, it is no consolation to know that most people get this problem wrong; in the initial study with Sheila Jones that was reported in *Psychology of reasoning* in 1972, the people concerned were 14–15-year-old schoolchildren: 60% of them produced this characteristic error, the 'intuitive error' as it came to be known. Which means that 40% of them did not. Psychologists, of course, love this sort of thing, and in December 1976, Wason reported that studies of Thog were going on in several British psychology labs; Ryan Tweney and his colleagues in the USA would also latch on to it, although they never went further than a few pilot studies and did not publish on it. However, despite this activity, it took a long time for the problem to make it into the pages of the research journals: Wason's 1979 paper (co-authored by Phil Brooks) was the first one, following the

1978 conference paper. And the pattern established with his work on the 2-4-6 task repeated itself: it was the only genuine experimental paper on the problem that he ever published. It was left to others to continue the work on it. Paolo Legrenzi and Vittorio Girotto are among the many who followed it up.

Thog is one of a class of phenomena now known as illusory inferences. Their signal property is that they produce a powerful intuitive but erroneous answer which feels so right that it is very hard to see past it. In this, they are an illustration of Wason and Evans' idea of dual processes: a fast intuitive process and a slow reasoning process. Wason's selection task is another example. But perhaps the most powerful illusory inference of all was discovered by Johnson-Laird, who coined the term. Here are two sentences about your opponent in a card game; one is true and the other is false.

Either:
1. If there is a king in the hand then there is an ace in the hand.
Or:
2. If there is a not a king in the hand then there is an ace in the hand.
Is there an ace in his hand?

It's got to be yes, hasn't it? Just about everyone who has ever been given this problem says so. But it isn't, it's no, definitely no. Once again, you are confronted with an exclusive disjunction, this time between two sentences: either the first is true and the second is false, or the second is true and the first is false. As with Thog, consider each possibility and follow it through. Take the first one: it is false when there is a king but not an ace (remember the logical solution to the selection task). Now take the second one. It is false when there is not a king and not an ace. It does not matter which sentence is the false one: either way, there is not an ace.

I said Johnson-Laird discovered this illusory inference, but in reality, it was a computer program he had written that discovered it. When he saw its output, Johnson-Laird was so sure it was wrong that he concluded that there must be a bug in the program, and spent hours trying to find it. Then it dawned on him: the bug was in his own mind, not the computer. When you find something that exerts such power even over one of the world's foremost experts on human reasoning, you know you have a deep problem on your hands. And an exciting one.

# 18

# TURNING TIDES

## The times

Original experimental work and book and journal editing were not the only things continuing apace during Wason's late 1970s. There were also invitations to talk about his work in other departments, sometimes in other countries, which he was usually happy to take up, as we have seen. Increasingly, he was also in demand to write review papers, introductions, prefaces and popular works about not just reasoning but the other things he was interested in too, such as writing, and the process of doing research. Sometimes he accepted these, such as when he was invited by the leading British psychologist Richard Gregory in 1976 to contribute to his monumental psychological encyclopaedia, *The Oxford companion to the mind* (published in 1987). Sometimes he turned them down, as he did when invited to review the psychology of reasoning in 1975 by the prestige American journal, *Annual review of psychology*. This would have entailed an enormous amount of work, including wide reading, which perhaps explains why he passed the assignment up. Johnson-Laird did it instead.

Wason was also invited by a publisher to write a biography of his former student, the chess champion Jonathan Penrose. That too went by the board. However, the following year, 1977, he did start thinking about his book about the psychology of chess, with the English international master William Hartston, shortly after appearing on a BBC2 TV programme about chess. It would be published in 1983.

For someone with Wason's ruminative approach to thinking, and propensity for numerous drafts and re-drafts when writing, these demands on his working time must have come to seem hectic. So it was no surprise that he and his family bowed to the inevitable and conceded that they had to move from their bijou Queen Anne house in Frognal. Wason's daughters were now in their teens, and he himself had no secluded study space. They moved to a new house, one with more space, in Swains Lane in nearby Highgate. It is the road that bisects Highgate Cemetery, fairly busy, but the new house was set back from the road with another in between and so screened from most traffic noise. It was roomy and bright, with big windows overlooking the historic western half of the cemetery, which is no longer used for new burials. Crucially, it had room for a separate study for Wason, in which he set out a large chessboard on which to rehearse his latest moves.

The house move did not proceed smoothly, and it took some time and trouble to offload the Frognal cottage; for a time, while the rest of the family settled in at Swains Lane, Wason himself would sometimes stay at Frognal. Partly this was because he had been unsettled by the arrival of squatters in a nearby house; this made it, he said, impossible either to sell or rent out theirs. He felt he had to stand guard on it, at least some of the time. They did at last manage to rent it out, to some visiting Americans, and finally, in the summer of 1975, succeeded in selling it. As if all that were not enough, while this was going on Marjorie was involved in a road accident which wrote off their car; she was badly shaken up but not injured. She had also suffered an allergic reaction to some skin cream, and was recovering from that too. It was a challenging time.

Into this mix of a hectic working life and disrupted living arrangements was thrown something that all families must confront: the children's entry into their teenage years. Doubtless no family has ever found this easy. In the Wason girls' case, they had very different experiences of their lives in the family. We have already seen that each identified more strongly with a different parent, as children often do: the elder, Armorer, with her father, the younger, Sarah, with her mother. Wason and Marjorie had little to go on when it came to parenting, neither having experienced what we would today regard as a normal family life themselves: each was cared for largely by staff in their younger years and then sent off to boarding schools. The deprivation of parental contact was especially severe in Marjorie's case.

Consequently, they were feeling their way when their first child came along, and it is not surprising that the experience of the second was so unlike hers. That tends to be the way of it with second and subsequent children in any case; it was just more acute with the Wasons than it might have been for families in more usual circumstances, by today's standards. There is also the matter of the times: the girls were born in the late 1950s and so spent their childhoods in the 1960s, and their adolescence and young adulthood in the 1970s, in London. These were times when the older generation regarded the attitudes and behaviours of their children's with at best puzzlement and at worst outright hostility; boys were expelled from school because they refused to get their hair cut, girls for refusing to lengthen their skirts. What were the consequences for their careers and places in society? From our present point of view, such punishments hardly seem to fit whatever crimes they were deemed to have committed. For the Second World War generation, however, it was as if this period was the end of the world as they knew it. They were right: it was.

Not that Peter and Marjorie Wason were troubled in this way. Their children remember them as being not just tolerant but welcoming of the ways of the young. They were a bohemian, unconventional couple, not ones to lay down rules for rules' sake; "hopelessly un-strict", as one daughter put it. Age 16, Armorer travelled to Marseille for a student exchange with a French family. Her parents had made no provision for how she was to get from the airport to the home in question, in Avignon; she had to work it out for herself. Such liberality did have its limits, though. There was one occasion when a boyfriend arrived at the family home to see one of their daughters; Marjorie did not entirely approve of him, and worked out a script for Wason to follow when the boy arrived. "In future you are only to come here when my wife requests it!" he boomed. "But I didn't come here to see your wife", said Jeremy, and strode past and up the stairs, leaving Wason open-mouthed and floundering: challenging someone in this way was quite out of character. They had neglected to prepare a follow-up line.

When Marjorie had her car accident and adverse reaction to cosmetics, she was not long past her 50th birthday; Wason's was yet to come, in 1974. Hardly elderly, and yet these setbacks were an unfortunate harbinger of what lay ahead. As the late 1970s turned into the early 1980s, health and its vicissitudes would increasingly intrude into their lives. Wason's health had always been shaky. There were the ever-present aftereffects of his war injury, and also his tendency to what we would now call bipolar mood states. He could sink into dark depressions; Christmas was a reliable trigger, as were the rather too frequent angry spats with Marjorie and ir-ritation over his perceived under-valuation by the powers-that-be at University College London (UCL). He had been a psychoanalytic client, shortly after the War, but now sought psychiatric treatment, which was provided for many years by Peter Dally, who prescribed antidepressant drugs, to add to his daily cocktail of analgesics.

Against that, he was enthused by the validation he increasingly got from outside the workplace: his admirers were now legion, and world-wide, as evidenced by invitations such as the one from Bowling Green, and to numerous national and international conferences. The generous review of the new *Thinking* book in the *QJEP* by Donald Broadbent, perhaps the most eminent of all British cognitive psychologists (and who was present at the December 1978 conference when Wason described Thog to a waiting world) must have helped. Broadbent aptly described the book, with its unusually extensive introductory sections, as "a short crisp book of 100 page length, in which key references are supplied in full". "The technique is outstandingly successful, because the editors have something important to say", he added (p. 737).

Increasingly, though, it would be Wason's physical rather than his mental health that would cause problems. He was about to enter the most difficult period of his life so far, more difficult even than his immediate post-war experience, because he now mattered to more people, more people mattered to him, and he had more to lose. As he did so, he managed one last flash of creativity. It came about through a twitch from his noticing faculty, picking up once again on a quirk of language. In 1977, he had spotted, in a newly published book by Jonathan

Bennett, the following sentence, and he wrote to Johnson-Laird asking him to say what he thought it meant:

No head injury is too trivial to be ignored.

Did it mean what it was intended to mean, he asked? Presumably, that all head injuries should be treated, however minor. "You are not a 'subject' in an experiment", he added, "but I do have an experiment in mind". He carried out that experiment, with the help of an assistant, Shuli Reich, and published his findings in a paper in 1979. As the leading American psycholinguist Herb Clark, a friend of Wason's, had noted, the sentence contains four negatives, one explicit (No) and three implicit (too, trivial, ignored). That alone, as Wason well knew from his own pioneering work on negation 20 years earlier, would be enough to sow confusion in a listener, but the clinching factor was that it is pragmatically anomalous: its semantics (it literally means that the more serious an injury is, the less it should be treated) are out of tune with its pragmatics, that all should be treated, no matter how small.

Once again, as with the selection task, the Thog problem, and the 2-4-6 task, we have an intuitive answer that jumps out, while the reality can only be arrived at by a slow thinking process. The title of the paper was 'A verbal illusion', which nicely anticipates Johnson-Laird's coinage of 'illusory inference' to describe a similar phenomenon with his king/ace sentences. The paper caused a ripple of interest, but as usual, no follow-up from Wason was forthcoming. There was another distant echo of his earliest work too: it had only one reference at the end. It was one of his last original pieces of published research. Since the mid-1970s, there had been a shift in his output, from peer-reviewed research papers to book chapters, prefaces, popular articles and suchlike, as the Table 18.1 below clearly shows; the spurt of 'other' papers in 1977 consists largely of the introductions for the *Thinking* book, some of which had been mainly written by Johnson-Laird. This shift is a mark of the esteem his work from his peak period had garnered, and also of the decline in his production of original work. Wason was well aware that his best days in research were behind him.

## Let down

And now, towards the end of the 1970s, when he was in his mid-50s, his physical health began to let him down seriously. He started to suffer from urinary tract infections (UTIs). These are not just unpleasant, but can be life-threatening. Although they are usually cleared up by antibiotics, in Wason's case, this was not completely effective, and he had to resort to surgery. In the end, he underwent several procedures for this problem; it was a problem he would never be entirely free of. In the summer of 1982, straight after his return from Bowling Green, he reported to Tweney that he had suffered from back trouble, perhaps as a result of lack of legroom on the long flight home (he was a tall man, over 6 feet). This was

**TABLE 18.1** Wason's papers in time: peer-reviewed scientific papers (left column) and others (right; b = book)

| Year | Peer-reviewed | Others |
|---|---|---|
| 1954 | ★ | |
| 1955 | | |
| 1956 | | |
| 1957 | | |
| 1958 | | |
| 1959 | ★ | |
| 1960 | ★ | |
| 1961 | ★ | |
| 1962 | ★ | ★ |
| 1963 | ★ | |
| 1964 | ★ ★ | |
| 1965 | ★ | |
| 1966 | ★ | ★ |
| 1967 | ★ | |
| 1968 | ★★ | b ★ |
| 1969 | ★ ★ ★ ★ | ★ ★ |
| 1970 | ★ ★ ★ ★ | ★ ★ |
| 1971 | ★ | |
| 1972 | ★ ★ | b ★ ★ |
| 1973 | | |
| 1974 | ★ ★ ★ | ★ ★ |
| 1975 | ★ | |
| 1976 | ★ | |
| 1977 | ★ | b ★ ★ ★ ★ ★ ★ |
| 1978 | ★ | ★ |
| 1979 | ★ ★ | ★ |
| 1980 | ★ | |
| 1981 | ★ | ★ ★ ★★ |
| 1982 | ★ | |
| 1983 | | b ★ |
| 1984 | ★ | |
| 1985 | | |
| 1986 | | ★ |
| 1987 | | |
| 1988 | | |
| 1989 | | |
| 1990 | | |
| 1991 | | |
| 1992 | | |
| 1993 | | |
| 1994 | | |
| 1995 | | ★ |
| 1996 | | ★★ |

quickly followed by one of his damaged knees falling prey to severe arthritis, a condition that would in the end require more surgery.

In 1978, his mother, the Hon. Kathleen, was still alive and well and living in an apartment in Bath, with her 84-year-old very long-serving housekeeper. But in November of that year she had a fall, and for someone in their mid-90s, this is a serious matter. She never fully recovered, and two years later, just before Christmas 1980, she died. She was 96. Her eldest son, Jim, had predeceased her. Her second son, the handsome, upstanding journalist and editor Eugene, had retired to Bath to be near her, and was also living in an apartment. He would not long survive her. In November 1981, at the age of 67, he was diagnosed with liver cancer, and was treated at St Thomas's Hospital in London. He died there the following month, almost exactly a year after his mother. His funeral was held in Barrhill, the village nearest to the Corwar farming estate that was home to the brothers' forebears; Wason attended, and was intrigued to meet several of the extended family, some for the first time.

With the loss of his mother and brothers, his immediate childhood family was now all gone. But worse was to follow before very long. In late 1979 or early 1980, Marjorie had noticed a lump in her breast and had consulted her GP about it, only to be told it was nothing. In early 1981, shortly after the death of Wason's mother, she went back again, and this time was referred to a specialist. Following a biopsy that May, she was diagnosed with breast cancer, and began treatment for it. The treatment seemed to have been successful, and life resumed its usual pattern, to Wason's great relief. She started to undergo radiotherapy, suffering a nasty incident, a radiation burn, in the process. But the treatment seemed to work, and in a letter to Johnson-Laird at the end of the year, Wason declared that "Marjorie is <u>much</u> better ... she has now finished the treatment and is as active as ever".

It was a false dawn. The following year, it was discovered that the cancer had metastasised, so she was put on a course of hormone treatment. She was now diagnosed with secondary cancer in her liver, and it was also found to have spread to her lungs. "If the [treatment] fails, then she will have chemotherapy", wrote Wason. It did fail, and she was admitted to the Whittington hospital for the chemotherapy. While she was undergoing this treatment, Wason suffered a burst appendix and contracted peritonitis. He was admitted to the same hospital. His daughters were told it was potentially fatal and to prepare for the worst. "Never mind", he told them at his bedside. "I've had a very good life. But how are you two?" But despite the odds against him, he began after a few days to recover, at the price of two hernia operations, to add to the treatment for his UTIs. The daughters visited both parents in their different hospital wards.

Despite all these setbacks, Marjorie remained, Wason reported, in very good spirits, and in the new year, 1984, the chemotherapy was discontinued; as before, it seemed to have worked. This crisis did have one good effect: it brought them closer together, and dampened down the arguments that had peppered their relationship. Wason himself was under additional strain not just from Marjorie's and his own health, the conditions themselves and the invasive treatments for them; he found his recovery from them "depressingly slow", and that he tired easily. There were also the pressures of his work: he was continuously in demand for speaking engagements and contributions to books. It was a moment of crisis, and of decision.

A few years earlier, he had been on the receiving end of a general memo that had gone round to all UCL staff over the age of 55, inviting them to consider taking voluntary redundancy. This was nothing particular to UCL; it was the early days of the Thatcher government, and pressure on public service spending was acute, with many higher education institutions feeling the strain and looking to cut costs. The pressure on higher education was so intense that a campaign group, called Save British Science, was set up. Wason did not think much of the terms on offer, and in any case, his department head had urged him not to go; his presence still added lustre to the staff group. But things were different now, five years later. Marjorie did not want him to retire but she was ill, and so was he, and he was ever more conscious that he was no longer making any real contribution to science, or to his university. So were his managers in the Linguistics department; his erstwhile protector, Frieda Goldman Eisler, had died early in 1982, and Wason attended her funeral. The situation was not helped by Wason's habit of giving departmental colleagues, none of whom had any connection to or interest in the psychology of reasoning, his problems to solve. He liked it when they failed to do so, as Diana Shapiro had observed many years earlier, and was careless enough to let this show. It did not make him popular.

He still had a room in the department; he would give up his office at Wolfson House and move to a smaller one in Gordon Square, nearer to the Psychology department, which he shared with a Japanese professor. But he was beginning to wonder what he was going to do with his days there, with little new work to be getting on with. So when an invitation to consider early retirement came along, seeing the writing on the wall he took it, and bowed out at the end of the academic year, at the age of 60.

He had not so much been pushed out as gently helped towards the door; he had become a problem that the department needed to solve, no longer 'earning his keep', as one of his former managers put it. His aversion to the daily academic grind of admin and teaching was a large part of this, and without producing new research he had turned, as far as the department was concerned, from an asset to a liability. He knew it was his time to go, and did not resist, except to argue about the arrangements, including financial, for his departure. Still niggled by the denial of a professorship, he insisted that he would go as long as he was given the courtesy title 'emeritus', usually conferred on retired professors. The university readily agreed, and henceforth he was to be known as 'emeritus reader'. It is a rare but not unique designation, though unprecedented at UCL at the time. A party was held in his honour at the University in June, to mark the end of his time there. It had been quite a long time, since his undergraduate days in the early 1950s, through his PhD programme to his work with the Medical Research Council research units and the end of its support for him in 1972, to his transfer to the Phonetics and Linguistics department.

Three months later, in September 1984, he had his fifth operation for UTI, and was able to report that "Marjorie (touch wood) is well and active", but with the caveat that she was "always a source of anxiety". The sky darkened. "I am worried about Marjorie", he confided to Johnson-Laird, after his sixth urinary tract operation, in October. On November 14th, six days before her 63rd birthday, she died.

## Carry on

It scarcely needs emphasising what effect this tragedy had on Wason and his family. "It really finished him off", said a contemporary. Not quite: he still had more to give, if not in terms of contributions to psychological knowledge, then to the work of those psychologists who had followed his lead. But the sense of an ending was palpable. Besides the obvious emotional shattering that comes from losing the love of one's life, there was the question of how he would now cope with day-to-day things. He was, as he had always been, hopelessly impractical, and had relied on Marjorie for just about everything in terms of everyday life management; they had laughed about it. Their daughters were adults, and no longer living at home. Everyone around him was worried about how he would cope, especially given his own health challenges. Those close to him rallied round, and somehow got him through this immediate phase of loss and grief, but everyone knew, he knew himself, that he would not be able to survive, let alone thrive, on his own for very long.

Despite the difficulties that his worsening health, loss of his academic position, and the decline and death of Marjorie had brought him, through these hellish years of the early 1980s he carried on working. There was the book on chess with William Hartston, which they had been thinking about since 1977; in 1982, they finally got down to writing it, meeting for lunches to discuss the drafts each had written, and produced a completed manuscript well within a year. It was published in 1983, and sold well, despite production and distribution problems that caused Wason considerable anger. The publisher was Batsford, the imprint that had put *Psychology of reasoning* out. Initially, he was not proud of the new book, and the future has not been kind to its predictions of the unlikelihood that computers would ever beat human champions (they have) or the provocative claim that women would never ascend to the same heights as male grandmasters (the Polgar sisters and others give the lie to that idea: the youngest of the three, Judit, was the youngest player, male or female, ever to attain the title of grandmaster). But he mellowed in his view of it quite quickly, to the extent that within a year of its publication, he was saying to Johnson-Laird that "I should like to be remembered [for] this book".

Hartston, besides being a renowned chess player, twice British champion, also wrote the Beachcomber column in the *Daily Express* – where Wason's first paper, on the soap wrappers' jig, had been featured – and would regularly convey stories about Wason's work and ideas to his readers. In one such column, he related a verbal puzzle which Wason liked to deploy at social gatherings; he never used it in an actual experiment. Suppose, he would ask, you have a four-legged table that wobbles. What do you do? The company would give their answers: fold some cardboard and put it under the 'short' leg, and so on. Then he would follow this question up with a second one about a three-legged table that wobbles: what would you do? It is a catch question, because three-legged tables cannot wobble; they can, at worst, only tilt. Wason claimed to have observed a sex difference in responses to the three-legged question: women try to fix the problem as described, while men are more likely to spot the flaw in the premise, that it is a non-problem because three-legged tables never wobble. Wason attributed this difference to women's tendency to address problems straight away, while men tend to theorise about them; this was, he thought, also behind women's lesser abilities in chess. Hartston himself failed to replicate it.

Then there was the work with David Green on the reduced-array version of the selection task, resulting in the publication of Wason's last research paper, written mainly by Green, in the fateful year of 1984. Also during this time, he accepted an invitation from Jonathan Evans to contribute a chapter to a planned book of readings that Evans was compiling, on the psychology of reasoning. He argued with Evans a lot over the contents of this chapter, these arguments taking place both before and after Wason's last trip to the USA, the one that included the diversion to Bowling Green; "I will withdraw my paper if he blocks my opinions", he wrote to Johnson-Laird. Evans was wise enough to back down in the end.

The chapter was a retrospective piece about the selection task, in which Wason confronts his critics. He had always believed that performance on the task, especially the kind associated with the Mensa protocol (which he reproduced in this chapter), where some participants engage in denial and self-contradiction when asked to explain themselves, was *prima facie* evidence of human irrationality. His earlier work on the 2-4-6 task, characterised by him as showing confirmation bias, he regarded as fully in tune with such results. Claiming that, at least as far as these results are concerned, people are, to some degree, fundamentally irrational was bound to attract a critical response from those who take the opposite view that humans must be fundamentally rational, otherwise, as the American psychologist David O'Brien put it, how come we got to the moon? Fundamental irrationality was an idea quite consistent with Wason's covert, sometimes overt, Freudianism, but it was then and is still a controversial claim in the study of reasoning.

The most direct such criticism of Wason came from the Oxford philosopher L. Jonathan Cohen, in a paper published in the journal for which Wason was a founding editorial board member, *Behavioral and brain sciences,* in 1981. Wason, following the journal's practice, provided a critical commentary, as did two dozen other experts (including Evans, Kahneman and Wetherick). Can human irrationality be experimentally demonstrated? asked Cohen. No, he argued: any apparent demonstrations of irrationality are down to misconceptions on the part of the experimenter, or inappropriately designed experiments – he compared the selection task to a visual illusion. On the contrary, says Wason in his chapter for the Evans book, "it could be argued that irrationality, rather than rationality, is the norm" (p. 59). Look not just at the selection task, he says, and at the phenomena revealed by the selection/evaluation experiments, but at widespread irrationality in argumentation, for which he provides references from the philosophical literature.

Cohen had argued that "a few moments' prompted reflection" would reveal to participants in Wason-style experiments that their thinking had been invalid. But that is precisely what does not happen in cases such as the Mensa protocol, where an intelligent participant all but denies the evidence of his senses in defending his initial illogical response. Life is full of cognitive illusions, says Wason, and we can learn a lot from them and from the irrationality that they reveal, just as we can learn a lot about vision from visual illusions. He also takes the opportunity to extol the reduced-array selection task, as he did to anyone who would listen. He would carry on doing so long into his retirement, in the letters that he continued to pour out to the many people who never forgot him and kept in contact. In those pre-internet days, this was the prime link (he was not a great telephone user) to the outside world for a person in declining health.

At the end of the Evans chapter, he thanks some of the people you would expect him to thank for helping him complete the task of writing it: Evans (through gritted teeth, perhaps), Johnson-Laird, Green. And a fourth person, a surprising inclusion in this company: Joan Williams.

# 19

# THE FINAL CHAPTER

## Second time around

Wason had known Joan Williams since at least the early 1970s, when she was working at University College London (UCL). She was an educational psychologist. They began working together, conducting, as we saw in Chapter 16, their research on collaborative writing games, although they only ever managed to write this work up as a working paper, never as a peer-reviewed publication in a recognised journal. After that, they tried to develop research on children's reasoning, and put a lot of work into it: "I must give all my time to Joan Williams", Wason wrote to Johnson-Laird in early 1976, postponing a possible meeting where they were to discuss the *Thinking* book. Little came of this effort to develop joint research with her. An attempt to run the 2-4-6 task with schoolchildren produced nothing worth recording, and no account of this experiment ever appeared in print.

Their relationship quickly became more than a working one, and it seems that around this time, Wason and Joan had a love affair; both friends and family recall 'something' going on between them. Devoted as he was to Marjorie, Wason was not above falling for the attractions of another woman, a story as old as the human race. She was also married, so any guilt they may have felt was evenly shared. In 1985, after the body-blow, the previous year of Marjorie's cruel apparent relief from her illness and then her rapid decline, he turned to Joan again.

Joan was by now a widow, with five surviving children, another having died in childhood, so she, like Wason, had had her share of tragedy. Fittingly for someone with Wason's Freudian inclinations, she reminded people of his mother: tall, beautiful and stately in her manner, which sometimes shaded into haughtiness, to some eyes. She made use of these attributes as an actress in local theatre groups. Wason was already profoundly lonely, and struggling to cope with day-to-day living, as he had done throughout his life; his nannies, his schools, the army and then Marjorie had taken care of everything until now. He proposed marriage and, early in 1986, they announced their engagement. The wedding was initially set for June, but took place eventually in July. Wason broke the habit of a lifetime and wore a suit; instead of making a speech, he continued another custom and recited, from memory, a passage from *Piers Plowman*.

Joan was living and working in Reading, half an hour by train to the west of London, and not far from Aldermaston, starting point for the anti-nuclear marches that Wason and Marjorie had joined a quarter of a century earlier; and from Sandhurst, where he had undergone part of his military training. Wason was now rattling around the family home in Highgate alone. Neither he nor Joan was prepared to move to the other's house, and so they decided to sell them and set up home together in a location in between the two: Wason still needed to get in to London for occasional work-related meetings, as he still had use of a room in Gordon Square, while Joan needed easy access to Reading. They found somewhere they liked in the pretty, prosperous little riverside town of Goring-on-Thames; Joan knew people in Goring. The house, an elegant 1930s mock-Tudor place, neither new nor old, was called Greycourt. Wason described living there, in the early days, as "wonderful".

Although she was a psychologist herself, and had worked with Wason years before, she was not interested in his work, or in the people he met through it. While Marjorie would happily ferry visiting scholars and their partners in her car around London to see the sights, and host receptions for them, charming them all in the process, Joan preferred to step back from this aspect of Wason's professional life; in any case, she could not drive. Even as a retiree, he kept up many contacts in the academic world, and was still in demand for contributions to books and meetings. Stately she may have been, but she was also warm and vivacious and shared Wason's sense of humour. That was how it had been with Marjorie too.

It did not take long for cracks to appear in the marriage. Each had been devoted to, and supported by, their previous spouses, even allowing for the extra-marital dalliance that had first brought them together, and each expected more from the other than either was prepared to give. This problem was particularly grave for Wason, with his long-standing difficulties from his wartime leg injuries now compounded by other health issues, such as the persistent urinary tract infections that blighted his final times with Marjorie. To that, of course, can be added his wholesale dependency on her for everyday practicalities. He needed a housekeeper as much as a partner, and that was not the role Joan had thought she was signing up for. She also expected more support from him than he was equipped to provide. Neither of them could drive, but Joan gamely, in her 60s, set about trying to learn. She did not take to it naturally. On one occasion, trying to reverse out of the garage at Greycourt, she selected a forward gear, ran full-tilt into the back wall, and brought the whole thing crashing down. She could have been forgiven for seeing it as an omen.

Holidays were another issue. Wason simply refused to go on holiday with Joan. Partly this was through fear, fear of not being able to be looked after in the way he was used to, especially in the light of his ever-worsening health. He would not have been able to manage bookings, or the actual process of travelling; this had always been done for him in the past, from his early childhood to his overseas speaking trips as a distinguished academic. Joan would have had to do it all, and she was not inclined to. There was also the matter of his impaired mobility, of course, and this was also getting worse. It had been getting worse even in the lead-up to their marriage: around the time of their engagement, a piece of the patella in one of his shattered knees broke away, causing him intense pain. There was only one course of action: he had to have an operation. It took place in early March. Unlike his urinary tract infection treatments, it proved a success, and he was now able to bend his knee more than he had been able to since sustaining the injury in 1944. Then just before their wedding, he had a problem with arthritis in his hip, which began to get steadily worse. Joan herself had health concerns, and had an operation three months later. She recovered well, this time; but both would continue to suffer health problems as the years went by, he more than she.

## Coming of age

The radical changes in his circumstances had not done anything for Wason's chess game. He still kept up correspondence matches, but not long after his marriage, he confessed to Johnson-Laird that "my chess has gone to pieces". This situation was remedied by the acquisition of his first chess computer – the only computer that he ever got to any kind of grips with. To his own surprise, he rather enjoyed playing it, noting how its moves would have led it to fail the Turing test: they would not have been mistaken by any competent player as emanating from a human. This intrigued him, and he wrote an article about his impressions of the program and his experiences playing it; it would be published in *Correspondence Chess* magazine in early 1989. The computer had the effect of reviving not just his enthusiasm but also his skill, and he threw himself back into correspondence chess: in 1987, he reported that he would soon have 40 games in play; this number would go up to 52. One dreads to think what the cost of pursuing this compulsion would have been, given all the stamps and specially designed little chess postcards that would have had to be bought. And one wonders what Joan thought of it, especially as she also had no interest in this other centrally important aspect of his life.

It was perhaps a price worth paying to maintain his equanimity in view of his ever-present health problems, now joined by the dismal prospects for his second marriage. The onset of arthritis had resulted in his being given steroid treatment, and Wason blamed this for a new problem. Early in 1989, he began losing his teeth; they would all be removed in hospital in August that year. Notwithstanding this latest setback, in March, he sent out invitations for a lunch party that he and Joan were putting on: "to celebrate Peter's coming of age", it said. He would be 65 in April.

At around this time, mid-1989, Wason was delighted by a visit from his old friend Paolo Legrenzi, accompanied by his young protégé, Vittorio Girotto. They were visiting the Open University in Milton Keynes where they were involved in a joint research project with a professor there, Paul Light. Paolo hired a car and drove with Girotto to Goring. Joan made her excuses and left them to their own devices, and the three of them set off on an outing. Quite by chance, they stumbled upon a shop selling Conservative Party artefacts. It was the tenth anniversary of Margaret Thatcher's accession to prime ministerial office and Paolo, being something of a fan of hers, wanted to buy a souvenir. So in they went. "Oh, Christ!" exclaimed Wason, and after a few minutes, he added "I need some air" and went outside. The whole thing amused Paolo and Vittorio greatly, and became a legend between them, told and re-told over the following years. Whenever one of them was fed up about something, he would say "I need some air" to the other.

## A Festsprache?

It would not be long before Legrenzi and Girotto would meet with Wason again. As the 1980s shaded into the 1990s, Jonathan Evans had an idea. In 1988, at Aberdeen University, Scotland, there had been the inaugural International Conference on Thinking. Evans was one of the organisers and keynote speakers, and the conference had been very well attended, featuring on its programme most of the names that would be expected from the now well-established research field of the psychology of reasoning, along with several new ones who would go on to prominence in the field, such as Ruth Byrne and Mike Oaksford. But not Wason. This was not surprising, given that he was infirm, and had been retired for four years, not to mention his helplessness when it came to travel; it would have meant a very long train journey from London, longer even than the flight from Washington DC that had caused him problems before. But now, there was a further instalment in prospect: the Second International Conference on Thinking was to be held at the university where Evans spent almost his entire academic career, Plymouth, in the summer of 1992.

Evans, like so many people in the field, was keenly aware of the debt owed to Wason by people like him (and in his case, the debt was personal, as one of Wason's former PhD students). He began, along with a fellow Plymouth professor, Steve Newstead, to plan a tribute meeting as part of the conference. It is quite common for collections of papers written in honour of an academic eminence to be published in book form – Evans has had one devoted to himself, as have Johnson-Laird and Legrenzi – and we use the German loan word Festschrift for them. Sometimes, you see this term also applied to meetings like the one that Evans and Newstead were planning, but that does not seem quite right, since the schrift part of the word comes from the German for 'write'. Festsprache (celebration-speech), perhaps? The word does not exist, yet.

Whatever you want to call it, the all-day symposium took place on the middle one of the conference, July 29, 1992, and was called, with a directness that Wason himself must have appreciated, 'The Wason symposium'. It featured contributions from many of the names that should now be familiar, along with many others: David Green, Jonathan Evans and David Over and myself spoke about the selection task, as did Vittorio Girotto, who gave an account of his work on running the task with children (it has been used, in its reduced form, with kids as young as three since then); Ryan Tweney, in a paper entitled 'Wason meets Faraday', talked about the hypothesis-testing research that Wason had inspired, as did another American psychologist who had met Wason during his visit to Bowling Green ten years earlier, Michael Gorman; Girotto and Paolo Legrenzi, along with Newstead and another US researcher, Richard Griggs, presented their research on Thog; and Phil Johnson-Laird summed up 'The contribution of Peter Wason to research on reasoning' at the end.

After the papers, Wason, who had begun the session by outlining the three major reasoning tasks he had invented, took to the stage along with Evans and Johnson-Laird, and Legrenzi had the presence of mind to take a couple of photos; one is reproduced below (Figure 19.1). Wason was 68 years old, but looked a lot older; he had his walking stick with him even on the stage. Very few people realised how poor his health was. He had arrived at the start of the day with a question for the small group of acquaintances gathered outside the lecture theatre: "Do you know what today is?" he asked. It happened that one of them did: it was Karl Popper's 90th birthday. Very fitting. On the stage at the end of the day, he subjected himself to a question-and-answer session, which went on for the best part of an hour before Evans, aptly describing him as a great man, forced the audience to let him go. Someone asked him what his favourite was of all the papers he had written. "*In real life negatives are false*", he replied. It had been

**FIGURE 19.1** Taking the stage at the Wason symposium, Plymouth, July 29, 1992: Johnson-Laird (left), Wason (centre) and Evans (right); photo by, and courtesy of, Prof. P. Legrenzi

published 20 years earlier and summed up his earliest psychological research, originating before he even began to study reasoning.

Daniel Kahneman, who ten years later would become the first person with a Psychology degree to be awarded a Nobel Prize (for economics), was also at the conference; his own keynote address was interrupted by a fire alarm and evacuation, which made it memorable for more than just its contents. He attended the Wason symposium, and recalled more than 30 years later the atmosphere of "affectionate admiration" that there was in the hall. Affectionate admiration: that was exactly how everyone who was there remembered it. The convenors of the symposium, Newstead and Evans, set about collecting the contributors' papers into a genuine Festschrift – a book. Everyone who had spoken at Plymouth duly complied, and the volume appeared in 1995. Wason himself added a final chapter, a reflective, partly autobiographical account of his experience of a research career. There would only be two more pieces of published writing from him after this, prefaces to Johnson-Laird's Festschrift and to a book co-written by Evans, the following year.

In the spirit of his volume, and rather in the manner of the traditional Oscar-winners' performance, he added an unusually lengthy list of thank-yous at the end: to Evans and Johnson-Laird, his star pupils and now two giants of the research field he had been foremost in creating; to Sheila Jones and the Legrenzis; to his American hosts at his visit to Harvard over 30 years before, George Miller and Jerome Bruner; to the Medical Research Council, whose support in his early years as a researcher had enabled him to establish himself while evading the normal academic duties; and to lost Marjorie, whom he called Ming, and his daughters. Not, unlike in 1983, to Joan.

There was a good reason for this. Around the time his Festschrift was appearing, Joan had instituted divorce proceedings. "I am looking forward to the divorce", he wrote to Johnson-Laird in June 1995, although he got round to mentioning this only after talking about chess.

## Blowing in the wind

The final collapse of Wason's second marriage – it had been a long time coming – added to the sense of walls closing in, from all sides. Despite the successful removal of the floating piece of patella from one of his knees, his mobility had become ever more restricted, and early in 1991, he had been referred to an orthopaedic surgeon for treatment on them. Later that year, the surgeon recommended a double replacement. The surgeon's name will be familiar to some: it was Art Themen, famous as a jazz saxophonist in addition to his day job as a high-ranking medic. (Phil Johnson-Laird, coincidentally, is also a proficient jazz musician, on piano, and has written about the psychology of musical improvisation.) It would not be for another four years that the second of these knee operations would be carried out, in the summer of 1995, the first having been done in December 1992, though it had to be re-done also in 1995. So although it was clear to all at the Plymouth conference that Wason's mobility was impaired, it was not clear just how much discomfort he was enduring, and hence how much effort it took to maintain his good humour; the three-hour train journey from London itself must have been a trial for him.

There was another difficulty to contend with, something that may have caused mere double-takes at the time but which, in hindsight, takes on a more ominous hue. In a letter to Johnson-Laird in 1988, he had straightforwardly repeated material from a previous letter, without any apparent awareness of doing so, and never having done so before. We can all have little memory lapses like this, of course, and they usually mean nothing, but in Wason's case, it begins to look like a straw in an ill wind. It would not be the only time it happened from now on.

Further straws were to follow. In August 1992, just after the Plymouth conference, Wason wrote to Johnson-Laird, thanking him for "the elegance of your presentation at my symposium". However, he then "take[s] issue at one point: negatives"; Johnson-Laird had said that, despite Wason's important work on what he had memorably called 'plausible denial', we still do not have a complete account of the use of negation in natural language. Wason then writes a two-page defence of his work on negation, which had come to an end 20 years before, but as Johnson-Laird notes in his reply, he never really spells out just what point he is really taking issue with. Although the tone of Wason's letter was friendly, Johnson-Laird thought it prickly, and wondered why Wason would want to rake over these old coals, or feel the need to go on the defensive like this. He continued to do so in a further reply, adding to this second one a postscript, asking if Johnson-Laird had had "Wetherick trouble" at the conference; Norman Wetherick had presented a paper at another symposium, but not, unsurprisingly, at Wason's, and they managed to avoid each other. It seems that the old bitterness between them, dating back 30 years at that time, was still there.

Evans also found himself on the receiving end of Wason's increasing tetchiness in the mid-1990s. Evans now occupied a role with the *Quarterly journal of experimental psychology* that Wason had earlier had, that of managing editor for papers in the field of thinking and reasoning. He had, on the advice of two referees and also after his own reading, approved for publication a paper which contained criticism of Wason's work. He did not expect what happened when this paper appeared: an irate phone call from Wason demanding to know why this paper had been accepted, saying that it meant that Evans must have approved of the criticism it contained.

As a consequence, Evans began to avoid sending things to Wason, who was still reading the psychological research literature, as this episode shows, lest he spark off another of these rages. It put distance between them, though perhaps not enough: in 1995, Evans was writing a book on rationality with a philosophical colleague, David Over, and when, early the next year, they had a complete manuscript, they sent it to Wason, asking him to write a foreword. Wason was, after all, one of the first cognitive psychologists to confront the question of the nature of human rationality, something that led to controversy, as we saw in the last chapter with the appearance of Jonathan Cohen's critical paper in 1981. When Wason sent his foreword to them, Evans and Over were appalled: it was full of Freudian arguments and hardly related to the contents of their book at all. They did something that is not often done with invited pieces like this: subjected it to some fairly severe editing. Wason was not amused, and once again vented his anger at Evans; but the cut-down version was what ultimately appeared. Sadly, this was effectively the end of the personal relationship between Evans and Wason: there were very few contacts after that. Evans has, though, written admiringly of him and his work since then.

Straws of a very different kind were also blowing in this wind: Wason had begun to 'have falls', which is the expression we seem to use whenever elderly people take a tumble. At first, he was inclined to blame this on the state of his knees, but as the falls became more frequent, it was hard to maintain this pretence, and in 1996, he was diagnosed as suffering from Parkinson's Disease. Although it was not appreciated for some time, this turned out to be a misdiagnosis. But not in a good way.

## A wish

Around the time of Wason's 70th birthday, his elder daughter Armorer overcame his reluctance to take holidays and organised a trip for the two of them (he was still married to Joan, but her participation was out of the question) to his old haunts in Ireland, in and around County Clare. They had been there years before, as a family, with the Miévilles, and of course Wason and Marjorie had had their slightly clandestine trip there in their very early days, before they were married. For this new trip, they stayed in Connemara and saw some of the sights, such as Yeats's Tower, in south Galway, a place of pilgrimage for Wason, having once been owned by his favourite poet of all, W.B. Yeats. There was a matchmaking festival at Lisdoonvarna – it is still held today – which happened to be taking place while they were there, in early September, and they attended it. To general astonishment, Wason danced in the street with a woman from Dublin, who urged him to throw his stick away. He didn't. They then visited Quin, the town nearest to the house at Ballykilty, the place where Wason had probably been happiest, as a lanky, tennis-playing youth, in the days before the War and its aftermath made everything complicated.

Ballykilty was now a hotel, and initially Wason was reluctant to see it. Armorer went alone, and told the proprietors that she wanted to bring her father, but that he wouldn't come. They of course knew of the house's provenance with the Blood family, and were aware of Wason's connection to it through his Aunt Gladys's marriage to Fitzgerald Blood. They said they would invite a man who still lived in the area and had done so during Wason's halcyon times there, in the 1930s. When Armorer told him about this, Wason relented, and they went to Ballykilty the following day, to be greeted with the cry, "Welcome home, Mr Wason". The old man the proprietors invited was now 86, and had been a member of Sinn Fein. He had regularly been chased off the grounds of Ballykilty by Wason's Uncle Fitz ('Old Fitzy', he called him), but remembered how the young Wason had delighted in helping the workers at the house; in those days, water had to be carried, it was not yet piped. They sat and talked (Wason remarked on how the people there never seemed to stop talking) in what had been his Aunt Gladys's drawing-room. The workers' communality, their friendliness towards him, repeated now, and the dismissive way they were treated by the Anglo-Irish nobility in the old days had played a large part in engendering Wason's strong Republican sympathies. He returned from Ireland nursing a wish that he could go and live there, coupled with an acknowledgement that he never would.

There is a sad coda to this part of the story. Ballykilty became derelict, the company that owned it having gone into liquidation as a result of the economic crash that wrecked Ireland's financial system, and property market, in the late 2000s. In 2016, it was offered for sale at €550,000, and was still listed at that price two years later (Figure 19.2). I can find no record of its having been bought.

There were to be two more such trips, but in between the first and second, there was the matter of his split from Joan, and its consequences. These centred not just on where he would now live, but how. Even without his infirmities, he would have struggled to look after himself, but with his physical difficulties, it was clear that he would need some paid professional care. His daughters talked to him about where he should relocate to after leaving, and selling, Greycourt in Goring; this, in the nature of these things, was not going smoothly. Rather impulsively, he told them he would like to go to Oxford, scene of another fondly-remembered period, the immediate postwar years and his encounters with some of the most important and influential people in his life: Marjorie, above all, but also Claude Miéville and his greatest intellectual mentor (alongside A.R. Jonckheere and John Whitfield), Lord David Cecil.

They found him a flat in a sheltered block with a warden, in the centre of the city, called Pegasus Grange, and he moved there in 1994, before the divorce had

FIGURE 19.2 A sad coda: Ballykilty, Wason's spiritual home, in 2016. Courtesy of Sherry, FitzGerald & McMahon, Ennis, Co. Clare, Ireland; thanks to Diarmuid McMahon

been finalised. Initially, he led a mainly independent life: he could visit the shops, go to church. He was visited by Paolo Legrenzi and his son, Matteo, who had a place at the university, studying political science. Wason and Matteo struck up an instant rapport, once again showing his non-generational, open attitude to younger people. He kept up correspondence with former colleagues and admirers, and heard from one of them, his former doctoral student Liz Valentine, that she was writing a biography of the earliest female British psychology PhD, Beatrice Edgell. It so happened that one of Edgell's own students was also a resident of Pegasus Grange. Wason was due to give a talk to the residents, so Valentine arranged to attend it and to visit Edgell's student. Wason's half-hour talk was called 'The evolution of a problem', was about the selection task, and featured his daughter Sarah as page-turner of a flip-chart. It was, recalled Valentine, a mixture of intellect, anecdote and humour, received in at atmosphere of slightly baffled congeniality. The healthy attendance at the talk indicated that Wason was a popular member of the Pegasus Grange community; his increasing vulnerability resulting from his physical deterioration had made him more attuned to the people around him and made him more empathetic, as well as good-humoured.

Despite Wason's intellectual vigour, his falling increasingly became a problem, and he needed constant attention from carers. Looking back, the daughters realised that his moving to Oxford had been a mistake: they both lived in London, so became very familiar with the M40 motorway, and both had busy working lives. It would have been better if he had been closer to hand. He did, though, stay there for several years, and they had no choice but to keep on clocking up the miles.

Armorer was the one who took charge of his medical needs, shuttling him to various hospitals and clinics, while Sarah oversaw the financial and administrative aspects of his living arrangements. Strangely, he seemed to love hospitals, and particularly nurses and carers, with whom he had great personal chemistry; perhaps he looked back to his months in the orthopaedic ward in Nottingham at the end of the War, where he fell in love with at least one of the nurses – there was a photograph of her, unnamed, in his wallet until the end. Now, in Oxford, he would often joke around with them and with the doctors and other patients; he was not one to mope or wallow. This was an extension of his approach to his war injuries: he was generally uncomplaining, despite the never-ending pain, discomfort and inconvenience.

While resident in his new flat in Oxford, Wason must have started having intimations of his mortality, as he took his regular church-going to a new level: he arranged to be received back into the Catholic church. He had joined the Church before, in his youth, partly as a way of needling his mother, and had often attended mass in the intervening years, mainly over his love for the aesthetics of its liturgy; late in life, he would sometimes attend a service with one of his daughters and, as it neared the end, jump up and urge her to come with him to a nearby church to attend another. Never having professed a serious religious faith before, his decision to be formally received into the Church at this stage marked a definite change in his position.

When his falling resulted in a broken hip, it was clear that he would have to move again, to a facility where he could be looked after; his doctors were adamant that any kind of independent living was no longer an option. It was time to move him back to London, nearer his family. They found an ideal nursing home on Vicarage Gate in Kensington, run by the picturesquely named charity, the Distressed Gentlefolks' Aid Association (it has changed its name twice since then): it was a home for retired professionals, and prospective clients had to provide a curriculum vitae to show that they were the right kind of person. Wason was pleased to have to do this, and had nothing to fear from it, given his eminence as a research psychologist. He moved there late in the year 2000. It was perfect for him, comfortable, with a pleasant garden to which he could retreat to smoke his pipe. He was still able to be taken for outings round London, now in a wheelchair; one of these was to the Globe theatre on the South Bank, where he and Armorer saw Macbeth, and he spent much of the time reciting the lines to her as it went along. It was a delight for him to be able to do things like this. He also enjoyed the company of the other residents: on one occasion, a peer of the realm, learning that they were both associated with the Reform Club (Wason, although not actually a member, was a descendent of one of its founders) related how he had lunched there with the spy Guy Burgess the day before Burgess's flight to the Soviet Union.

There had to be a catch, and there was: in less than a year, the charity decided to sell its Kensington holdings – the value of land and property in this, one of the richest parts of London, can hardly be overstated. He had been happy at Kensington, and took a particular interest in the lives of the staff there, who were from a variety of national and ethnic backgrounds. They responded with affection as well as friendliness. And so in 2001, he had to move again, and his daughters were faced with the task of finding another nursing home for him. They could not find anywhere in London suitable, and so in the end opted for one back in Oxfordshire, in the country rather than the city this time: Rush Court, in the pretty Thames-side town of Wallingford. This time, there was more of a monoculture among the staff; the only non-British members were two Irish nurses. They were nowhere near as interesting to Wason as the Kensington staff had been, and he began to try to aggravate the matron, just as he used to do things to annoy his mother. It was the time of the 2001 general election, and she had arranged for a poster for the Conservative candidate for the local constituency, one Boris Johnson, to be put up at the front of the property. Wason was infuriated, and one of his daughters was dispatched to take it down in the night. It ended up in a ditch. Unlike Johnson himself, despite his promise, when Prime Minister 18 years later, to die in one should he fail to pilot Britain out of the European Union by a set date.

## His last bow

It was becoming increasingly clear that Wason's initial diagnosis of Parkinson's Disease needed to be reconsidered. Partly, this was indicated by an increase in delusional thinking on his part, which is not something associated with

Parkinson's; it had been the falling that had originally led to the misdiagnosis. The delusions took the form of visual and auditory hallucinations and, particularly, paranoia. There had been signs of paranoid thinking beforehand; Johnson-Laird reckoned that this lay at the root of Wason's dispute with him over his laudatory address at the Plymouth conference, where he had taken exception to an otherwise innocuous remark over psycholinguists' less than complete understanding of negation. It was a contributory factor in the breakdown of his second marriage: Joan cited his suspicions that she was plotting against him in her divorce petition. There was also the rupture of his relationship with Evans. In another example, he objected to the use by a young researcher in a published paper of the term 'Tower of London' instead of 'Tower of Hanoi' as the name of a well-known puzzle, seeing in it evidence of American political influence. There were little things too: on finding it increasingly difficult to open jars, he would attribute it to the manufacturers making them too tight, and fulsomely congratulate his daughters when they opened them for him; he would keep asking for new nibs for his favourite pens, again citing faulty manufacture as a reason for his writing becoming more difficult.

In the face of these psychological problems, Rush Court's general practitioner referred Wason to a psychiatrist, but there was a delay as the psychiatrist was himself on long-term sick leave. Armorer tried to get a replacement referral, but in the end a locum was appointed, and went to the nursing home to examine him. The locum realised that the difficulties Wason was having with his movements – the frequent falling – and his delusional thinking together indicated that he was suffering not from Parkinson's or Alzheimer's but from a condition known as dementia with Lewy bodies (DLB). It was understandable that this had been missed before, since DLB shares some of the symptoms both of Parkinson's Disease and Alzheimer's; according to the Alzheimer's Society, about 4% of dementia diagnoses are of DLB, but this may be a considerable underestimate of its true prevalence, because of these overlaps. One consolation is that DLB is not characterised by the destruction of the patient's memory, and hence their sense of self, that so distresses those close to someone with Alzheimer's. There are cognitive problems associated with DLB, such as delusional thinking and hallucinations, both of which occurred with Wason, but, as the Society says, it is possible to live (relatively) well with DLB, as long as the appropriate care is provided.

One part of this care is the provision of appropriate drug treatments, and the locum recommended trying to get a prescription for Aricept. However, she could not prescribe it herself, having diagnosed DLB, since it was only licensed by the National Health Service (NHS) for use with Alzheimer's; a private prescription was the only option. Armorer agreed with the locum that she would approach the psychiatrist Wason had been seeing while he was living at Pegasus Grange in Oxford for a private appointment. In an act of extraordinary generosity, this psychiatrist waived his consultancy fees and also changed Wason's diagnosis from DLB to Alzheimer's, so that Aricept would be available via the NHS, obviating the enormous cost that a private prescription would have entailed.

The drug made an immediate and profound positive difference to Wason's condition. It improved his mental functioning to the extent that he was now able to resume playing correspondence chess. However, although he could make the moves himself, he could not write the letters: Armorer or Sarah had to do this. His last letter to Johnson-Laird, in October 2001, was dictated to Armorer, who typed it up. Anyone who wrote to him during these last years would get a letter back telling them that Wason could no longer write. A letter he did type, to Mo Johnson-Laird, Phil's wife, was so riddled with mistakes that it was almost as illegible as those he wrote in his own hand.

His movements may have been impaired but his mind was revived: he was able to think more clearly not only about his world but the world outside as well. In that last letter to Johnson-Laird, he commented on the September 11 attack on New York, where the Johnson-Lairds were living. Earlier, during the 2001 election campaign, Armorer arranged for him to have a postal vote. Since he could not read any more, as well as not write, she read him the list of candidates. The first one represented Alliance of Socialist Labour. "I'll have that one!" She said she would read out all 20 names, and did so, as Wason listened patiently. She went back to the top: Alliance of Socialist Labour. "Yes, I want them!" You know it's not the Labour Party, said Armorer. "Darling, the Labour Party's not the Labour Party", Wason replied. It was the peak time of the Tony Blair New Labour project, and many Labour people had come to the same conclusion. Wason's mind was still sharp enough for him to sympathise with this view.

Wason did indeed continue to live well with DLB, helped by his drug treatment, and did not appear to be in any kind of distress. One reason for this was that he avoided finding out about his diagnosis, even though he had the opportunity: he became adept at explaining away his symptoms, as with the jars and pens, and his daughters did not tell his friends about it, lest they should shock him by mentioning it. He was, however, full of remorse over the rows that he had had with Marjorie, and wished he had treated her better; his general approach to other people continued to mellow as well, a process that had begun as soon as he retired from UCL. Partly, this was achieved by talks with his daughters. He reported to Armorer what was clearly a hallucination, that there was a nasty man in the home, a brilliant young research fellow, he said, who was cruel to the nurses and made them cry. She realised that the nasty man was him, and that this was part of the remorse he was feeling. She consulted a psychotherapist friend, who advised on how to respond: forgive the nasty man. At the next visit, he reported that there was now a nice man in the home, who was kind to the nurses. It was a brilliant therapeutic coup on her part.

It was not all introspection and painful recollection; he was, as he had been in his Oxford home, a cheerful and popular resident. He entertained the residents and staff by giving talks on Yeats and on Shakespeare, reciting from memory. He was given a Chuck Berry tape and liked to play it loud; the nurses came in and he 'danced' with them in his wheelchair. "It's Doc Pete and the Rush Court sisters!" he would say. He took great interest in their lives and backgrounds, and they reciprocated. This shows one of the characteristics of DLB: the problems associated with it fluctuate quite markedly from day to day, hour to hour even. The patient's grip on reality can tighten or loosen with it.

DLB is progressive and irreversible, and Wason's condition declined, less steeply than it might have done because of the drug treatment, happily. He managed one last outing with his daughters: to Bath, his birthplace. They took him to see his family home, Grafton Lodge, and they had tea in the gardens nearby, one of the places he had enjoyed as a child. Catering was now becoming a problem, because he was having difficulty swallowing, and it was also not easy manoeuvring him in and out of a car. They asked him what he would like to do next: "Go to Marks & Spencer and buy a belt". Another trip to Ireland was planned but abandoned, and the wish he expressed for a trip to the seaside had to be put aside too.

During his last year, he told the nurses that he was expecting a visit from three eminent professors. Whether they dismissed this as deluded rambling is uncertain, but if they did, they were about to be put right: Phil Johnson-Laird, Paolo and Maria Legrenzi duly turned up. Wason was perfectly lucid with them, although Johnson-Laird had the distinct impression that he was not entirely sure who they were. Paolo did not share this impression, but he was shocked to see the person he had loved and admired in the condition he was now in. He was the designated driver for the visit, and on the way out of Rush Court was so preoccupied with what he had just experienced that, in an eerie reminiscence of the jeep at Turnhout in 1944, he drove for a short distance on the wrong side of the road, before realising his mistake. Phil and Maria, engrossed in talking about the experience, did not notice.

Armorer and Sarah increased the frequency of their visits as, even though his mind was still fairly sound, Wason's physical decline was obvious. When it was clear that he was dying, they stayed at a cottage nearby, and Armorer slept for a week in the library at the nursing home. She went back to London for a brief break. The day after, April 17, 2003, a Thursday, was the day that he died. It was as if he had waited for them to leave before allowing himself to go. Just as with Marjorie, it was less than a week before his next birthday, which would have been his 79th.

His funeral took place on April 30th; it was a Catholic service, which did not sit well with some of his former colleagues, held at the beautiful Georgian St Mary's Church in Hampstead. The order of service was illustrated with the Miéville portrait (see Chapter 6), the drawing of him by 10-year-old Sarah, and a photo of him, and his pipe, taken outside the Blackheath house with the girls as toddlers. Some of the nurses from his care homes, whom he had got to know so well and who loved him in return, were there too. He was committed to Highgate Cemetery, almost within sight of the final home he had shared with Marjorie, and he rests with her there. The grave is close to the entrance to the eastern part, a few metres to the right as you go in.

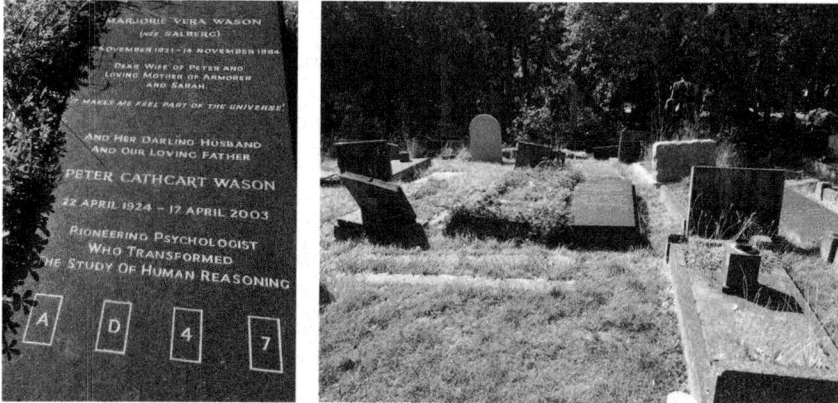

**FIGURE 19.3** Marjorie and Peter Wason's gravestone in Highgate Cemetery – illustrated with the selection task. Photos by K. Manktelow

## Afterword

There is a species of *If* sentence that has become increasingly popular as an object of study by researchers in the psychology of reasoning. It is called a counterfactual conditional, and the name comes from its role in enabling us to hypothesise about things that have not yet happened, or which might have happened but did not: things which, in other words, are counter to the facts of what actually did happen. They often use the subjunctive mood: *If E were to happen*, or *If E had happened…* We use them all the time, because thinking about possibilities rather than actualities is something that the human mind is uniquely fitted to do. And it's fun, not least because counterfactuals cannot be decisively proven to be true or false, unlike the ordinary conditionals that Peter Wason pioneered research into. If E had been there, then 7 would have been there? We cannot say for sure.

So here is one, or at least, the *If* half of one, and we can enjoy speculating about what the *then* part would contain: If Peter Wason had not survived his jeep accident… Well, a lot of things in psychology that did happen would not have happened. Some kind of psychology of reasoning would have evolved, because reasoning is such an important part of human cognition, and there had been some pre-Wason gropings towards studying it. But it would not look the way it has done since 1960, or does now. Someone would have started studying hypothesis testing; but would the 2-4-6 task have been invented? People would have studied reasoning with *If* sentences; but would the most popular method used in doing so, the Wason selection task, have been invented by someone other than Wason? Would there be Thogs stalking the earth even now?

If your answer is 'yes' to these questions, you're welcome: you can't be disproved. But even if you in your parallel world are right, consider this. Two of the greatest names in research on reasoning, Phil Johnson-Laird and Jonathan Evans, were pupils of Peter Wason. They happened to have been Psychology students at his university, which was how they came to meet him. Neither had had any thoughts of an academic career before they met him; in Evans' case, this meeting occurred almost on a whim, or rather on two whims: to go to his talk on negation, and then to trek to Wolfson House, knock on his door and ask him about it. The pair of them have produced hundreds of published research studies, heaven knows how many books, and revolutionary theoretical ideas. Each has supervised dozens of research students (who have then had students of their own, and so on) and worked with uncountable numbers of colleagues across the world. And that is just those two; there are dozens of others who either worked with Wason, worked with someone who had worked with him, or were inspired by him. Or who just used the methods he devised. The psychology of reasoning has turned from a maverick's quirk to a scientific industry and produced profound ideas about human mentality that have migrated into the common culture. What it would have looked like without Wason and his disciples is unimaginable. And perhaps those official forms you have to fill out would be even more horrendous than they are, without his earliest research.

Plenty of people therefore have cause to be grateful to Peter Wason, and in the interests of full disclosure, I had better admit that I am one of them. He was my PhD examiner. I passed, though not without a moment of heart-sinking trepidation. After little more than an hour of the oral examination, a very short time for one of these, in his spacious office at Wolfson House, Wason looked over his glasses and intoned, "I think we have heard enough". He meant that he was perfectly satisfied, but that's not how I heard it. I can laugh about it now...

One more little snapshot. In 1993, I was giving a paper at a meeting in London, in a session that also featured one by Evans. At the coffee break, Wason, wearing a beret as he had done in the 1940s, tottered in on his stick; he had come in from Goring. He reached into his rather shapeless overcoat, pulled out a brown envelope, and said, "I thought you would like to have these". They were a set of his original selection task cards, the ones used in the study that produced the Mensa protocol; the ones pictured in Chapter 13.

# APPENDIX 1

## WASON'S FAMILY TREE: PATERNAL LINE

**Wason's family tree: paternal line**

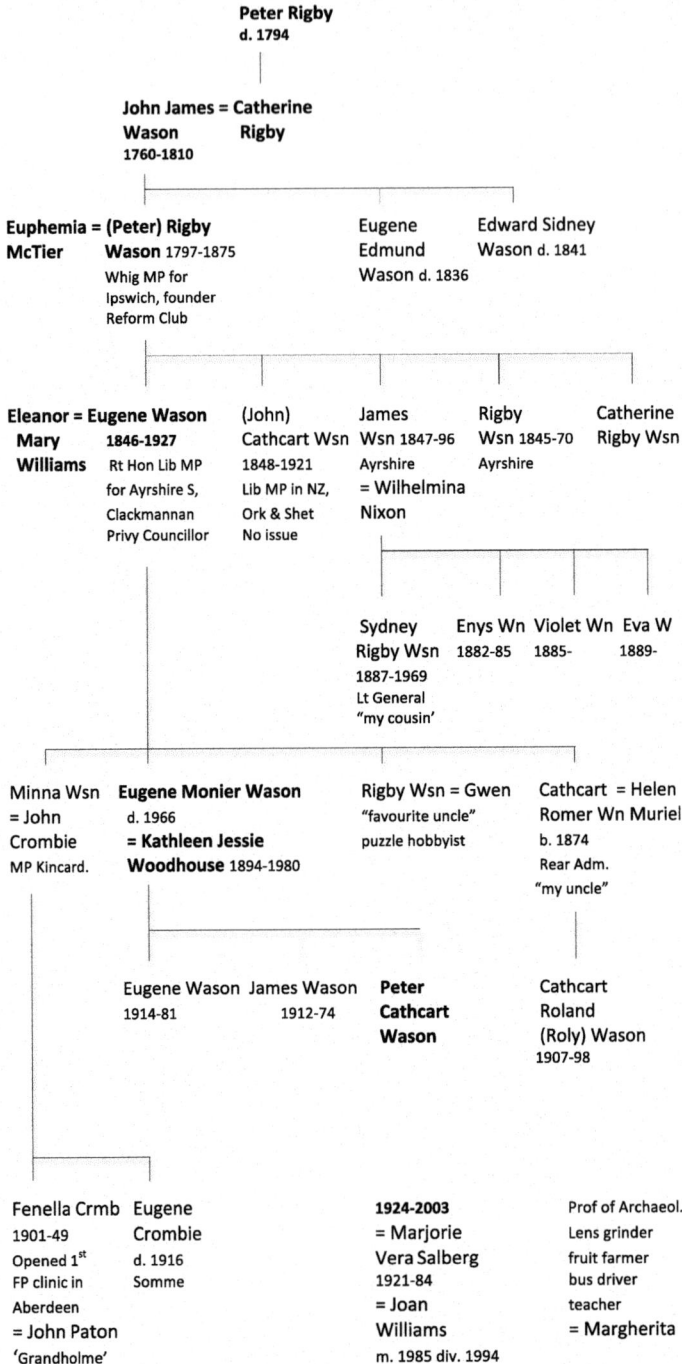

Peter Rigby
d. 1794

John James = Catherine
Wason        Rigby
1760-1810

Euphemia = (Peter) Rigby          Eugene          Edward Sidney
McTier        Wason 1797-1875      Edmund          Wason d. 1841
              Whig MP for          Wason d. 1836
              Ipswich, founder
              Reform Club

Eleanor = Eugene Wason    (John)            James            Rigby           Catherine
Mary        1846-1927     Cathcart Wsn      Wsn 1847-96      Wsn 1845-70     Rigby Wsn
Williams    Rt Hon Lib MP 1848-1921         Ayrshire        Ayrshire
            for Ayrshire S, Lib MP in NZ,   = Wilhelmina
            Clackmannan     Ork & Shet      Nixon
            Privy Councillor No issue

                                            Sydney          Enys Wn    Violet Wn  Eva W
                                            Rigby Wsn       1882-85    1885-      1889-
                                            1887-1969
                                            Lt General
                                            "my cousin"

Minna Wsn   **Eugene Monier Wason**   Rigby Wsn = Gwen      Cathcart = Helen
= John       d. 1966                  "favourite uncle"     Romer Wn  Muriel
Crombie     **= Kathleen Jessie**     puzzle hobbyist       b. 1874
MP Kincard.  **Woodhouse** 1894-1980                        Rear Adm.
                                                            "my uncle"

            Eugene Wason James Wason    **Peter**            Cathcart
            1914-81      1912-74        **Cathcart**         Roland
                                        **Wason**            (Roly) Wason
                                                             1907-98

Fenella Crmb Eugene                    **1924-2003**         Prof of Archaeol.
1901-49      Crombie                   = Marjorie            Lens grinder
Opened 1st   d. 1916                   Vera Salberg          fruit farmer
FP clinic in Somme                     1921-84               bus driver
Aberdeen                               = Joan                teacher
= John Paton                           Williams              = Margherita
'Grandholme'                           m. 1985 div. 1994

Names in bold indicate direct line of ancestry; = married. Notes refer to items mentioned in the text. Items in double quotes are as Wason referred to them.

# APPENDIX 2

## WASON'S FAMILY TREE:
## MATERNAL LINE

**Wason's family tree: maternal line**

James  =  Dorothy
Thomas      Marton
Woodhouse

Sir James  =  Jessie
Thomas      Reed
Woodhouse   "Grandmother
1852-1921    Terrington"
1st Baron    d. 1942
Terrington                                     John Blood
Huddersfield                                    1849-1912
Lib MP                                         = Jane
                                              Studdert

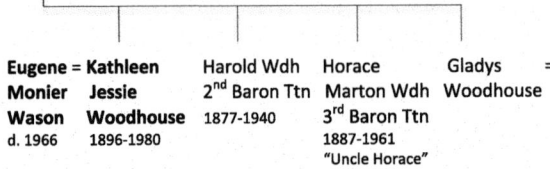

Eugene = Kathleen    Harold Wdh    Horace      Gladys  =  Charles
Monier   Jessie       2nd Baron Ttn   Marton Wdh   Woodhouse    Fitzgerald
Wason    Woodhouse   1877-1940      3rd Baron Ttn                Blood
d. 1966    1896-1980               1887-1961                     1879-1953
                                    "Uncle Horace"                "Uncle Fitz"

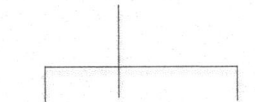

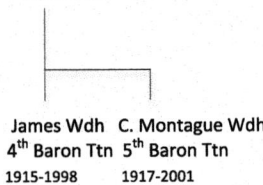

Peter      James     Eugene       James Wdh   C. Montague Wdh    Bindon
Cathcart   Wason    Wason       4th Baron Ttn   5th Baron Ttn      Fitzgerald
Wason     1912-74   1914-81     1915-1998    1917-2001         Blood Lt Col
1924-2003                                                1915-1972
= Marjorie                                              "1st cousin"
Vera Salberg
1921-1984

Names in bold indicate direct line of ancestry; = married. Notes refer to items mentioned in the text. Items in double quotes are as Wason referred to them.

# APPENDIX 3

## WASON'S PUBLICATIONS: CHRONOLOGICAL LIST

Wason, P.C. (1954). Soap wrappers' "jig". *British journal of industrial medicine*, vol. 11, pp 279–283.

Wason, P.C. (1959). The processing of positive and negative information. *Quarterly journal of experimental psychology*, vol. 11, pp 92–107.

Wason, P.C. (1960). On the failure to eliminate hypotheses in a conceptual task. *Quarterly journal of experimental psychology*, vol. 12, pp 129–140.

Wason, P.C. (1961). Response to affirmative and negative and negative binary statements. *British journal of psychology*, vol. 52, pp 133–142.

Wason, P.C. (1962). Psychological aspects of negation; an experimental enquiry and some practical applications. Working paper, Communication Research Centre, University College London.

Wason, P.C. (1962). Reply to Wetherick. *Quarterly journal of experimental psychology*, vol. 14, p 250.

Wason, P.C. (1962). The retention of material presented through précis. *Journal of communication*, vol. 12, pp 26–43.

Wason, P.C. & Jones, S. (1963). Negatives: denotation and connotation. *British journal of psychology*, vol. 54, pp 229–307.

Wason, P.C. (1964). The effect of self-contradiction on fallacious reasoning. *Quarterly journal of experimental psychology*, vol. 16, pp 30–34. Reprinted in P.C. Wason & P.N. Johnson-Laird (eds.) (1968), *Thinking and reasoning*. Harmondsworth: Penguin.

Wason, P.C. (1965). The contexts of plausible denial. *Journal of verbal learning and verbal behaviour*, vol. 4, pp 7–11.

Wason, P.C. (1966). Reasoning. In. B.M. Foss (ed.), *New horizons in psychology 1*. Harmondsworth: Penguin.

Wason, P.C. & Kosviner, A. (1966). Perceptual distortion induced by reasoning. *British journal of psychology*, vol. 57, pp 413–418.

Wason, P.C. (1967). Effect of self-instruction on perceptual judgement. Nature, vol. 213, p 848.

Wason, P.C. (1968). Reasoning about a rule. *Quarterly journal of experimental psychology*, vol. 20, pp 253–281. Reprinted in J.A. del Val (ed.) (1977), *Investigaciones sobre logica y psicologia*. Madrid: Alianza Universidad.

Wason, P.C. (1968). On the failure to eliminate hypotheses … a second look. Chapter in P.C. Wason & P.N. Johnson-Laird (eds.) (1968), *Thinking and reasoning*. Harmondsworth: Penguin.

Wason, P.C. (1968). The drafting of rules. *New law journal*, vol. 118, pp 548–549.

Wason, P.C. & Johnson-Laird, P.N. (eds.) (1968). *New horizons in psychology 1.* Harmondsworth: Penguin.

Wason, P.C. (1969). Structural simplicity and psychological complexity. *Bulletin of the British Psychological Society*, vol. 22, pp 281–284.

Wason, P.C. (1969). Regression in reasoning? *British journal of psychology*, vol. 60, pp 471–480. Reprinted in P. Legrenzi & A. Mazzocco (eds.) (1973), *Psicologia del pensiero*. Milan: Alto Martello.

Wason, P.C. & Johnson-Laird, P.N. (1969). Proving a disjunctive rule. *Quarterly journal of experimental psychology*, vol. 21, pp 14–20.

Wason (1970) On writing scientific papers. *Physics bulletin*, vol. 21, pp 407–408. Reprinted in J. Hartley (ed.) (1980), *The psychology of written communication*. London: Kogan Page.

Wason, P.C. (1970). Psychological aspects of inference. Chapter in G.B Flores d'Arcais & W.J.M. Levelt (eds.), *Advances in psycholinguistics*. Amsterdam: North-Holland.

Wason, P.C. & Johnson-Laird, P.N. (1970). A conflict between selecting & evaluating information in an inferential task. *British journal of psychology*, vol. 61, pp 509–514.

Cornish, E. & Wason, P.C. (1970). Recall of affirmative and negative sentences in an incidental learning task. *Quarterly journal of experimental psychology*, vol. 22, pp 109–114.

Greene, J.M. & Wason, P.C. (1970). Negation: a rejoinder to Wales & Grieve. *Perception and psychophysics*, vol. 8, pp 238–239.

Johnson-Laird, P.N. & Wason, P.C. (1970). Insight into a logical relation. *Quarterly journal of experimental psychology*, vol. 22, pp 49–61.

Johnson-Laird, P.N. & Wason, P.C. (1970). A theoretical analysis of insight into a reasoning task. Cognitive psychology, vol. 1, pp 134–148. Reprinted in P. Legrenzi & A. Mazzocco (eds.) (1973), *Psicologia del pensiero*. Milano: Alto Martello; and in P.N. Johnson-Laird & P.C. Wason (eds.) (1977), *Thinking: readings in cognitive science*. Cambridge: Cambridge University Press.

Wason, P.C. (1971). In real life negatives are false. Communication and cognition, vol. 4, pp 239–253. Reprinted in *Logique et analyse*, vol. 57–58, pp 17–38 (1972), and in L. Apostel (ed.) (1972), *Negation*. Leuven: Nauwelaerts.

Wason, P.C. (1971). Problem solving and reasoning. *British medical bulletin*, vol. 27, pp 206–210. Reprinted in G. Mosconi & V. D'Urso (eds.) (1973), *La soluzione di problemi*. Firenze: Giunti-Barbera.

Wason, P.C. (1971). Logical reasoning. Chapter in F. Novak (ed.), *Lexicon der Psychologie*. Freiburg: Verlag Herder.

Wason, P.C. & Shapiro, D.A. (1971). Natural and contrived experience in a reasoning task. *Quarterly journal of experimental psychology*, vol. 23, pp 63–71.

Wason, P.C. (1972). The psychology of chess. *New Scientist*, July 20.

Wason, P.C. & Johnson-Laird, P.N. (1972) *Psychology of reasoning; structure and content.* London: Batsford. Translated into Italian by A. Mazzocco as *Psicologia del ragionamento*. Milano: Alto Martello (1977); and into Spanish by J. del Val Marino as *Psicologia de Razionamento*. Madrid: Editorial Debate (1980).

Goodwin, R.Q. & Wason, P.C. (1972). Degrees of insight. *British journal of psychology*, vol. 63, pp 205–212.

Wason, P.C. (1974) The psychology of deceptive problems. *New scientist*, vol. 62, pp 382–385.

Wason, P.C. (1974). Notes on the supervision of PhDs. *Bulletin of the British Psychological Society*, vol. 27, pp 25–29.

Wason, P.C. & Golding, E. (1974). The language of inconsistency. *British journal of psychology*, vol. 65, pp 537–546.

Wason, P.C. & Uren, O. (December 26, 1974). The semantics of semiotics. *New society*, pp 812–814.

Golding, E., Reich, S.S. & Wason, P.C. (1974). Inter-hemispheric differences in problem solving. *Perception*, vol. 3, pp 231–235.

Wason, P.C. & Evans, J.StB.T. (1975). Dual processes in reasoning? *Cognition*, vol. 3, pp 141–154.

Evans, J.StB.T. & Wason, P.C. (1976). Rationalization in a reasoning task. *British journal of psychology*, vol. 67, pp 479–486.

Wason, P.C. (1977). The theory of formal operations: a critique. In B. Geber (ed.), *Piaget and knowing*. London: Routledge.

Wason, P.C. (1977). Self-contradictions. Chapter in P.N. Johnson-Laird & P.C. Wason (eds.), *Thinking; readings in cognitive science*. Cambridge: Cambridge University Press.

Johnson-Laird, P.N. & Wason, P.C. (eds.) (1977). *Thinking; readings in cognitive science*. Cambridge: Cambridge University Press.

Johnson-Laird, P.N. & Wason, P.C. (1977). Introduction to Conceptual thinking. Chapter in P.N. Johnson-Laird & P.C. Wason (eds.), *Thinking; readings in cognitive science*. Cambridge: Cambridge University Press.

Johnson-Laird, P.N. & Wason, P.C. (1977). Introduction to Deduction. Chapter in P.N. Johnson-Laird & P.C. Wason (eds.), *Thinking; readings in cognitive science*. Cambridge: Cambridge University Press.

Johnson-Laird, P.N. & Wason, P.C. (1977). Introduction to Hypotheses. Chapter in P.N. Johnson-Laird & P.C. Wason (eds.), *Thinking; readings in cognitive science*. Cambridge: Cambridge University Press.

Johnson-Laird, P.N. & Wason, P.C. (1977). Introduction to Conceptual thinking. Chapter in P.N. Johnson-Laird & P.C. Wason (eds.), *Thinking; readings in cognitive science*. Cambridge: Cambridge University Press.

Johnson-Laird, P.N. & Wason, P.C. (1977). Introduction to Imagery and internal representations. Chapter in P.N. Johnson-Laird & P.C. Wason (eds.), *Thinking; readings in cognitive science*. Cambridge: Cambridge University Press.

Johnson-Laird, P.N. & Wason, P.C. (1977). Introduction to Inference and comprehension. Chapter in P.N. Johnson-Laird & P.C. Wason (eds.), *Thinking; readings in cognitive science*. Cambridge: Cambridge University Press.

Johnson-Laird, P.N. & Wason, P.C. (1977). Introduction to Language, culture, and thinking. Chapter in P.N. Johnson-Laird & P.C. Wason (eds.), *Thinking; readings in cognitive science*. Cambridge: Cambridge University Press.

Johnson-Laird, P.N. & Wason, P.C. (1977). Introduction to Problem solving. Chapter in P.N. Johnson-Laird & P.C. Wason (eds.), *Thinking; readings in cognitive science*. Cambridge: Cambridge University Press.

Lowenthal, D. & Wason, P.C. (June 24, 1977). Academics and their writing. *Times literary supplement*.

Williams, J. & Wason, P.C. (1977). *Collaborative writing games*. Washington DC: Educational Resources Information Center Clearing house.

Wason, P.C. (1979). Novelty and tradition in cognitive research: a case study. *Italian journal of psychology*, vol. 6, pp 1–8.

Wason, P.C. & Brooks, P.J. (1979). THOG: the anatomy of a problem. *Psychological research*, vol. 41, pp 79–90.

Wason, P.C. & Reich, S.S. (1979). A verbal illusion. *Quarterly journal of experimental psychology*, vol. 31, pp 591–597.

Wason, P.C. (1980). Specific thoughts on the writing process. Chapter in L.W. Gregg & E.R. Steinberg (eds.), Cognitive processes in writing. Hillsdale, NJ: Erlbaum.

Wason, P.C. (1980). The verification task and beyond. Chapter in D.R. Olson (ed.), The social foundations of language and thought. New York: Norton.

Wason, P.C. (ed.) (1980). Dynamics of writing. *Visible language 14*. Cleveland, OH: Cleveland Museum of Art.

Wason, P.C. (1980). Conformity and commitment in writing. Paper in P.C. Wason (ed.), *Visible language 14*. Cleveland, OH: Cleveland Museum of Art.

Wason, P.C. (1981). The importance of cognitive illusions (reply to L.J. Cohen). *Behavioral and brain sciences*, vol. 4, p 356.

Wason, P.C. (1981). Understanding the limits of formal thinking. Chapter in H. Parret & J. Bouveresse (eds.), *Meaning and understanding*. Berlin: Walter de Gruyter.

Wason, P.C. & Johnson-Laird, P.N. (1981). The discovery of a general rule. Chapter in R.D. Tweney, M.E. Doherty & C.R. Mynatt (eds.), *On scientific thinking*. New York: Columbia University Press. Originally published as Chapter 16 of Wason & Johnson-Laird, Psychology of reasoning (1972).

Lowenthal & Wason (1981). Academics and their writing. *Leonardo*, vol. 14, p 57.

Green, D.W. & Wason, P.C. (1982). Notes on the psychology of writing. *Human relations*, vol. 35, pp 47–56.

Wason, P.C. (1983). Realism and rationality in the selection task. Chapter in J.StB.T. Evans (ed.), *Thinking and reasoning: psychological approaches*. London: Routledge and Kegan Paul.

Wason, P.C. (1984/5). How to write an essay. The new psychologist (annual journal of the Open University Psychological Society), May 1985, pp 2–5.

Wason, P.C. & Green, D.W. (1984) Reasoning and mental representation. *Quarterly journal of experimental psychology*, vol. 36A, pp 597–610.

Wason, P.C. (1986). Trust in writing. Chapter in M.E. Wrolstad & D.F. Fisher (eds.), *Toward a new understanding of literacy*. New York: Praeger Scientific.

Hartston, W.R. & Wason, P.C. (1984). *The psychology of chess*. London: Batsford.

Wason, P.C. (1987). Problems: their appeal. Entry in R.L. Gregory (ed.), *The Oxford companion to the mind*, pp 639–641. Oxford: Oxford University Press.

Wason, P.C. (1987). Problems-solving. Entry in R.L. Gregory (ed.), *The Oxford companion to the mind*, pp 641–644. Oxford: Oxford University Press.

Wason, P.C. (1995). Creativity in research. Chapter in S.E. Newstead & J.St.B.T. Evans (eds.), *Perspectives on thinking and reasoning: essays in honour of Peter Wason*. Hove: Erlbaum. Reprinted in G. Bunn, A.D. Lovie & G. Richards (eds.), *Psychology in Britain: historical essays and personal reflections*. Leicester: BPS Books (2001).

Wason, P.C. (1996). Early impressions of a research worker (1963–1980). Foreword to J. Oakhill & A. Garnham (eds.), *Mental models in cognitive science; essays in honour of Phil Johnson-Laird*. Hove Psychology Press.

Wason, P.C. (1996). Foreword. To J.StB.T. Evans & D.E. Over, *Rationality and reasoning*. Hove: Psychology Press.

# NOTES AND SOURCES

Chapter 1

Little paperback: Foss, B.M. (ed): *New horizons in psychology 1.*
  Harmondsworth: Pelican, 1966.

Milgram's experiments: see, e.g. Milgram, S. 'Behavioral study of
  obedience.' *Journal of abnormal and social psychology*, vol. 67,
  pp. 371–378, 1963.

Divisional Inspector: much of the material in this and the next two
  chapters comes from a testimony written (in longhand) by Wason
  in 1989, called *Not much to declare.*

Not to be quite sane: Churchill Archive CHAR 2/62/123. Thanks to
  David Wason for this item.

Monty Woodhouse: Obituary, *The Guardian*, 20.02.2001

Chapter 2

By his own account: Wason, E.: *Banned*. London: Hamish Hamilton, 1976.

He was respected: e.g. *Belfast Telegraph*, 04.04.2105

Fenella was a notable person: *Mapping memorials to women in Scotland*,
  website, 19.11.2014

Hazlewood House: not to be confused with Hazelwood House, Sligo.

Chapter 3

National Socialist et seq.: see Evans, R.J.: *The coming of the Third Reich.*
  New York: Penguin Press, 2004.

The Wason household et seq.: *Not much to declare.*

Fell foul of the law: thanks to Jane Evans for finding this record.

We have chosen: quoted by Stamp, G.: *Britain's lost cities*. London:
  Aurum, 2007.

At the age of 24: Obituary, *The Herald*, Scotland, 03.02.1998
followed by a book: Wason, C.R.: *Busman's view*. London: George Allen
    & Unwin, 1958.

Chapter 5

Black Death: details from Ziegler, P.: *The black death*. Stroud: The
    History Press.
Lord David Cecil: much of the information in this section comes from
    Cranbourne, H. (ed.): *David Cecil, a portrait by his friends*. Wimborne:
    Dovecote Press, 1990.
The historian David Kynaston: see *Austerity Britain*. London: Bloomsbury,
    2007.
"Posturing quack": quoted in Kynaston, D: *Austerity Britain*. London:
    Bloomsbury, 2007.
Cruel and futile extension: see Kershaw, I.: *The end*. New York:
    Penguin Press, 2011.
Amis did remark: quoted in Kynaston, D.: *Family Britain*. New York:
    Penguin Press, 2009.

Chapter 6

Almost doubled: figures from House of Commons Library report
    no. SN/SG/4252
New 'redbricks': these were the universities of Nottingham,
    Southampton, Hull and Exeter.
350,000 first degrees: figure from House of Commons Library report
    no. SN/SG/4252
R.D. Laing: see Clay, J.: *R.D. Laing: a divided self*. London: Hodder &
    Stoughton, 1996.
Sorry to see him go: from a reference in Wason's personal file at UCL.

Chapter 7

John B. Watson. See 'Psychology as the behaviorist views it.'
    *Psychological review*, vol. 20, pp. 158–177, 1913.
Serious theoretical question: search online for 'imageless thought
    controversy'.
"Medieval conceptions": Watson, J.B.: *Behaviorism – the modern note
    in psychology*, 1929.
*Cargo cult science*. Caltech commencement address reprinted in
    *Surely you're joking, Mr Feynman!* London: W.W. Norton & Co., 1985.
His reputation was damaged: see e.g. Mackintosh, N.: *Cyril Burt: fraud
    or framed?* Oxford: Oxford University Press, 1995; Joynson, R.B.: *The
    Burt affair*. London: Routledge, 1989.
'The imaginary questionnaire': *Quarterly journal of experimental
    psychology*, vol. 2, pp. 76–87, 1950.

Sequences of four or five: see Blastland, M & Dilnot, A.: *The tiger that isn't*. London: Profile Books, 2007, for more on people's flawed Understanding of randomness.

'An experiment in problem solving': *Quarterly journal of experimental psychology*, vol. 3, pp. 184–197, 1951.

'Soap wrappers' "jig"': *British Journal of industrial medicine*, vol. 11, pp. 279–283, 1954.

Chapter 8

Western Daily Press: thanks to Jane Evans for finding this cutting.

Returned the compliment: thanks to Neil Limbert and the BCCA for Information about the Potter-Wason prize.

*The psychology of chess*: by W.R. Hartston and P.C. Wason. London: Batsford, 1983.

Defeat of a world champion: see the first-person account by the champion in question: Kasparov, G: *Thinking deeply: where machine intelligence ands and human creativity begins*. London: John Murray, 2017.

The latest such engine: see the review of Kasparov's book by Wason's former PhD student, Jonathan St.B.T. Evans, 'Human versus machine thinking: the story of chess,' published online in *Thinking & reasoning*, February 2018.

Chapter 9

Chomsky's destruction: Chomsky, N.: 'A review of B.F. Skinner's *Verbal Behavior*.' *Language*, vol. 35, pp. 26–58, 1959.

Wrote up this work for publication: Wason, P.C., 'The retention of material presented through précis.' *Journal of communication*, vol. 12, pp. 36–43, 1962.

A book with Piaget: Jonckheere, A., Mandelbrot, B. and Piaget, J.: *Etudes d'épistémologie génétique, V: La lecture de l'expérience*. Paris, Presses universitaires de France, 1958.

Tim Shallice, writing in an obituary: *The Independent*, 12 October 2005.

Several of Wason's accounts: e.g. Wason, P.C.: *Psychological aspects of negation*, Communication working group, UCL, 1962; Wason, P.C. and Johnson-Laird, P.N.: *Psychology of reasoning: structure and content*. London: Batsford, 1972.

Another example: see Wason, P.C. and Johnson-Laird, P.N.: *Psychology of reasoning: structure and content*. London: Batsford, 1972.

An official publication: Lewis, B., Horabin, I. and Gane, C.: 'Flow charts, logical trees and algorithms for rules and regulations.' HM Treasury Centre for Administrative Studies occasional paper number 2, HMSO, 1967.

As Peggy Duff recounts: Duff, P.: *Left, left, left: a personal account of six protest campaigns 1945-65*. London: Allison & Busby, 1971.

Groundbreaking book: Chomsky, N.: *Syntactic structures*. The Hague: Mouton, 1957.

Other researchers: e.g. Gough, P.: Grammatical transformations and speed of understanding.' *Journal of verbal learning and verbal behavior*, vol. 4, pp 107–111, 1965; Slobin, D.: 'Grammatical transformations in childhood and adulthood.' *Journal of verbal learning and verbal behavior*, vol. 5, pp 219–227, 1966.

A paper that summed up all this work: Wason, P.C.: 'In real life negatives are false.' *Logique et analyse*, vol. 57–58, pp. 17–38, 1972.

In a later book: Wason, P.C. & Johnson-Laird, P.N.: *Psychology of reasoning: structure and content*. London: Batsford, 1972.

The reference to and quotation from Freud is on p. 230.

Richard Nixon: see Clark, H. and Clark, E.: *Psychology and language*. New York: Harcourt Brace Jovanovich, 1977, p. 100.

A recollection unfortunately not shared: Noam Chomsky, personal communication, February 21 2018.

Chapter 10

"Rather above my head": in Wason, P.C.: 'Creativity in research.' Chapter in S.E. Newstead & J.St.B.T. Evans: (eds.): *Perspectives on thinking and reasoning; essays in honour of Peter Wason*. Hove: Erlbaum, 1995.

"Scintillating": in Wason, P.C.: 'Creativity in research.' Chapter in S.E. Newstead & J.St.B.T. Evans (eds.): *Perspectives on thinking and reasoning; essays in honour of Peter Wason*. Hove: Erlbaum, 1995.

Published in 1960: Wason, P.C.: 'On the failure to eliminate hypotheses in a conceptual task.' *Quarterly journal of experimental psychology*, vol. 12, pp. 129–140, 1960.

Later ones: Wason, P.C.: "On the failure to eliminate hypotheses…' – a second look.' Chapter in P.C. Wason & P.N. Johnson-Laird (eds.): *Thinking & reasoning*. Harmondsworth: Penguin, 1968. Also Wason, P.C. & Johnson-Laird, P.N.: *Psychology of reasoning: structure and content*. London: Batsford, 1972, chapters 16 & 18.

Delusional thinking: see Galbraith, N. (ed.): *Aberrant beliefs and reasoning*. Hove: Psychology Press, 2015.

Psychoanalytic language: see Wason, P.C.: "On the failure to eliminate hypotheses…' – a second look.' Chapter in P.C. Wason & P.N. Johnson-Laird (eds.): *Thinking & reasoning*. Harmondsworth: Penguin, 1968, p. 174.

His 1966 book chapter: Wason, P.C.: 'Reasoning.' In B.M. Foss (ed.): *New horizons in psychology 1*. Harmondsworth: Penguin, 1966.

A second paper: Wason, P.C.: "On the failure to eliminate hypotheses…' – a second look.' Chapter in P.C. Wason & P.N. Johnson-Laird (eds.): *Thinking & reasoning*. Harmondsworth: Penguin, 1968.

Psychotic breakdown: this incident is reported in Wason, P.C.: "On the failure to eliminate hypotheses..." – a second look.' Chapter in P.C. Wason & P.N. Johnson-Laird (eds.): *Thinking & reasoning.* Harmondsworth: Penguin, 1968; and in Wason, P.C. & Johnson-Laird, P.N.: *Psychology of reasoning: structure and content.* London: Batsford, 1972, chapter 18.

Wetherick published a critique: Wetherick, N.E.: 'Eliminative and enumerative behaviour in a conceptual task.' *Quarterly journal of experimental psychology,* vol. 14, pp. 246–249, 1962.

Jonathan Evans remarks: in 'Reasoning, biases and dual processes: the lasting impact of Wason (1960).' *Quarterly journal of experimental psychology.* Vol. 69, pp. 2076–2092, 2016.

American psychologists: Klayman, J. & Ha, Y-W.: 'Confirmation, disconfirmation, and information in hypothesis testing.' *Psychological review,* vol. 94, pp. 211–228, 1987.

One of his last pieces: Foreword to Evans, J.St.B.T. & Over, D.E.: *Rationality and reasoning.* Hove: Psychology Press, 1996; last paragraph.

## Chapter 11

As Wason tells it: Wason, P.C.: 'Creativity in research.' Chapter in S.E. Newstead & J.St.B.T. Evans (eds.): *Perspectives on thinking and reasoning; essays in honour of Peter Wason.* Hove: Erlbaum, 1995.

An earlier review piece: Wason, P.C.: 'Realism and rationality in the selection task.' Chapter in J.St.B.T. Evans: (ed.): *Thinking and reasoning; psychological approaches.* London: Routledge and Kegan Paul, 1983.

Quine, in a book: Quine, W.v.O.: *Methods of logic.* London: Routledge and Kegan Paul, 1952.

"An amusing puzzle": see Wason, P.C.: 'Realism and rationality in the selection task.' Chapter in J.St.B.T. Evans (ed.): *Thinking and reasoning: psychological approaches.* London: Routledge and Kegan Paul, 1983, p. 45.

Wason's 1972 book: Wason, P.C. & Johnson-Laird, P.N.: *Psychology of reasoning: structure and content.* London: Batsford, 1972, p. 173.

Wason was adamant: letter to the author, December 1993. An example of such an interpretation occurs in Chapter 5 of Steven Pinker's monumental *How the mind works* (London: Penguin, 1997).

"After some thought": Wason, P.C.: 'Creativity in research.' Chapter in S.E. Newstead & J.St.B.T. Evans: (eds.): *Perspectives on thinking and reasoning; essays in honour of Peter Wason.* Hove: Erlbaum, 1995, p. 296.

Published in 1964: Wason, P.C.: 'The effect of self-contradiction on fallacious reasoning.' *Quarterly journal of experimental psychology,* vol. 16, pp. 30–34, 1964.

"A small study": Wason, P.C.: 'Reasoning.' Chapter in B.M. Foss (ed.): *New horizons in psychology 1.* Harmondsworth: Pelican, 1966, p. 145.

Peer-reviewed scientific paper: Wason, P.C.: 'Reasoning about a rule.' *Quarterly journal of experimental psychology,* vol. 20, pp. 273–281, 1968.

In 1965, he published: Wason, P.C.: 'The contexts of plausible denial.' *Journal of verbal learning and verbal behavior,* vol. 4, pp. 7–11, 1965.

A letter from Himsworth: much of the material in this section was retrieved by Richard Rawles, who is warmly thanked.

Environmental shame: see Stamp, G.: *Britain's lost cities.* London: Aurum, 2007.

Book on spontaneous speech: Goldman Eisler, F.: *Psycholinguistics: experiments in spontaneous speech.* London & New York: Academic Press, 1968.

Chapter 12

'How to write an essay': *The new psychologist,* annual journal of the Open University Psychological Society, May 1985.

A best-seller: Valentine, E.R.: *Conceptual issues in psychology.* London: Routledge, 1982; 2nd edition, 1991.

Chapter 13

An early review paper: Wason, P.C.: 'Structural simplicity and psychological complexity: some thoughts on a novel problem.' *Bulletin of the British Psychological Society,* vol. 22, pp. 281–284, 1969.

His *New horizons* chapter: Wason, P.C.: 'Reasoning.' Chapter in B.M. Foss (ed.): *New horizons in psychology 1.* Harmondsworth: Pelican, 1966.

The first of these published therapy studies: Wason, P.C.: 'Regression in reasoning?' *British journal of psychology,* vol. 60, pp. 471–480, 1969.

He compared: this imaginary dialogue appears in Wason's 1969 'Regression' paper, and in his 1983 'Realism and rationality' chapter (see above for full references).

A new book by Piaget: Beth, E.W. & Piaget, J.: *Mathematical epistemology and psychology.* Dordrecht: Reidel, 1966.

A profitable sideline: see e.g. Wason, P.C.: 'The theory of formal operations – a critique.' Chapter in B. Geber (ed.): *Piaget and knowing.* London: Routledge, 1977.

A follow-up paper: Wason, P.C. and Johnson-Laird, P.N.: 'A conflict between selecting and evaluating information in an inferential task.' *British journal of psychology,* vol. 61, pp. 509–515, 1970.

Write a rejoinder: Shapiro, D: "Representativeness', structure and content in a reasoning problem.' *Bulletin of the British Psychological Society,* vol. 24, pp. 43–44, 1971.

The paper that resulted: Wason, P.C. & Shapiro, D.A.: 'Natural and contrived experience in a reasoning problem.' *Quarterly journal of experimental psychology*, vol. 23, pp. 63–71, 1971.

'Weak facilitator': so termed by Jonathan Evans in his chapter, 'A brief history of the Wason selection task', in N. Galbraith, E. Lucas & D. Over, *The thinking mind*. Hove: Psychology Press, 2017.

## Chapter 14

A book of proceedings: Flores D'Arcais, G.B. & Levelt, W.J.M. (eds.): *Advances in psycholinguistics*. Amsterdam: North-Holland, 1970.

The paper reporting it: Johnson-Laird, P.N., Legrenzi, P. & Legrenzi, M.S.: 'Reasoning and a sense of sense of reality.' *British journal of psychology*, vol. 63, pp. 395–400, 1972.

The rule they were presented with: this is a considerably simplified account of the Johnson-Laird et al. postal experiment. In the original, alternative wordings and different currencies and amounts were used, and there was also a fifth, unstamped envelope. These details are not crucial to the argument, but anyone seeking to replicate this study should consult the original source (see previous note).

Reassessment by subsequent researchers: this now large literature is reviewed in Manktelow, K.I.: *Thinking and reasoning*. Hove: Psychology Press, 2012.

He and Johnson-Laird had published: Johnson-Laird, P.N. & Wason, P.C.: 'Insight into a logical relation.' *Quarterly journal of experimental psychology*, vol. 22, pp. 49–61, 1970.

Reported in a co-authored paper: Goodwin, R.Q. & Wason, P.C.: 'Degrees of insight.' *British journal of psychology*, vol. 63, pp. 205–212, 1972. As with the postal experiment, the account given here is much simplified.

Evans ran the experiment: see Evans, J.St.B.T. & Lynch, J.S.: 'Matching bias in the selection task.' *British journal of psychology*, vol. 64, pp. 391–397, 1973.

## Chapter 15

His grand theory: Johnson-Laird, P.N.: *Mental models*. Cambridge: Cambridge University Press, 1983; also *How we reason*. Oxford: Oxford University Press, 2006; and Johnson-Laird, P.N. & Byrne, R.M.J.: *Deduction*. Hove: Lawrence Erlbaum Associates, 1991.

'Cognitive psychology': Neisser, U.: *Cognitive psychology*. New York: Appleton-Century-Crofts, 1967.

"Immense offence": letter to Johnson-Laird, June 1974.

Several peer-reviewed papers: examples are Bracewell, R.J. & Hidi, S.E.: 'The solution of an inferential problem as a function of the stimulus materials.' *Quarterly journal of experimental psychology*, vol. 26, pp.

480–488, 1974; Gilhooly, K.J. & Falconer, W.A.: 'Concrete and abstract terms and relations in testing a rule.' *Quarterly journal of experimental psychology*, vol. 26, pp. 355–359, 1974; Smalley, N.S.: 'Evaluating a rule against possible instances.' *British journal of psychology*, vol. 65, pp. 293–304, 1974; Van Duyne, P.C.: 'Realism and linguistic complexity in reasoning.' *British journal of psychology*, vol. 65, pp. 99–67, 1974.

Large-scale monograph: Miller, G.A. & Johnson-Laird, P.N.: *Language and perception*. Cambridge, MA: Harvard University Press, 1976.

Hypothetical thinking theory: Evans, J.St.B.T.: *Hypothetical thinking; dual processes in reasoning and judgement*. Hove: Psychology Press, 2007.

The RAST: see Wason, P.C. & Green, D.W.: 'Reasoning and mental representation.' *Quarterly journal of experimental psychology*, vol. 36A, pp. 597–610, 1984. The experiment referred to here is Expt. 2, of four, and these experiments address additional variables to the one described. The earlier experiment appeared in Johnson-Laird, P.N. & Wason, P.C.: 'Insight into a logical relation.' *Quarterly journal of experimental psychology*, vol. 22, pp. 49–61, 1970.

Evans recently found: see Evans, J.St.B.T.: 'A brief history of the Wason selection task', in N. Galbraith, E. Lucas & D. Over (eds.): *The thinking mind*. Hove: Psychology Press, 2017.

Evans had found that: Evans, J.St.B.T. & Lynch, J.S.: 'Matching bias in the selection task.' *British journal of psychology*, vol. 64, pp. 391–397, 1973.

In a retrospective paper: Evans, J.St.B.T.: 'Reasoning, biases and dual processes: the lasting impact of Wason (1960).' *Quarterly journal of experimental psychology*, vol. 69, pp. 2076-2092, 2016.

Publishing their report: Wason, P.C. & Evans, J.St.B.T.: 'Dual processes in reasoning?' *Cognition*, vol. 3, pp. 141–154, 1975.

A study that has given Evans pangs of guilt: Evans, J.St.B.T. & Wason, P.C.: 'Rationalisation in a reasoning task.' *British journal of psychology*, vol. 63, pp. 205–212, 1976.

Stanley Milgram: Milgram, S.: 'Behavioral study of obedience.' *Journal of abnormal and social psychology*, vol. 67, pp. 371–371, 1963. Milgram reviews his research and the furore it excited in *Obedience to authority: an experimental view*. New York: Harper & Row, 1974. See also Miller, A.G.: *The obedience experiments: a case study of controversy in psychology*. New York: Praeger, 1986; and Blass, T.: *The man who shocked the world*. New York: Basic Books, 2004.

Dissenting voices: one of the loudest is that of the German psychologist Gerd Gigerenzer, e.g. in Kruglanski, A.W. & Gigerenzer, G.: 'Intuitive and deliberate judgments are made on common principles.' *Psychological review*, vol. 118, pp. 97–109, 2011. Their criticism, and others', were addressed in a reply by Jonathan Evans and Keith Stanovich: 'Dual process theories of cognition: advancing the debate.' *Perspectives on psychological science*, vol. 8, pp. 223–241, 2013.

Detailed and wide-ranging accounts: e.g. Evans, J.St.B.T.: 'Dual-process accounts of reasoning, judgment and social cognition.' *Annual review of psychology*, vol. 59, pp. 255–278, 2008; *Thinking twice: two minds in one brain.* Oxford: Oxford University Press, 2010; *Thinking and reasoning: a very short introduction.* Oxford: Oxford University Press, 2017.

Chapter 16

Two instances: Girotto, talking to the author in 2015, pointed to Malcolm Gladwell's *The tipping point* (London: Little, Brown, 2000) and Michael Gazzaniga's *The mind's past* (Berkeley & Los Angeles: University of California Press, 1998). Neither mentions Wason's name as inventor of the selection task; Gladwell credits Cosmides with having "dreamt up" (p. 160) a version actually devised by Richard Griggs and James Cox: see 'The elusive thematic-materials effect in Wason's selection task.' *British journal of psychology*, vol. 73, pp. 407–420, 1982.

Evans' canonical publications: Evans, J.St.B.T.: *Reasoning, rationality and dual processes: selected works of Jonathan StB.T. Evans.* Hove: Psychology Press, 2013.

Bugbears: these are summarised in Wason, P.C.: 'Notes on the supervision of PhDs.' *Bulletin of the British Psychological Society*, vol. 27, pp. 25–29, 1974.

Deceptively simple: see for instance his chapter in J.St.B.T.Evans (ed.): *Thinking and reasoning: psychological approaches.* London: Routledge, 1983.

The article reporting it: Wason, P. & Uren, O: 'The semantics of semiotics.' 194 *New society*, December 1974, pp. 812–814.

Write about writing: Wason, P.C.: 'On writing scientific papers.' *Physics bulletin*, vol. 21, pp. 407–408, 1970; reprinted in J. Hartley (ed.): *The psychology of written communication.* London: Kogan Page, 1980.

Published book chapter: Wason, P.C.: 'Specific thoughts on the writing process.' Chapter in L.W. Gregg & E.R. Steinberg (eds.): *Cognitive processes in writing.* Hillsdale, NJ: Lawrence Erlbaum Associates, 1980.

It would appear: Lowenthal, D. & Wason, P.C.: 'Academics and their writing.' *Times literary supplement*, June 24, 1977; *Leonardo*, vol. 14, p. 57, 1981.

An extensive review paper: Wason, P.C.: 'Conformity and commitment in writing.' *Visible language*, vol. 14, pp. 351–363, 1980. The quoted passages are from Parsons, T.: *The social system.* Glencoe: Free Press,

1951; and Wright Mills, C.: *The sociological imagination.* Oxford: Oxford University Press, 1959.
A later paper: Green D.W. & Wason, P.C.: 'Notes on the psychology of writing.' *Human relations*, vol. 35, pp. 47-56, 1982.
Elbow: Elbow, P: *Writing without teachers.* Oxford: Oxford University Press, 1973.
A report: Williams, J.E. & Wason, P.C.: 'Collaborative writing games.' Educational resources information center, US National Institute of Education, 1977.

Chapter 17
Two major journals: these were the long-established and prestigious *Quarterly journal of experimental psychology*, and the newly-established (in 1976) *Behavioral and brain sciences.* The latter was unique in inviting large-scale review papers followed by commentaries from other specialists and the authors' riposte. It has become one of the foremost journals in Psychology, with a very high impact factor, which is what counts these days.
The paper in question: Mynatt, C.R., Doherty, M.E. & Tweney, R.D.: 'Confirmation bias in a simulated research environment: an experimental study of scientific inference.' *Quarterly journal of experimental psychology*, vol. 29, pp. 85-95, 1977.
Its follow-ups: see e.g. Mynatt, C.R., Doherty, M.E. & Tweney, R.D.: 'Consequences of confirmation and disconfirmation in a simulated research environment.' *Quarterly journal of experimental psychology*, vol. 30, pp. 395-406, 1978.
Research on Faraday: Tweney, R.D.: 'Faraday's discovery of induction: a cognitive approach.' in D. Gooding & F. James (eds.): *Faraday rediscovered: essays on the life and work of Michael Faraday, 1791-1867.* London: MacMillan, 1985. See also Gorman, M.E.: 'Confirmation, disconfirmation, and invention: the case of Alexander Graham Bell and the telephone.' *Thinking and reasoning*, vol. 1, pp. 31-53, 1995 for related work, and Gorman's *Simulating science: heuristics, mental models, and tech-noscientific thinking.* Bloomington: Indiana University Press, 1992, for a general review of psychological studies of scientific thinking.
When it was tried at Bowling Green: Tweney, R.D., Doherty, M.E., Worner, W.J., Pliske, D.B., Mynatt, C.R., Gross, K.A. & Arkkelin, D.L.: 'Strategies of rule discovery in an inference task.' *Quarterly journal of experimental psychology*, vol. 32, pp. 109-123, 1980.
Evans' recent review: Evans, J.St.B.T.: 'Reasoning, biases and dual processes: the lasting impact of Wason (1960).' *Quarterly journal of experimental psychology*, vol. 69, pp. 2076-2092, 2016.

A paper on a disjunctive form: Wason, P.C. & Johnson-Laird, P.N: 'Proving a disjunctive rule.' *Quarterly journal of experimental psychology*, vol. 21, pp. 14-20, 1969.

Paper published in 1979: Wason, P.C. & Brooks, P.G.: 'THOG: the anatomy of a problem.' *Psychological research*, vol. 41, pp. 79-90, 1979.

A conference audience: the London conference of the British Psychological Society, December 1978. Wason's paper, entitled 'THOG: a preliminary account of a looking-glass world', was part of a symposium on deductive reasoning convened by Jonathan Evans; Phil Johnson-Laird was the discussant, and the current author was a contributor.

To continue the work: the most extensive review of this work is given by Cynthia Koenig and Richard Griggs: 'Facilitation and analogical transfer on a hypothetico-deductive reasoning task.' In K.I. Manktelow, D.E. Over & S. Elqayam (eds.): *The science of reason: essays in honour of Jonathan StB.T. Evans.* Hove: Psychology Press, 2010.

Legrenzi and Girotto: see the above review by Koenig & Griggs, and also their own earlier review: Newstead, S.E., Legrenzi, P. & Girotto, V.: 'The THOG problem and its implications for human reasoning.' In S.E. Newstead & J.St.B.T. Evans (eds.): *Perspectives on thinking and reasoning: essays in honour of Peter Wason.* Hove: Lawrence Erlbaum Associates, 1995.

Discovered by Johnson-Laird: Johnson-Laird, P.N. & Savary, F.: 'Illusory inferences: a novel class of erroneous deductions.' *Cognition*, vol. 71, pp. 191-229, 1999.

## Chapter 18

Generous review: Broadbent, D.E., *Quarterly journal of experimental psychology*, vol. 31, pp. 737-747, 1979.

A book by Jonathan Bennett: Bennett, J.: *Linguistic behaviour.* Cambridge: Cambridge University Press, 1976.

A paper in 1979: Wason, P.C. & Reich, S.S.: 'A verbal illusion.' *Quarterly journal of experimental psychology*, vol. 31, pp. 591-597, 1979.

In one such column: '90 years old and still far from wobbly.' *Daily Express*, November 15 2007.

The work with David Green: Wason, P.C. & Green, D.W.: 'Reasoning and mental representation.' *Quarterly journal of experimental psychology*, vol. 36A, pp. 597-610, 1984.

A chapter to a planned book: Wason, P.C.: 'Realism and rationality in the selection task.' In J.St.B.T. Evans (ed.): *Thinking and reasoning: psychological approaches.* London: Routledge & Kegan Paul, 1983.

David O'Brien: O'Brien, D.P.: 'Mental logic and human irrationality: we can put a man on the moon, so why can't we solve those logical-reasoning problems?' Chapter in K.I. Manktelow & D.E. Over (eds.):

*Rationality: psychological and philosophical perspectives.* London: Routledge, 1993.

L. Jonathan Cohen: Cohen, L.J.: 'Can human irrationality be experimentally 224 demonstrated?' *Behavioral and brain sciences*, vol. 4, pp. 317-370, 1981; Wason's reply, entitled 'The importance of cognitive illusions', a term Cohen had used to disparage the Wason selection task, appears on p. 356.

Chapter 19

Ruth Byrne: see for instance Johnson-Laird, P.N. & Byrne, R.M.J: *Deduction.* Hove: Lawrence Erlbaum Associates, 1991.

Mike Oaksford: Oaksford, M.R & Chater, N.: 'A rational analysis of the selection task as optimal data selection.' *Psychological review*, vol. 101, pp. 608–631, 1994. This is a radical reinterpretation of performance on the selection task in terms of justified belief updating rather than faulty reasoning. It has been highly influential, but Wason himself, in a letter to the author, was not persuaded.

Evans has had one: Manktelow, K., Over, D. & Elqayam, S (eds.): *The science of reason: a Festschrift for Jonathan StB.T. Evans.* Hove and New York: Psychology Press, 2011; Oakhill, J. & Garnham, A. (eds.): *Mental models in cognitive science: essays in honour of Phil Johnson-Laird.* Hove and New York: Psychology Press, 1996; Girotto, V. & Johnson-Laird, P.N. (eds.): *The shape of reason: essays in honour of Paolo Legrenzi.* Hove and New York: Psychology Press, 2005.

With kids as young as 3: Cummins, D.D.: 'Evidence of deontic reasoning in 3- and 4-year-old children.' *Memory & cognition*, vol. 24, pp. 823-829, 1996. Denise Cummins adapted the form of task invented by Girotto and colleagues using not cards, but concrete objects, in her case some toy mice, a marauding toy cat and a mouse-house. The children had to select mice to test whether any were violating the queen mouse's injunction that all squeaky mice must stay in the house. The correct mice to test, to see if they squeaked, are just the ones outside the house, and two-thirds of the three-year-olds did so.

His favourite: Wason, P.C.: 'In real life negatives are false.' *Logique et analyse*, vol. 57-58, pp. 17-38, 1972.

"affectionate admiration": Daniel Kahneman, personal communication, June 1 2017.

The volume appeared: Newstead, S.E. & Evans, J.St.B.T. (eds.): *Perspectives on thinking and reasoning: essays in honour of Peter Wason.* Hove and Hillsdale, N.J. USA::awrence Erlbaum Associates, 1995.

A book co-written by Evans: Evans, J.St.B.T. & Over, D.E.: *Rationality and reasoning.* Hove and New York: Psychology Press, 1996.

Evans was writing a book: see above.

According to the Alzheimer's Society: 'What is dementia with Lewy bodies?' Web article from alzheimers.org.uk, 2013.

# SUBJECT INDEX

Titles of articles are given in single quotes; titles of books are in italics

army; *see* military service

Baedeker air raids 21–3, 25, 69
Ballykilty *see* Ireland, Co. Clare
behaviourism 13, 59–61, 78, 84–5, 149

Catholicism 15, 16, 30, 39, 40, 50, 52, 194, 198 *see* religion
chess 11, 13, 14, 24, 25, 26, 29–30, 31, 32, 35, 36, 40, 48, 57, 72–83, 122, 124, 135, 148, 165, 170, 175, 176, 182–3, 187, 190, 197
children 70–2, 122, 123–4, 176–7, 180, 182, 198
clinical method; *see* Qualitative data
CND (Campaign for Nuclear Disarmament) 91–3, 117, 123
conferences: International, on thinking (1988) 188; International, on thinking (1992) 188–90, 191, 196; Trento, on selection task 149–50, 166
confirmation bias 101–4, 143, 145, 183
content effect (in selection task) 137–8, 141–2
correspondence: *see* Letter-writing

deception 100, 154
dementia 196–8
deontic reasoning 142
dual processes 2–3, 134, 150–5, 158, 165, 174

evaluation, in selection task 130–4, 137, 140, 142–3, 150, 153–4; *see also* dual processes

facilitation effect: *see* content effect
falsification 98–9, 101, 103, 107–8, 110, 143
friends and friendship 15, 17, 45, 57, 71, 75, 125
Freudian theory: *see* psychoanalysis

Harvard visit 94, 95–6, 102, 105, 108, 110, 111, 150, 190
holidays 15–8, 125, 165–6, 187, 192, 198
homes: Blackheath (flat) 58, 70; Blackheath (house) 70, 121–3, 135, 198; Frognal 122–3, 127, 141, 175–6; Goring-on-Thames 186, 188, 193, 200; Grafton Lodge, Bath 9, 20, 22, 31, 37, 42, 54, 55, 56, 57, 75, 121, 198; Highgate 176, 186; retirement 193–8
hypothesis testing 97–100, 103–4, 167, 168–70, 189; *see also* tasks, 2–4–6

illness and health: Marjorie's 176, 177, 180, 182, 185; mental 56–7, 71–2, 177, 191, 195–7; physical 71, 177, 178–80, 182, 184, 186, 187, 188, 189, 190–1, 192, 194–5, 198; *see also* Dementia; Injuries (war)
impracticality 4, 69, 111, 123, 149, 170, 182, 185–6
injuries (war) 36–8, 39–41, 69, 71–2, 74, 93, 121–2, 141, 177, 186–7, 192, 194
Ireland: Co. Clare 8, 15, 16–8, 21, 37, 42, 52, 69, 124, 192–3, 198; Northern Ireland 10, 124; republican sympathies 8, 17, 124, 193
irrationality: *see* Rationality

# NAME INDEX